TRANSNATIONAL PALESTINE

WORLDING THE MIDDLE EAST

Transnational Palestine

MIGRATION AND THE RIGHT OF RETURN BEFORE 1948

Nadim Bawalsa

STANFORD UNIVERSITY PRESS
STANFORD, CALIFORNIA

STANFORD UNIVERSITY PRESS
Stanford, California

Printed in the United States of America on acid-free, archival-quality paper

Library of Congress Cataloging-in-Publication Data

Names: Bawalsa, Nadim, author.
Title: Transnational Palestine : migration and the right of return before 1948 / Nadim Bawalsa.
Other titles: Worlding the Middle East.
Description: Stanford, California : Stanford University Press, [2022] | Series: Worlding the Middle East | Includes bibliographical references and index.
Identifiers: LCCN 2022004001 (print) | LCCN 2022004002 (ebook) | ISBN 9781503629110 (cloth) | ISBN 9781503632264 (paperback) | ISBN 9781503632271 (ebook)
Subjects: LCSH: Palestinian Arabs—Latin America—Politics and government—20th century. | Palestinian Arabs—Latin America—History—20th century. | Citizenship—Palestine—History—20th century. | Palestinian Arabs—Legal status, laws, etc.—Palestine—History—20th century. | Palestinian Arabs—Ethnic identity—History—20th century. | Transnationalism—Political aspects—Palestine—History—20th century. | Palestine—Emigration and immigration—History—20th century. | Latin America—Emigration and immigration—History—20th century.
Classification: LCC F1419.P35 B39 2022 (print) | LCC F1419.P35 (ebook) | DDC 305.892/7408—dc23/eng/20220202
LC record available at https://lccn.loc.gov/2022004001
LC ebook record available at https://lccn.loc.gov/2022004002

Cover design: Rob Ehle

Cover map: *kharitat rasm al-ard* (Map of the world), 1835, from the Rex Nan Kivell map collection, National Library of Australia.

Typeset by Newgen North America in 11/14 Arno Pro

For Teta, Mama, and Baba

Contents

Author's Note

Unless indicated otherwise, all translations in this book, including from Arabic, French, and Spanish, were completed by the author. Arabic transliterations follow the *International Journal of Middle East Studies* guidelines, including for hamzas and ʿayns, but complex diacritics were omitted.

This book makes frequent reference to the Middle East and its peoples using different categories of geographic, racial, national, colonial, and linguistic affiliation. The region, which today includes Syria, Lebanon, Jordan, Palestine, and Israel, is historically referred to as Greater Syria, the Middle East, and the Mashriq. The book uses the five identifiers interchangeably.

Historically, residents of Greater Syria were collectively referred to as Syrians and Arabs, and, as this book shows, Lebanon and Palestine were always recognized as geographic regions within Greater Syria. Unless indicated otherwise, the terms Syrian, Mashriqi, Arab, and Arabic speaker are used interchangeably in the book to refer to residents of and migrants from Greater Syria, including Palestine and Lebanon. However, this book makes particular note of the ways in which the terms Syrian, Lebanese, and Palestinian acquired new legal and political meanings after the ouster of the Ottomans and instatement of European rule in the region following the end of World War I. The book deliberately shifts to naming migrants by their new nationalities to reflect this significant transition in colonial powers across the Mashriq.

Citizenship and nationality are also significant themes in the book. Palestinian migrants seeking Palestinian citizenship in the interwar period used both terms interchangeably in the sources, and European authorities did too. This book treats citizenship and nationality similarly for the purposes of the historical analysis.

TERMS

mahjar: the abode of migration; the diaspora
Mashriq: the Levant; Greater Syria, including the present-day nations of Syria, Lebanon, Palestine, Israel, and Jordan
Mashriqi: a person from the Mashriq
watan: the homeland; the motherland; the fatherland; the nation (pl. *awtaan*)
jaaliya: a community of migrants in the diaspora (pl. *jaaliyaat*)

Prologue

I traveled to Santiago, Chile, in August 2014 to conduct research related to the Palestinian community in that country and in Latin America more broadly. Chile is home to the largest number of Palestinians outside the Middle East. Figures vary, but reliable estimates place the number at approximately five hundred thousand, mostly Christians, and predominantly from the townships of Beit Jala, Bethlehem, and Beit Sahour in Palestine. The historical narrative of their centuries-old migration to the continent was the missing piece to my book, and what I found in Chile was more than what I had bargained for. In addition to the multitude of primary source documents from the early migrant community housed at the national library in Santiago and the oral histories of their descendants, I discovered a diaspora community that has maintained substantive and multifarious connections with its ancestral homeland despite persistent exile. The experience was foundational for me as a diaspora Palestinian. To travel so far from Palestine—to the end of the world, as many referred to Chile—and connect profoundly with a community so geographically and linguistically disparate from me was hitherto inconceivable.

Today, Chile's Palestinians are bounded by a mode of group identification that they proudly proclaim to be both Palestinian and Chilean. And unlike the experiences of diaspora Palestinians in North America, this connection is largely recognized and celebrated by non-Palestinian Chileans and their government as part of the country's social, political, and economic fabric.

Descendants of Palestinians in Chile today, many of whom have achieved considerable economic and political clout, are included in a national narrative that highlights the historic successes and ingenuities of the country's diverse migrant communities.

But the summer of 2014 was tragic. The Israeli bombardment of Gaza killed over two thousand Palestinians and left entire neighborhoods flattened, many to this day. On 9 August 2014, with the Egyptian-brokered ceasefire between Hamas and Israel looming, I joined a march in support of Palestinians in Santiago de Chile. I was unprepared for what I witnessed. Tens of thousands of people took to the streets of the capital, marching peacefully down one of Santiago's main thoroughfares, Avenida Libertador O'Higgins, halting traffic for several hours, chanting, dancing, and calling for the severance of ties between Chile and Israel. The protest ended on the lawn across the avenue from La Moneda, the country's presidential palace and famed governmental building.

Giant banners and flags were paraded throughout the crowds calling for, among other things, an end to the massacre of Palestinians, the closure of Israel's embassy in Chile, and the return of refugees to their homes in historic Palestine. These chants were not unfamiliar to me, having just been in Amman, Jordan, a few days prior, where protests—albeit on a smaller scale—had been held daily during the assault on Gaza. But what struck me about the Santiago protest were its demographic composition and its idiom. Children, teenagers, adults, and senior citizens alike joined in the march; they donned the symbolic black and white *kuffiyyaat* and other accessories celebrating Palestinian heritage and political resistance; Chile's Communist Party members as well as its more conservative groups were present; native groups from the north of the country, dressed in traditional costumes with instruments in hand, traveled to the capital to take part in the event; the police stood by calmly, some even cheering along with the crowds; and various youth took the opportunity to publicly proclaim their love, sexuality, or libertarian ideals. This was by all means a community event, and not an irregular one. The marches had been organized weekly for some time before that day.

In addition to the diversity of the marchers, the event was entirely in Spanish. All the slogans and banners were written in Spanish, and all the chants and cheers were yelled in Spanish—it was quite difficult to find anyone who spoke Arabic. I tried. Evidently, most of the marchers were not of Palestinian or even Middle Eastern descent. The protest was by Chileans and for Chileans. The plight of Palestinians and the role the Chileans believed they and their government could play in showing support meant a great deal to them. The scene moved me to tears. A few nights later, I attended an evening of poetry, storytelling, and music organized by different Palestinian groups in Santiago celebrating Palestinian culture following the summer's dramatic events. Most of the attendees were of Palestinian descent, but again, almost none spoke Arabic and the event was held entirely in Spanish. The practice of solidarity, in all its facets, with Palestine and Palestinians, is well entrenched in Santiago and in local vernaculars.

There was a sense of regularity about the events I attended, and surprisingly, the groups and platforms involved were predominantly mainstream politically and socially, except for the communist factions. Palestinians in Chile are considered wealthy and cosmopolitan, and many among the older generations are more conservative and inclined to right-wing politics. This was effectively the first time in my life I had witnessed and participated in anti-Israeli occupation activism with a predominantly non-Arab collective that was supported politically by a country's liberals and conservatives alike. Who were these Palestinian descendants who had come to occupy these privileged positions in Chilean society? What is their history in Chile? Considering their comparatively small number, how did the continued occupation of Palestine by Israel since 1967 come to represent such a powerful and unifying social cause in their Chilean society? I had many questions, and many of them remain unanswered, but the answers I found were significant, both personally and intellectually.

A PERSONAL STORY

In writing this book, I thought deeply about what I could present that would add significance to my readers' understanding of the history of Palestinians. The contribution would need to offer scholarly insight, yet I could not help but feel connected to my topic personally and perhaps existentially. Since my earliest thoughts growing up in Amman, Jordan, and Cairo, Egypt, I recall feelings of discomfort and stress linked to who I am: on the one hand, a descendent of exiled Palestinians and, on the other, a Jordanian citizen. Though my story fits into a familiar narrative of displacement and assimilation among Palestinians worldwide, especially among Palestinians in Jordan, my brother and I were different on another level. We are also "native Jordanians," a reality we were often compelled to articulate and believe, whether at school, with our extended families, or at border crossings.

My father's family, originally from the city of Kerak on the east bank of the Jordan River, moved to Beit Jala on the West Bank in 1946. My grandfather, who had been an army civilian in the Arab Legion, had been stationed in neighboring Bethlehem, where he worked as a nurse and then a postal worker and where he raised eight children with his wife in a single-room dwelling that I would later come to know through my doctoral fieldwork. Growing up as Kerakis from the east side of the river and in poverty in Beit Jala, my father and his siblings had found a welcoming and close-knit community of Bajjaalis with whom they developed strong bonds. But following a series of conflicts and losses in Palestine, the Bawalsas in Beit Jala chose to "return" to Jordan, though most of them had never been there. One after the other, they trickled into Jordan starting in the mid-1970s, received Jordanian passports, and gradually began to let go of their memories from the west side of the river. Much like the hundreds of thousands of Palestinians who had been seeking refuge in Jordan since 1948, the Bawalsas grew to become Jordanians by no longer being Palestinians. But they had it easier than many; their name was "originally" Jordanian.

Some of my father's family members chose to remain in Palestine for professional reasons. Driven by opportunity in the tourism sector, they moved to Jerusalem from Bethlehem to work as tour guides of Christian holy sites, and they subsequently weathered decades of occupation, humiliation, and loss. Although they have visited Jordan only for family events and vacations since the bulk of the family left Palestine in the 1970s, to this day, they continue to express their loyalty to the Jordanian crown. For them, as I discovered during my research in Jerusalem, identifying as Jordanians worked to their advantage when it came to living in occupied East Jerusalem. As non-Palestinian Arabs scattered throughout Jerusalem's non-Jewish environs, they proclaim their east bank origins while maintaining a sense of civic duty to remain law-abiding residents of the Israeli state. So, while they may be critical of the Israeli government's behavior, they feel a sense of relief and gratitude that they reside in occupied East Jerusalem as foreigners and as Christians who benefit from what the Israeli state has to offer. This, of course, has largely been attributed to their ability to work in Jerusalem, receive subsidized healthcare, and travel with relative ease. In fact, over the years, these members of my family have come to represent a type of cosmopolitanism among the extended family in Jordan for their ability to be at once Jordanian Kerakis and residents of Israel, a regional economic and social anomaly that is at once loathed and admired.

But the Bawalsa family in Jordan also pitied their kin on the West Bank for leading such stressful lives under military occupation. They never quite understood why anyone who had the chance to enter the Kingdom of Jordan and assume rights as a Jordanian would not do so immediately. To receive national rights and privileges, including a ubiquitous repertoire of Arab tribal patriotism and imagery by an Arabic-speaking government, was to them obviously preferable to life under Hebrew-speaking Jewish occupiers. To them, there was no reason to not fully enjoy the option of assimilation as nationalized Jordanians in a country that welcomed their help economically, politically, and socially and that protected them as Christians. In some senses, like the Bawalsas in Jerusalem, the Bawalsas on the east bank have considered themselves privileged, living as a protected minority in a kingdom that recognizes their tribe and religion as native to the land.

As for my father, he continues to cherish the publicly precarious sentimentality—hence why he remains fairly quiet about it—of having Jordanian parents but feeling "completely Palestinian," as he once told me. "Before I came to Jordan in 1976, I had never been nor thought to come. I was working and studying, and even though many of my friends and siblings were leaving, I wouldn't have left if I didn't have to." My father had to leave Palestine after he was arrested and jailed by Israeli authorities on more than one occasion for his student activism while at Bethlehem University. He never completed his university degree. I thus came to see my father's sense of self-understanding while living in Jordan to be incontrovertibly still linked to Palestine. Whether in his ability to seamlessly switch between Jordanian and Palestinian vernaculars—always preferring the latter—depending on the context and with whom he is speaking; in his childlike excitement at reconnecting with friends from Beit Jala whom he invariably called his "closest friends who know me best"; or in his acerbic critiques of the Israeli state and US administrations, my father has always been Palestinian in his own way. This came to greatly impact my understanding of my family, our history, and myself.

But the same spread of loyalties, as it were, does not apply to my mother and her family. In their minds, the Said family has always been and will forever be Palestinian from Jerusalem. Whether at one point in time, centuries ago, they were less urban and could locate their roots in larger Bedouin, Muslim, or even Jewish communities (there has been speculation about all these), there was no doubt that they were, in their and their parents' lifetimes, Anglicans from Jerusalem, a city that was located in a Palestine to which they could no longer return. My grandparents impressed on my mother and her siblings a conviction that a wrong had been committed against them by the Jews, the Arabs, the British, and the Americans—although the latter two were somehow also to thank for our aristocratic sensibilities. Fleeing Jerusalem in 1948, my grandparents raised their three children in Cairo, Egypt; Manhasset, New York; and finally, Beirut, Lebanon. It was in Beirut that they came to develop an even stronger sense of being dispossessed Palestinians, especially after the assassination in 1973 of my grandmother's cousin, Kamal Nasser, a leading figure in the Palestine Liberation Organization, at the hands of the Israeli Mossad.

In addition to the politically active Nasser branch of the family, my maternal grandfather's family, the Saids, would come to acquire a significant reputation for intellectualism and, undeniably, Palestinianness. My grandfather's cousin, Edward Said, had already been devoting his career to lecturing and writing about the wrongs committed against us as a family and a people. The pervasiveness of the "Palestine Question" among members of my mother's family thus made it simple for them to identify with it, wherever it was and whatever it meant, such that in the three years after my grandfather's untimely death in 1980, when my mother, her siblings, and their mother finally settled in Amman, Jordan, there was no doubt in their minds that they were displaced and originally from Palestine. Notwithstanding, they assumed their places as Christian Palestinian business owners who were considered an asset to the Jordanian crown relative to the majority of the Palestinian refugee population in the country.

Today, the Said family is scattered. The majority of its members reside in Amman, with several branches of the family settled in Lebanon, Switzerland, Canada, and the United States, but not a single Said remains in Palestine. Dwindling in numbers, my mother's family has borne the brunt of exile. Christmases and incomplete family reunions are always marked by a measure of sorrow and nostalgia, perhaps exacerbated by what seems to be the inevitability of our extinction as a family. This is to say, apart from my brother, none among the younger generations has had children, and the prospects for traditional families appear more distant as the rates of our educational and professional accomplishments continue to increase. The legacy our grandparents secured for us, both in economic profit and education, is rooted in that trauma of exile from Jerusalem, our home. To doubt it, deny it, or supplant it with Jordanian jingoism is, for many Saids, a betrayal. What, after all, did so many of our ancestors live and die for?

My maternal grandmother, Sylvia, who was responsible for our upbringing for several years during our childhoods, spent much of the 1980s and 1990s on her couch in her apartment in Amman too afraid and too depressed to leave her home. She was born in 1934 in a peaceful Ramallah that would gradually transform with the loss of Palestine. Her father, Hannah Salah, an engineer, died when she was ten, and so her widowed mother, Lamia Nasser, an elegant and sophisticated English teacher at Ramallah's Quaker school, raised her children alone in Ramallah. During 1948, Lamia fled with Sylvia to the mountains of Lebanon, where they took refuge in a Christian school. Her older children had already married and left home. During those months, Sylvia experienced hunger and crippling fear, and when they returned to Ramallah, she was unable to withstand further trauma. By the time she married my grandfather Albert at the age of seventeen, she was ready for a life of stability, but that was never to come. Sylvia, Albert, and their three children were expelled from Egypt by Gamal Abd al-Nasser in 1962; they fled Ramallah for Beirut during Israel's 1967 occupation of Palestine; they suffered immense bigotry and racism in Long Island, New York; and they somehow managed to escape death during the Lebanese Civil War, which brought a rocket through their apartment while they slept. When Albert died at fifty-one, Sylvia was a traumatized woman, and by the time my brother and I were born, in 1982 and 1985, she had resigned herself to a life spent on her couch, avoiding unnecessary risks, including travel or leaving her apartment.

Every day throughout my childhood, I sat beside her on her couch, our eyes directed toward the television screen. Between meals, naps, and the occasional guests, this is how Teta Sylvia chose to spend her last years. During the daytime, we watched un-dubbed American and British soap operas and television shows. As a member of Ramallah's elite, Teta Sylvia's English was perfect, after all, and I learned much of mine with her. We watched the news nightly, and like clockwork, she chain-smoked two cigarettes with her head looking down between her legs as we learned of Palestine's continued destruction. In those early years of my life, Teta Sylvia was my caretaker, and she was Palestine to me. Her exhaustion with life would develop over the years, especially as the memories of the traumas she endured throughout her life were not eased with the ongoing suffering and loss in Palestine she witnessed nightly on the news.

I spent almost every day of my childhood with Teta Sylvia, but I also spent weekends with the Bawalsas in Fuheis, a modest and predominantly Christian town in the western hills of Amman, singing and dancing to Jordanian songs in living rooms often adorned with pictures of King Hussein—and, since 1999, Abdullah II. I tried not to sound too Palestinian with the soft dialect I spoke at home with my grandmother and to hide my dislike for the strong taste and smell of *mansaf*, the traditional dish made of rice, lamb, and *jameed* (dried goat's milk yogurt). But there was no hope; I was decidedly more Palestinian than Jordanian in all but name.

Experiencing this inconsistency surrounding my identity was taxing, but I was always sure that my choices to pursue a career in Middle Eastern studies at the graduate level were deeply associated with those uneasy feelings with which I grew up talking about myself, my family, and our origins. As Palestinians, we have never had an autonomous state to call our own, yet we have never stopped identifying as Palestinians and with Palestine as a geography, a politics, a lived and imagined past, and a future site of literal or symbolic return. For the millions of us across the world today who identify as Palestinians, nothing and no one can deny us this connection, yet it is anomalously unverifiable legally or by our presence in Palestine. Our ongoing exile as Palestinians continues to fundamentally shape our Palestinianness. It is from this vantage point that I chose to study the historical lives of Palestinian migrants who could not be in Palestine but who refused to detach from it, in part in order to understand how I see myself and why I continue to identify, fundamentally, as a Palestinian.

TRANSNATIONAL PALESTINE

INTRODUCTION

"WE SHALL ALWAYS BE Palestinians, never admit change of nationality."[1] On 2 January 1927, Jesus Talamas, a Palestinian migrant in Saltillo, Mexico, ended a petition he wrote to Herbert Plumer, second British high commissioner for Palestine, with these words.[2] Talamas sent the petition on behalf of the Comité Hijos de Palestina in Saltillo, whose members represented a growing number of Palestinian migrants who were being denied Palestinian citizenship by the Government of Palestine in Jerusalem following the promulgation of the Palestinian Citizenship Order-in-Council in July 1925, legislation enacted as part of the new British mandate over Palestine. Weeks later, on 5 February 1927, members of the Centro Social Palestino in Monterrey, Mexico, wrote a six-page petition to the high commissioner following the rejection of their applications for Palestinian citizenship. In their petition, members of the Centro declared: "Our firm conviction is that neither the authority of England's Mandate on Palestine, nor you personally, Lord High Commissioner, nor lastly the League of Nations would ever reduce us to such an ignominious extremity."[3]

With the Government of Jerusalem's refusal to grant them citizenship and with their Ottoman citizenship documents defunct following the collapse of the Ottoman Empire in 1918, these Palestinian migrants were rendered stateless. Without citizenship in the new interwar world order, they lacked consular and legal representation while abroad; they could not request travel permits; and, most disastrously, they lost any claim to inheritance and ownership in Palestine. They refused this undignified status and expressed their steadfastness in the face of what they considered a grave injustice against the rightful heirs of Palestinian citizenship. By 1930, the citizenship ordinance affected roughly thirty thousand Palestinian migrants throughout the Americas.

This book explores the history of Palestinian immigration to Latin America starting in the late nineteenth century, the struggles of Palestinian migrants to secure a legal and permanent means to remain connected to geographic Palestine through citizenship in the interwar period, and the ways in which these challenges contributed to the formation of a Palestinian diaspora that was intimately connected to the emergence of Palestinian national consciousness. In other words, the book argues that Palestinian national consciousness developed transnationally throughout the interwar period in spite of and in response to exclusionary British policies. It thus expands the study of modern Palestinian history to embrace transnational analysis through the lenses of migration and diaspora; it demonstrates how the governance of Palestine during the so-called liberal interwar period was thoroughly lopsided in favor of the Zionists; and it repositions the start of the narrative of a Palestinian struggle to secure a right of return to Palestine from 1948, the year of the permanent dispossession of over 750,000 Palestinians upon the creation of the state of Israel, to 1925, the year of the promulgation of the Palestinian Citizenship Order-in-Council.

The book examines sources from archives, libraries, and private collections in England, Palestine, Israel, Mexico, and Chile to chart a new kind of history of Palestine and Palestinians. It uses the themes of migration and diaspora to investigate the ways in which migrants across Latin America who came from geographic Palestine began to speak of themselves more and more as Palestinians in petitions and periodicals as a result of exclusionary British citizenship policies. Whereas migrants from Palestine had identified more readily as Syrians, Ottomans, or Arabs in the years prior to the dissolution of the Ottoman Empire, the radical transformations in the geopolitics of Greater Syria following World War I saw the emergence and consolidation of new categories of national identification among migrants from the region, including "Lebanese," "Syrian," and "Palestinian." The emergence of "Palestinian" as a political identifier, although not alien to a community that had long known Palestine to be the southern region of Greater Syria, was thus inextricably connected to British colonial practices in Palestine, which started in the midst of the war and which favored Zionists and Jewish immigrants at the expense of Palestinians in Palestine and the diaspora, or the *mahjar*.

As Rashid Khalidi puts it, "World War I changed many things as far as Palestinian identity was concerned."[4] And what ensued from the war brought about permanent transformations in the ways Palestinians all over the world identified and related to their Palestinian homeland, or *watan*. In other words, by ensuring the permanent distancing of Palestinian migrants from Palestine, the 1925 Palestinian Citizenship Order-in-Council was critical for the development of distinctively Palestinian modes of self and group understanding among larger Arabic-speaking community of migrants, or *jaaliyaat*, across the mahjar. In thousands of petitions and hundreds of periodicals authored in Arabic, English, French, and Spanish, Palestinian migrants asserted and continually affirmed their Palestinianness in response to Britain's denial of their applications for Palestinian citizenship over the course of its thirty-year rule in Palestine. They also added their voices and contributed financially to the Palestinian nationalist movement developing in Palestine throughout the interwar years. Concomitantly, Palestinian nationalists in Palestine made the defense of the rights of Palestinian migrants to Palestinian citizenship a critical message in their anti-colonial struggle. Fundamentally, then, the growth of Palestinian national consciousness in the interwar period was invariably and thoroughly transnational.

The Palestinian Citizenship Order-in-Council was designed as part of the British Mandate for Palestine, which began in 1923 and under which Palestine was entrusted to Britain by the League of Nations following the collapse of the Ottoman Empire at the end of World War I in 1918. Yet unlike its other mandated territories, Britain had also promised Palestine to the Zionists. In a letter dated 2 November 1917, British Foreign Secretary Arthur Balfour promised Walter Rothschild, a prominent Jewish financier, to see to the establishment in Palestine of a "national home for the Jewish people." Balfour asked Rothschild to relay the message to the Zionist Federation of Great Britain and Ireland.

The letter, known as the Balfour Declaration, was fundamental to the British Mandate for Palestine and was the primary reason for Palestinian opposition to British rule throughout the interwar period. As part of the declaration,

Britain also promised to facilitate the acquisition of Palestinian citizenship by Jews. Article 7 of the text of the mandate stated: "The Administration of Palestine shall be responsible for enacting a nationality law. There shall be included in this law provisions framed so as to facilitate the acquisition of Palestinian citizenship by Jews who take up their permanent residence in Palestine." In order to implement this policy, British authorities saw to the yearly in-migration of tens of thousands of Jews to Palestine. In 1925 alone, the year of the promulgation of the ordinance, of a total of 34,641 immigrants to Palestine, including Christians, Muslims, and Jews, 33,801 were Jews.[5] These immigrants applied for Palestinian citizenship and most received it,[6] while non-Jewish applicants for Palestinian citizenship were regularly denied for a variety of reasons—chief among them being what British authorities referred to as Palestine's limited "economic absorptive capacity." The latter included thousands of Palestinian migrants who had left Palestine as subjects of the Ottoman Empire before the war, many of whom had settled across Latin America, effectively barring them from their rights to Palestinian citizenship and nationality.[7]

TOWARD A TRANSNATIONAL HISTORY OF PALESTINE

There has been a significant trend in writing Palestinian history whereby Palestine, as a geographically, historically, politically, and legally contested territory, is at the center of the historical narrative. This has been indispensable for various historiographic and political purposes, including refuting claims of the absence of Palestinian social, political, and nationalist awareness since the late nineteenth century and through the interwar period. The trend has also contributed to contextualizing the losses that Palestinians endured following the 1948 *nakba,* including the permanent displacement of hundreds of thousands of Palestinians from their homes. Yet it has also contributed to restricting Palestine and developments surrounding Palestine and Palestinians to a bounded space in which non-British and non-Zionist actors were routinely disadvantaged and frustrated. This book posits that examining the lives of Palestinian migrants in the early twentieth century with an eye to migration, diaspora formation, and group identification creates a space for discussing the experiences of Palestinian diaspora communities with historical contingency and for exploring the different symbolic and material connections Palestinians forged throughout the world.[8]

By decentering Palestine and the losses its inhabitants endured from the historical inquiry about the social and political lives of Palestinians in the interwar period, one might ask how the Palestinian migrants in the small mountain town of La Calera, Chile, reacted to the arrival of British forces into Jerusalem in December 1917 and the subsequent collapse of the Ottoman Empire months later. What did they think these developments meant for them? How did Palestinians in Monterrey, Mexico, respond to news of the rejections Syrian nationalists faced when they petitioned the 1919 Paris Peace Conference for redress regarding their rights, and how did they envision their counterparts' grievances affecting them in the diaspora? When Palestinian citizenship was officially promulgated in 1925, what did Palestinians in San Pedro Sula, Honduras, believe this entailed for them? Who among them would apply, and who would not? While the book does not purport to answer all these questions, posing them and reading the sources with an eye to them yields a compelling historical narrative about diaspora formation that expands the scope of the historical study of Palestine, Palestinian nationalism, and Palestinians.

This book fits into an existing literature that traces the development of Palestinian national consciousness in the twentieth century. Rashid Khalidi's book *Palestinian Identity* is critical among these works for examining the development of political Palestinian consciousness from the late Ottoman period through 1948 and into the 1960s. While Khalidi rightly asserts that "Palestinian identity . . . is not now and never has been defined solely by the conflict with Zionism and Israel," he does point out that, since the emergence of nationalism as a form of political and social organization in the nineteenth century, Palestinians have repeatedly had to define and defend a Palestinian mode of national identification against a series of uncompromising others, often backed by oppressive imperial armies.[9] From Ottomanism, which Istanbul and its loyalists used to quash separatist nationalisms throughout its imperial domains, to Syrianism and Arabism, which, to varying extents, eclipsed the unique experiences of inhabitants within different regions of Greater Syria, to Zionism, which often denied or simply overlooked the very existence of a population in Palestine, Palestinians have had to continuously define themselves vis-à-vis robust others throughout the modern period.

Khalidi's thorough analysis paints a dynamic image of the development of Palestinian national consciousness within Palestine throughout dramatically changing times. Yet within his analysis, Palestine, an entity whose exact boundaries and shape continue to be negotiated and reimagined by Palestinians and other imperial actors, remains roughly within the same geographic coordinates: the southern region of historic Greater Syria between the Mediterranean Sea and the Jordan River. That Palestinian national consciousness appeared and developed there in the first half of the twentieth century and in a continuous and often oppressed fashion should no longer be disputed. Yet Palestinian national consciousness was also appearing outside this geography during the same transformative periods. To see how and why, we must turn to transnational historical analysis and specifically to the themes of migration and diaspora.

Migration and Palestinian History

The ceaseless outpouring of Palestinians from their homes in geographic Palestine in the decades before World War I was part of a global movement—aided by the invention of the steamship in the mid-nineteenth century—of skilled workers and artisans, aspiring entrepreneurs, political dissidents, and adventurous youth from across Europe, the Mediterranean basin, and eastward into Asia to the Americas in pursuit of economic gain. The scholarly literature on these "great waves" of migration, as Nancy Foner has called them, has tended to focus on the various communities that settled in the Americas and contributed to their economic and cultural development over the course of the twentieth century.[10] This literature has also called attention to the impact that these migrants had on their homelands in the form of financial remittances, the flow of ideas, and periodic or permanent return, among others. Within this literature, several historians of the Middle East, notably Philip Hitti, Nadim Shehade, Alixa Naff, Albert Hourani, Evelyn Shakir, and Akram Khater, have secured for Lebanese and Syrian migrants their rightful place.[11] As Camila Pastor shows, "between 1870 and 1901 three hundred thousand estimated migrants circulated between Mashriq and Mahjar," the majority of whom are recorded as Lebanese or Syrian migrants in the historiography.[12]

While Palestinians were always part of these migrations from the Mashriq, or Greater Syria, their specific stories remain largely untold. This is related to a unique historical trajectory in which a distinct social, political, and legal reality emerged for Palestinian migrants in the interwar period. By 1936, the Palestinian Citizenship Order-in-Council, enacted on 24 July 1925, had left an estimated forty thousand Palestinians worldwide unable to secure a legal means to return to Palestine. The result was their permanent exile from Palestine and the concomitant formation of Palestinian diaspora communities throughout the Americas. This story has not been told, nor has the story of the historical connections these diaspora communities forged and maintained with Palestine. It is time to write the Palestinians into transnational histories, and the transnational into Palestinian history.

This approach is part of a greater effort to revisit key themes in Middle Eastern historical trajectories in the nineteenth and twentieth centuries through migration and diaspora studies. The journal *Mashriq & Mahjar*, for example, brings the themes and approaches of migration studies to the study of the Middle East. For its editors, the journal is important for the development of Middle Eastern studies because "the colonial and nationalist discourses" that have dominated much of twentieth-century historiography on the Middle East have produced static historical narratives of "bounded territories and populations, each one neatly delineated and differentiated from the next."[13] They continue: "Nowhere is this analytical stillness . . . more apparent than in the continuing disregard that scholars of 'the Middle East' have for migration and the worlds that migrants make."[14] In addition to an incomplete understanding of the region, the editors posit that the result has been a truncated perspective on global history "shorn of wider connections" that invariably included peoples from Middle Eastern regions.[15]

Applying a transnational lens to understanding the Middle East and its peoples can open new avenues for research. An approach that considers migration, settlement, and return as central to the historical narratives of Middle Eastern lives and territories since the nineteenth century can help construct a vision of the region as a "set of networks holding together, and held together by, people and things, places and practices."[16] Or as Pastor describes it, "making *Mashriqis in movement* the unit of analysis" can challenge reductionist and essentialist tropes that Middle Eastern lives have continuously been marked by "trails of suffering . . . outside the bounds of a broader history of global processes."[17] The editors of *Mashriq & Mahjar* point out:

> That the men and women who travelled away from the region were firmly part of such a broader history can be glimpsed in the aged, torn reams of ships' registers and naturalization records scattered in archives through the diaspora,

> which record the names of thousands of migrations from "Syria" alongside those of others from Italy, Armenia, Greece, Austria-Hungary and elsewhere.[18]

These men and women thus remind us of the "presence of the Middle East in the world, and the world in the Middle East."[19]

Moreover, the newspapers these "*Mashriqis in movement*" printed in the mahjar, the letters they wrote to one another and to their families back home, and the petitions they sent to European offices across the world evince the networks of communication and solidarity that connected Arabic-speaking migrants and that contributed to the consolidation of political categories of identification directed toward the homeland among these transnational communities. Diaspora communities are thus proof of lively and generative historical trajectories that are critical to comprehending a range of political, economic, and social developments both in the homeland and transnationally. It is now a matter of writing their stories.

Diaspora and Palestinian History

Can we classify the Palestinian migrant community in the interwar period as a diaspora? Scholars have debated the meaning and utility of the term for decades. As Rogers Brubaker points out, diaspora has been so discussed that it would be reasonable to speak of a "'diaspora' diaspora" where the term has proliferated to such an extent that it might mean everything and nothing at once. Yet even though it has been critiqued for being nondescript and unhelpful, it has continued to evoke considerable discussion in scholarly circles. But what, exactly, does the term signify? Is it simply, as Khachig Tololyan argues, a recent linguistic phenomenon used to describe a timeless act of population dispersion for a variety of scholarly reasons?[20] Is it a valid measure of "structures of identity and subjectivity,"[21] or, as Brubaker postulates, is it ultimately unhelpful as a "bounded entity" and instead ought to be considered "as an idiom, stance and claim"?[22] What, if anything, does the term *diaspora* denote historically? What does it leave out?

Scholars have proposed criteria for defining diaspora. These include an initial dispersion from the homeland, followed by an orientation toward that homeland "as an authoritative source of value, identity and loyalty,"[23] a preservation of a form of distancing or differentiation from the host society in spite of hybridity, fluidity, syncretism, and so on, and finally, a personal or collective engagement with return as a critical life decision.[24] While these criteria do not necessarily signal a recent historical phenomenon—what we would today consider as a diaspora has in fact been a central theme of human history for centuries—we would not readily refer to certain movements in human history as diasporas. How come? When and why were phenomena of population migrations, movements, displacements, and returns replaced with or further qualified as diasporas? How do the concepts of "'exile,' 'expatriation,' 'postcoloniality,' 'migrancy,' 'globality,' and 'transnationality'" shape our understanding of diaspora in the modern period?[25] The answers lie to a considerable extent in the development of nation-states in the nineteenth and twentieth centuries.

Brubaker's exposition of the limits of "diaspora" as an increasingly overused category of analysis highlights its political origins. As he puts it, when diaspora is discussed, it is often "informed by a strikingly idealist, teleological understanding of the nation-state" that is seen as the culmination of projects that aim at homogenizing population groups.[26] States prescribe sameness and inclusiveness while simultaneously defining difference and exclusion in relation to the nation. By defining nationals, therefore, nation-states have created non-nationals, and they have made these identifiers determinable by the state. They have monopolized access to the nation—the homeland—and in the case of exclusion from the homeland, they have influenced the subjective experiences of belonging and identification. As Tololyan puts it, the "nation-state is the primary conceptual 'other' against which diaspora is defined."[27]

Yet *nation-state* also should not be a catchall term that homogenizes and flattens diasporas, which are infinitely diverse in their stories. In other words, rather than speak of diasporas as coming into existence at the moment of dispersion or settlement away from or return to a nation-state, we should seek to investigate the "stances, projects, claims, idioms, practices"—briefly, the struggles—of a group of people who developed—or were forced to develop—new ways of thinking of themselves in relation to a geographically distant place of ethnic origin to which they desired to remain connected.[28] The messy and unstipulated process by which these people chose to develop and coalesce into a group with agreed-upon characteristics—whether national or otherwise—thus becomes the subject matter of the historical narrative. *Diaspora* is a useful term to designate and describe this process.

In order to examine the complex and subjective stances, projects, claims, idioms, and practices that make up the process of a given group's formation into a diaspora, we must consider diaspora to be a way of formulating both the material and symbolic characteristics of a given group.[29] This is particularly important when examining a diaspora community's experience with return. Scholars have argued that narratives of return are central in shaping sentiments of longing and belonging in the diaspora, but the return need not be literal; a symbolic discourse is sufficient. Erik Olsson and Russell King propose that the "image of a homeland" is an essential component of diaspora formation. They argue that "diasporas emerge from a collective construction of the significance of the homeland and what it means to return to the imaginary homeland."[30] In the context of permanent legal and physical exclusion from the imagined homeland, the sense of collectiveness is strengthened by the impossibility of return, and the collective's unique outward articulations and expressions of its experiences of longing for and solidarity and identification with that homeland define its diaspora. Daphne Winland posits that diaspora is a "critical and increasingly malleable, even sometimes murky term" that can be a useful way to speak of subjectivities like "longings and displacements."[31] Relieved of its nation-state imperatives, therefore, diaspora can be an informative unit of social historical analysis, and the Palestinian migrant experience is a telling example.

The experiences of Palestinian migrants in Latin America who sought to remain legally and permanently connected to Palestine through citizenship constitute their diaspora story. That is, the ways in which they went about protesting their exclusion from Palestinian citizenship, their claims and stances to rights and belonging articulated in thousands of petitions and dozens of periodicals, their use of increasingly distinctive and collective idioms that expressed steadfastness in the face of British injustice, and their nostalgic longing for a homeland that grew farther and farther from their reach—collectively, these stances, claims, processes, and articulations *are* the first Palestinian diaspora. How precisely these early Palestinian migrants came to conceive of themselves vis-à-vis a Palestinian watan that would never be theirs—as well as in relation to other communities in their host countries and other individuals and communities who identified as Palestinians locally, regionally, and transnationally—is effectively the story of the formation of a Palestinian diaspora in the interwar period. We can and we must consider the

Palestinian migrant community in the interwar Americas as the first Palestinian diaspora.

ASSUMPTIONS AND HISTORICAL SCOPE OF THE ANALYSIS

The pages that follow tell the stories of individuals and communities and the ways in which they came to identify during rapidly changing times. Accordingly, they posit methodologically that the emergence of a political mode of identification among Palestinian migrants during the interwar period can be ascertained from the sources. Palestinians within Palestine and throughout the diaspora increasingly identified politically as Palestinians throughout the interwar period in written documents scattered across a range of archives. Collectively, the documents in Santiago's Biblioteca Nacional, Jerusalem's Israel State Archives, and London's National Archives describe dramatic changes in social and legal structuring, political and economic organization, and territorial mapping that were unprecedented, at times unintended, yet often permanent consequences of imperial practices in a new world defined by legislated colonialism. The book thus assumes that the progression of these shifts during the interwar period was unpredictable and that the historiographic terminology used to describe them is inconclusive. Terms like *diaspora formation, transnational identification, self-determination, citizenship legislation, mandate sovereignty,* and so on are used in this book to reflect processes that were fluid and to demonstrate that ordinary people's reactions to them in Palestine, Latin America, and much of the world were also part of how they progressed. This book thus posits that migrants were active, albeit oppressed players in the processes that radically transformed their lives.

While the transformations that accompanied the instatement of European mandates in the Mashriq after World War I form the political and legal backdrop to much of the analysis in the book—indeed, Europe's unstoppable rise to global dominance in the interwar period meant continued colonization in a variety of forms for large populations across the world—the book considers the emergence of the nation-state as the universal standard for political and legal organization as a critical starting point. The rise of the nation-state formation throughout the nineteenth and twentieth centuries brought unprecedented and permanent changes to the lives of people worldwide that are evident not only in the ways states formed and consolidated their hold over their populations but also in the ways individuals and groups identified. These shifts in daily life were further cemented by the imposition of citizenship documents, passports, travel certificates, and residency permits that invariably signified the increasing importance of the nation-state in the everyday processes of self and group identification and in the movement of individuals and communities. Over the course of the twentieth century, the presence of the nation-state and its apparatuses in the lives of individuals and communities worldwide became increasingly visible and indelible.[32]

The dominance of the nation-state way of life, so to speak, was not an overnight development among individuals and communities from the Middle East. As historians have shown, it achieved gradual prominence with the establishment of the League of Nations in the aftermath of World War I and the concomitant propagation of a new world order characterized by what Keith Watenpaugh has described as a "moral and political reordering along modern liberal nationalist, Wilsonian lines."[33] The 1920s were therefore transitional years between an age of traditional empire and a new age of bordered legal territories defined by aspiring self-determined nationalisms entrusted, purportedly temporarily, to European powers through the mandates system. That is to say, with the end of the war and instatement of European rule in 1920, Middle Eastern individuals and communities began speaking about themselves in ways that reflected the liberal political and legal rhetoric—often voiced in the language of nation-states—that was characteristic of the interwar world order. These shifts in modes of identification were so pervasive that they became central to individual and collective understanding and to diaspora formation. The petitions, letters, and periodicals authored by transnational Middle Eastern migrants throughout the interwar period that are examined in this book point to the primacy of national sentiments and nation-centered forms of affiliation and identification among countless transnational communities in the interwar years. Since their ascension to global prominence, nation-states have thus insidiously appropriated the timeless characteristics of human mobility, relationality, and identification worldwide.

A fundamental premise of this book is that the sources demonstrate that after World War I, the category of Palestinian was increasingly articulated to mark the experiences of inhabitants of and migrants from geographic Palestine with the new world order—their specific struggle for self-determination against a mandate government that prioritized preparing Palestine for the Zionists. The 1917 Balfour Declaration, therefore, is a critical starting point for this book. The ways in which diaspora individuals and communities responded to British policies that challenged or denied their attachment to Palestine and that gave their watan to the Zionists is most evident in the first years of British rule in Palestine starting in December 1917. And although petitions and periodicals authored and printed by Palestinian migrant communities throughout the interwar period can be found in archives from Santiago de Chile to Jerusalem, this book focuses on the immediate postwar years during which Britain instated its mandate and its citizenship legislation. This book considers the promulgation of the 1925 Palestinian Citizenship Order-in-Council as a seminal event in this historical narrative, and the transnational campaigns it spurred among Palestinians and their allies in the few months and years after its promulgation form the core of this book's analysis. It is in these years that Palestinian migrants were most prolific in their political struggle to safeguard their rights to Palestinian citizenship and nationality, and consequently, it is in these years that transnational articulations of Palestinian national consciousness were most loudly and consistently voiced.

Finally, this book posits that accounting for mobility in studies of migration and diaspora is central to writing transnational historical narratives. "Creating a history of movement," in the words of Camila Pastor, "requires shifting the boundaries of analysis to recognize the spheres of action of various agents."[34] It requires us to make the agents of movement "central, rather than marginal," to human sociality.[35] That is, that Palestinian migrants were a minority of the total number of Syrian migrants in the Americas in the early twentieth century should not preclude an in-depth examination of their transnational experiences in the interwar period or of their impact on the larger Arabic-speaking migrant collective and their transforming watan. Nor does this suggest that the stories of Syrian migrants who applied for and received Lebanese and Syrian citizenship at French consulates throughout the mahjar should not be examined. It is to say, though, that an analysis of the unique struggles and successes of Palestinian migrants with British mandate citizenship policies introduces compelling dimensions to the discussion, including transnational political mobilization and resistance through print media and petitioning. As Pastor poignantly points out, "attending to the diversity of migrants and their trajectories and to the transformations of the discursive frameworks through which they narrate and enact their lives affords glimpses beyond hegemonies."[36] Palestinian migrants' narratives thus challenge the historiographic packaging of the so-called liberal interwar world order, or the bounded and geographically limited understandings of anti-colonial nation-state formations. "Moving people rub against the grain of the nation-state," Pastor says, "according to which subjects are members of one and only one state-nation-territory-language; those who live otherwise are represented and managed as deviant."[37] It is this deviancy that this book assumes is worth examining.

ARCHIVAL SOURCES

To find these migrants' stories and voices, the book draws on a range of sources. In addition to hundreds of documents in colonial archives in Jerusalem and London that describe the development of British citizenship legislation throughout the interwar period, the greatest wealth of sources about the social lives of Palestinian migrants struggling to secure their rights to remain legally connected to Palestine is the periodicals, correspondence, and petitions authored by Palestinian migrants themselves.[38] The national library in Santiago de Chile houses tens of Arabic and Spanish periodicals from the early twentieth century, preserved on microfilm. Printed by Chile's Arabic-speaking migrants, these periodicals convey the industrious lives of these migrants whose tales unfolded in Chile, as well as aboard ships and on land in three continents; they describe peripatetic stories of peddlers and merchants in San Francisco, Monterrey, Lima, and Illapel; of agents and creditors in the ports of Marseille, New York, Veracruz, and Buenos Aires; of newspaper editors and protestors outside British consulates from Santiago de Chile to Mexico City; and they chronicle sojourners in Port-au-Prince, Rio de Janeiro, and San Pedro Sula, as well as others as far away as the Philippines and some tucked away in the Chilean and Peruvian Andes.[39] The historical narratives of Syrian jaaliyaat in the late nineteenth and early twentieth centuries unfolded in a variety of settings. After all, they were part of a global trend of migration and settlement of diverse peoples that saw the exchange of resources, talents, languages, races, religions, and so on in various forms at a relatively fast and continuous pace.

This book explores two aspects of the formation of a diaspora of Palestinian migrants in the first decades of the twentieth century. First, it examines dispatches, memoranda, and policy documents from the British Colonial, Foreign, and Home Offices at the National Archives in London, as well as migrant petitions and letters found there and from the Israel State Archives in

Jerusalem, to make sense of the discussions, negotiations, and contestations that took place in London, Geneva, Jerusalem, and various British consulates in the Americas regarding the citizenship policies that contributed to the exclusion of Palestinian migrants from Palestinian citizenship. It thus builds on existing discussions among historians of the modern period whose work has offered critical analyses of the contradictory practices of the so-called liberal world order in the context of interwar colonialism.[40]

The story of Palestinian migrants contributes a compelling dimension to this literature. Their exclusion from citizenship by British mandate authorities during the 1920s could not be based on the migrants' racial, birth, or material connections to Palestine. Those connections, enumerated in the citizenship legislation itself, were incontestable: Palestinian migrants shared a race with the majority of the inhabitants of Palestine, many owned property in Palestine, and many were even born in Palestine. Rather, the documents indicate that British authorities were aware of these connections and were therefore strategic in the language used to reject Palestinian migrants' applications for citizenship. British authorities promulgated what Palestinians and their allies saw as unreasonable and arbitrary criteria for citizenship that were antithetical to the discourse about natives' rights included in the text of the British Mandate for Palestine. These criteria included the length of a migrant's stay abroad and his or her intention to return permanently to Palestine. Specifically, applicants for citizenship had to have left Palestine after 1920 and have presented proof of an intention to return for good, two prerequisites that Palestinian migrants pointed out were arbitrary and "impossible of fulfillment" for a variety of practical reasons. The sources are thus examined to elucidate how these requirements came to be meaningful mechanisms for exclusion and, in response, for the development of new modes of group identification among Palestinian migrants.

The second dimension of the book examines petitions, letters, and periodicals authored by the migrants themselves in order to trace the emergence of a specifically Palestinian mode of identification and of political claims making. As mentioned, prior to the dissolution of the Ottoman Empire in 1918 and the fragmentation of the Mashriq into mandates, most residents of Greater Syria identified as Syrians, and any qualifications were largely geographic or confessional.[41] To wit, a Syrian could be from Palestine, the southern territory stretching between the Jordan River and the Mediterranean Sea, and from Lebanon, the narrow strip of land located west of Mount Lebanon down to the Mediterranean. Syrians often also identified as Arabs and Ottomans, depending on their political leanings and where they were, especially in the turbulent years leading up to the war. However, the end of the war made these fluid categories increasingly untenable. British mandate policies brought hardship to thousands of Palestinians worldwide that isolated them in their experiences with mandate rule. Put differently, the exclusion of thousands of individuals from the Palestinian citizenship to which they believed they had natural and national rights contributed to their identification as Palestinians in enduring ways. Migrants' petitions, correspondence, and newspapers are examined to trace how the categories of Syrian, Arab, or Ottoman—although they did not disappear altogether as identifiers—were steadily replaced with the Palestinian designation.

The second dimension thus examines how Palestinian migrants in the interwar period engaged creatively and strategically with the liberal language of the interwar legal world order emerging from Europe to stake claims to Palestinian nationality and citizenship.[42] In doing so, they laid the foundations for a Palestinian diaspora that has maintained significant political, economic, cultural, and social clout transnationally to this day. Today, there are sizeable communities of Chileans, Hondurans, Peruvians, Mexicans, Colombians, Argentinians, Cubans, Brazilians, and others who celebrate a unique past as descendants of Palestinian migrants. While a handful of scholars of Latin America have taken an interest in the historical development of Palestinian and other Middle Eastern diasporas in Latin America, this book furthers the discussion of how these communities came to be with an examination of their hitherto unexamined periodicals and petitions.[43] The different instances in which these migrants came to write about themselves, their communities, and their homeland as Palestinian reflect the process of this community's formation into a diaspora. By examining the sources with an eye to these developments, this book brings both the history of Palestinians to the Americas and the themes of diaspora and migration to Palestine studies.

ORGANIZATION OF THE BOOK

The book is divided into six chapters. Chapter 1 situates emigration from Palestine within the broader literature on Ottoman Syrian immigration to the Americas. While emigration from Greater Syria in the late nineteenth and early twentieth centuries has received considerable scholarly attention, the specifically Palestinian migratory narrative has been markedly less developed relative to the Lebanese and Syrian narratives. In addition to investigating why, this chapter offers a more detailed portrayal of the Palestinian experience with migration. It offers examples from two case studies in particular, Mexico and Chile, hubs of Palestinian settlement, which reappear in more depth in chapters 4 and 5. And finally, chapter 1 ends with a discussion of the dramatic changes to migrants' lives that were brought on by the end of World War I and the instatement of the mandates system in the Mashriq.

Chapter 2 explores what was termed "pro-Palestina" activism among Palestinian migrants in Latin America between the end of the war in 1918 and the official instatement of the British mandate over Palestine in 1923. The chapter examines the ways in which Palestinian migrants in the Americas opposed a Zionist takeover of Palestine and demanded self-determination from European leaders *as* Palestinians, a category of identification that, while never separate from the existing categories of Syrian and Arab, was increasingly deployed in deliberately political displays. The chapter situates this pro-Palestina activism within the larger transnational political activism of migrants from Greater Syria across the Americas, especially in New York, São Paulo, and Buenos Aires, in the first two decades of the twentieth century. It thus points to the tradition of communication between Arabic-speaking migrants throughout the Americas and different European legal bodies before the British mandate and to the roots, as it were, of transnational Palestinian consciousness.

Chapter 3 provides the legal and political context for the dramatic changes Palestinian migrants experienced when it came to mobility, naturalization, and belonging as a result of the 1925 Palestinian Citizenship Order-in-Council, promulgated by British authorities in Jerusalem and London within the context of international law. The chapter examines colonial records from archives in Jerusalem and London, including the 1925 citizenship ordinance itself, as well as a series of declassified correspondence exchanged between British offices transnationally, to investigate the ways in which British authorities continually excluded Palestinian migrants from Palestinian citizenship. The chapter also offers a discussion of the long-term practice of excluding Palestinians from Palestinian citizenship during the 1930s, making particular note of the colonial and imperial legacies of British mandate rule in Palestine.

Chapters 4 and 5 explore the ways in which Palestinian migrants responded to what they considered to be unjust British policies embodied in the 1925 ordinance and how these responses formed an important part of transnational Palestinian national consciousness. Chapter 4 begins with an examination of petitioning as a transnational practice of colonized peoples in the interwar period and delves into petitions authored by Palestinian migrants in 1927 Mexico. Following the rejection of thousands of applications for Palestinian citizenship, members of the Centro Social Palestino in Monterrey and of the Comité Hijos de Palestina in Saltillo, among others, submitted petitions protesting Jerusalem's policy to various British consular and colonial offices throughout Mexico. These petitions, which were forwarded to the high commissioner, as well as to the Arab Executive in Jerusalem, signify the importance of petitions as a mechanism for social and political identification. The chapter posits that while the 1927 petitions—indeed, most petitions—did not secure their authors redress, they nonetheless convey the development of a Palestinian diaspora and of Palestinian national consciousness in the interwar period.

Chapter 5 takes the story of Palestinian migrants to cities and towns in Chile, today home to the largest number of Palestinians outside the Arab world. It introduces several Santiago-based Arabic newspapers that were in circulation starting in the first two decades of the twentieth century. Looking closely at two, *al-Watan* and *al-Sharq*,[44] it explores the ways in which the periodicals' editors and contributors focused on circulating content that, on the one hand, safeguarded the jaaliya's economic success in the mahjar and, on the other, strengthened its interconnectedness through edification in patriotic love for the watan. The periodicals' editors and contributors made the defense of Palestinian migrants' rights to Palestinian citizenship and nationality central in this edification. The chapter ends with a discussion of how these periodicals contributed to the emergence and consolidation of a specifically Palestinian mode of diasporic identification among palestinos-chilenos.

Finally, chapter 6 explores the transnational interconnectedness of Palestinians more closely by returning to Palestine. It examines the solidarity Palestinians within Palestine showed their diaspora counterparts in their struggle to secure Palestinian citizenship. Specifically, it examines the efforts of the Committee for the Defense of the Rights of Palestinians in Foreign Countries, formed in Beit Jala in 1927, and of the editors of the Jaffa-based *Filastin* newspaper in protesting the disenfranchisement of their diaspora compatriots. While their efforts would ultimately not sway British policy in their favor, they managed to stir debate and disagreement among European officials regarding the equity of denying Palestinian migrants their citizenship and to politicize the crisis of citizenship by lumping it with the Palestinian nationalist movement. This discussion makes note of the significant connections and networks of communication and solidarity that existed between Palestinians worldwide and of the importance of the plight of Palestinian migrants in the struggle for Palestinian national self-determination within Palestine. Significantly, then, the chapter shows that the development of Palestinian national consciousness in the interwar period was thoroughly transnational and that Palestinians' struggle to secure a right of return to Palestine began well before 1948.

CHAPTER 1

PALESTINIANS SETTLE THE AMERICAN MAHJAR

IT TOOK KAMEL Jarufe Jadue, a Palestinian from Beit Jala, forty-five days to reach Buenos Aires in the 1910s from Beirut. After leaving the port at Beirut, Jadue boarded several ships, which took him to Marseille, Barcelona, Dakar, the small, coastal town of Santos in Brazil, Rio de Janeiro, and finally, Buenos Aires:

> We first went to Lebanon to take the boat. We slept the night there. We boarded the boat, but not the one we had to take for the long trip; this boat was small, it was Turkish, and it went to Greece. There we took the other ship; it was gigantic. It was called *Bretain.* It was an Italian ship. It was immense. The first couple of days we could not eat anything. We were all seasick. The first port we came to was Marseille. There we stayed about five days, then to Barcelona, Spain. . . . There were few Palestinians on the boat, and from our town it was just us. After Spain, we arrived to Dakar. . . . In Dakar we stayed one more day, then on to Brazil. The boat stopped in Santos, a very old city. We slept a night there. Then we went to Rio de Janeiro. . . . From Rio de Janeiro we continued to Buenos Aires. It took five days. That completed the 45-day trip, with stops included.[1]

Six weeks, however, was not a particularly long journey for migrants traveling on limited budgets in the early period of migration. Migrants could often expect to be delayed in Europe for weeks at a time and then stop at several other ports in West Africa, the Caribbean, or Central America before making it to their final destination in South America. But what could impel a merchant with meager means from the small town of Beit Jala to undertake the arduous journey to a new and strange land?

THE NOT-SO-DIFFICULT DECISION TO LEAVE

Assaf Khater was a peasant from the silk-producing village of Lehfed in Mount Lebanon. By the mid-nineteenth century, silk had become a valuable Ottoman export following sweeping *tanzimat* reforms that introduced cash-crop economies in an attempt to strengthen the Ottomans' position in the burgeoning global economy.[2] By the 1870s, following a surge in global demand for silk, Mount Lebanon suffered from severe droughts that crippled the silk industry and destroyed villagers' livelihoods.[3] Assaf had no choice but to seek employment elsewhere, so he moved to Beirut to join the Ottoman gendarmerie. After several years with the gendarmerie, earning an unlivably low income, and with worsening inter-confessional relations across Mount Lebanon, Assaf left the gendarmerie and migrated to Uruguay in 1890.

Although at first he experienced challenges securing a stable income in Uruguay, within a few years, he amassed considerable wealth. He traveled back and forth between Uruguay and Lebanon from 1890 to 1933, the year of his death, remitting money to his family and eventually purchasing property in Lehfed, where he built the home in which he died. Throughout his travels back and forth to Uruguay, he made enough money to also secure an inheritance for his children. Assaf's peripatetic lifestyle offers an example of what a viable and attractive alternative would have looked like for farmers and workers from across Greater Syria who wished for economic success outside the Arab Ottoman provinces.

Assaf's story evinces what historians have been arguing about the motivations for migration among residents of Greater Syria around the turn of the twentieth century. Worsening political, social, and economic conditions in the Ottoman Empire left many with little choice but to pack up and leave. In the years leading up to World War I, the Ottoman Empire was notorious for its discontented subjects. In addition to exhausted economies and overstretched resources, the Young Turk Revolution of 1908; the spike in censorship, imprisonment, and exile; and new Ottoman conscription laws drove thousands to board ships at Beirut, Jaffa, or Alexandria in the hope of escaping, at least until things improved back home.[4] The 1908 revolution sought the reinstitution of the Ottoman constitution to limit the sultan's power and spurred an exclusivist form of Turkish nationalism. As a result, agitation for secession among nationalists increased across Ottoman domains, including the Arab provinces, and consequently, Istanbul issued repressive censorship laws on the press and freedom of expression.[5] Many intellectuals, writers, and journalists who were actively involved in the Arab literary *nahda* (renaissance) percolating in city centers across Greater Syria, particularly Beirut, Aleppo, and Damascus, were subjected to imprisonment, fines, and exile.[6] This atmosphere spurred an outpouring of many Syrians to more liberal destinations across the region and the Americas.

Escaping conscription in the Ottoman army was also central to migrants' decisions to leave, especially Christians and Jews. Starting with the conscription law of 1908, the Ottomans gradually began incorporating non-Muslims into the Ottoman army, and in 1914, conscription became mandatory.[7] Prior to 1914, Christian and Jewish subjects of the Ottoman Empire could obtain exemptions from military service by paying a fee. By 1914, however, the policy had been amended and non-Muslims were required to serve. The issue of conscription became particularly problematic for Christian Syrians during the First Balkan War between 1912 and 1913. With the majority of Christians in the Arab Ottoman provinces espousing Orthodox Christianity, fighting for the Muslim Ottoman army put many in a thorny position.[8] Therefore, instead of sending them off to fight for the Ottoman army, families across the region went to great lengths to ensure that their sons were not conscripted, including "spirit[ing] the young men out of the country."[9]

Assaf's story also shows that the promise of economic betterment in the Americas was enticing to new migrants, especially with the many stories of success reaching residents of Greater Syria from their migrant counterparts. As Kemal Karpat points out, successful migrants who returned home from the Americas "represented a strong argument in favor of bold initiative and enterprise on the part of their fellow Ottomans."[10] Those who heard their stories of success were driven to seek wealth in the Americas. Bidirectional travel was thus central to the lives of Syrians in the decades before World War I. Frequent return was mutually beneficial for migrants and their communities back home; while communities in the Mashriq benefited from migrants' remittances, successful migrants were sure to attract increasing numbers of their family members and friends to join them abroad, leading to further economic success.

Connected to this success was the possibility of partaking in world fairs across the United States. Held in Philadelphia in 1876, Chicago in 1893, and St. Louis in 1906, these fairs welcomed merchants from across the world.[11] For example, the Columbia Exposition of 1893, held in Chicago, attracted a large number of migrants from Jerusalem and Ramallah who were selling "olive wood articles and other curios."[12] Their success was so impressive that many young men in Palestine followed suit.[13] Indeed, in 1924, Philip Hitti remarked, "Once started," the decades-old wave of Syrian migration to the Americas "was never checked."[14] Starting in the last decades of the nineteenth century, therefore, thousands were leaving Greater Syria each month in the hope of improving their socioeconomic standing and securing more stable lives for themselves and their families. Tolerating the arduous six-week journey was a small price to pay for the sweet promise of wealth and prosperity in the Americas.

SITUATING PALESTINIANS IN OTTOMAN SYRIAN MIGRATION

In 1906, Abdullah Saade, an Orthodox Christian merchant from Bethlehem, moved his family to Kiev, in the Russian Empire, carrying in his luggage "Holy Land" items such as rosaries, incense, and olive wood.[15] Abdullah was drawn to Kiev in part by Tsar Nicolas II's support of the Russian Orthodox Church, which "ensured a large market for religious articles from the Holy Land."[16] Kathy Kenny, Abdullah's great-granddaughter, explained that her family lived relatively comfortably in Kiev, periodically making return trips to Palestine to collect more merchandise and to tend to their properties in Bethlehem (figure 1). However, they were forced to return permanently to Bethlehem in 1914 with Russia's entry into World War I. Katrina, Kenny's grandmother, described to her granddaughter their family's struggle leaving Kiev and resettling in Palestine in 1914:

> There were a lot of problems. [The Russians] started killing people. My family went to a priest who made some papers to allow them to escape. They had a lot of money—paper money. They were hoping that the money would regain its value, but they lost every cent.... When we returned to Palestine, we had a hard time surviving. My father had a lot of land. He was forced to sell to provide for the family. There were a lot of mouths to feed. The land helped them survive.[17]

Yet conditions in Palestine were also dire, especially with the Ottoman participation in the war on the side of the Central Powers and with the economic

FIGURE 1. The Saade family in Bethlehem, circa 1910. Katrina sits in the front row at her father Abdullah's feet. Source: Personal collection of Kathy Kenny.

calamities that swept through Greater Syria.[18] In 1914, within months of their return to Bethlehem from Kiev, and with conditions worsening in Palestine, fourteen-year-old Katrina was betrothed to a Palestinian Christian, Jamil (Emilio) Kabande, who had settled with his family in Mexico earlier that decade. Accompanied by her sister and future brother-in-law, she traveled halfway across the world to marry eighteen-year-old Emilio, a man she had never met.

Who were the Kabandes, and why did Abdullah believe that sending his fourteen-year-old daughter to marry a stranger would be a safe and worthwhile decision? What did he know about Mexico and its Palestinian jaaliya, especially having just returned from Kiev? The story of the Saade family suggests that religion was an important factor in the choice to migrate and, for that matter, to send children abroad. In the early period of migration, the largest proportion of Syrian migrants to the Americas were Christians.[19] These migrants, much like their counterparts back home, preferred endogamous marriage arrangements. With the news that the Kabandes—a Christian family—were seeking a bride for their son and with the knowledge among

Christian communities in Palestine that the Kabandes had made a fortune in Mexico, sending young Katrina to Mexico to wed Jamil was certainly preferable to struggling to feed her in Palestine on the eve of World War I. In short, as Saliba explained, emigration became popular for many in the region, especially in the years leading up to the war,[20] and it set in motion a social and economic trend that influenced the ways in which Ottoman Syrians ensured their livelihoods and self-identified. As Katrina's story suggests, some Palestinian migrants in the Americas may have never known life in Palestine. After all, Katrina left Bethlehem when she was six and grew up in Kiev.

The Kabandes of Ramallah and Saades of Bethlehem were part of a growing number of families in Palestine that were hoping for safety and prosperity in the Americas. They were also connected to Palestinian jaaliyaat in the Americas to which they sent their children. Who were these diaspora Palestinians? Where in Palestine did they come from, and where did they settle? How did they come to navigate the Americas so skillfully that within a few years, they could send bountiful remittances to and secure spouses from the homeland? Throughout these periods, how did they identify? As with most histories of Ottoman Palestine, we must expand the queries to include undivided Greater Syria. Ottoman migrants from Greater Syria were, in fact, all Syrians before the establishment of the European mandates.

It is generally agreed that approximately 600,000 persons emigrated from Greater Syria to both North and South America between 1860 and 1920.[21] In the United States alone, Alixa Naff points out, the US Department of Commerce and Labor estimated that between 1899 and 1907, 41,404 migrants from different locales in Greater Syria were admitted.[22] By 1910, she adds, "the figure swelled to 56,909, a veritable exodus from the homeland."[23] Philip Hitti's 1924 ethnography, *The Syrians in America,* is the earliest known scholarly work on the westward movement of peoples from Greater Syria. Having undertaken the journey west himself, Hitti's contribution functions as both a primary and a secondary source. Researchers make frequent reference to Hitti's observations on the motivations, destinations, settlement patterns, and contributions of Syrian migrants starting in the nineteenth century. With the help of migration records from across the diaspora from Ottoman archives and from Syrian and Lebanese state registries, Hitti and his successors have managed to isolate the experiences of migrants from Greater Syria who would become Lebanese and Syrian following the end of the Ottoman Empire. In doing so, they have shown that while Lebanese Christians formed the largest number of Ottoman Syrian migrants around the turn of the twentieth century, a significant number of Syrians from Palestinian locales had also been emigrating since the nineteenth century. As Hitti put it, while the Lebanese "furnished the pioneer migrants and the bulk of later emigration, . . . all portions of Syria and Palestine contributed to the westward-flowing stream,"[24] even, he adds, Bethlehem and Nazareth, relatively small towns compared to Damascus, Beirut, or Aleppo. Yet until recently, the stories of these Palestinian migrants have remained largely untold. It is worthwhile to question the dearth of scholarly material regarding the case of Palestinian migrants, who amounted to approximately ten thousand by the start of World War I and over forty thousand by 1936.[25]

The disparity in information regarding the Palestinian constituents of Ottoman Syrian migration is primarily due to the ways in which immigration records were kept in Latin America at the turn of the twentieth century and to issues of accessibility.[26] As Ottoman subjects carrying Ottoman travel documents, most migrants who arrived in the years before 1918 were indiscriminately registered as *turcos* (due to their Ottoman travel documents), *sirios*, or *arabes* in Latin American registries upon arrival; their specific origins were thus obscured.[27] Notwithstanding, estimates of Palestinian migrants are not entirely absent. Population estimates based on Ottoman censuses in the early twentieth century put the total population of Palestine in 1914 at approximately 797,000, with Muslims amounting to 657,000, Christians to 81,000, and Jews to 59,000. A French consular report published in 1907 put the number of Palestinian emigrants to the United States at 4,000 persons during ten years.[28] Data from the American consul in Jerusalem placed emigration from the Mutasarrifate of Jerusalem at 3,000 in 1913, of which the majority were young men.[29] Established in 1872 during Ottoman rule, the Mutasarrifate of Jerusalem was an administrative demarcation that designated the city of Jerusalem and a swathe of territory that stretched west from the city to the Mediterranean coast, south to the Naqab desert, and east across the Jordan River. It included Jerusalem, Bethlehem, Biʾr al-Sabiʿ, Gaza, Jaffa, and Hebron. Along with the Sanjaks of Nablus and Acre to the north, these three districts were collectively referred to as Southern Syria or Palestine. Half the migrants from these districts brought their families over afterward, mostly to Argentina, Brazil, Chile, Honduras, Mexico, and El Salvador.[30] In Chile, for example, Palestinian migrants amounted to 56 percent of the total number of Syrians in the country between 1905 and 1914.[31]

As for other Latin American countries, while the exact numbers of Palestinian migrants is virtually impossible to ascertain from the existing records, the proportions of Palestinian migrants in El Salvador and Honduras were relatively high, with the latter country receiving the most.[32] Until 1955, when the numbers were tallied, Honduras was overwhelmingly the most common destination for these early migrants, with 255 registered family names, followed by El Salvador (199), Nicaragua (25), Guatemala (23), and Costa Rica (2).[33] Notwithstanding unreliable, inaccessible, and often muddled migration registers, historians have been able to determine that by the time of the establishment of the British Mandate for Palestine in 1923, there was a sizable population of Palestinian migrants residing abroad who possessed only Ottoman travel papers and who were registered as *turcos*, *sirios*, or *arabes* upon arrival in Latin America.

THE JOURNEY BACK AND FORTH

Prior to World War I, migrants could expect monthly, and later weekly, departures to Marseille aboard European ships from the ports of Jaffa and Beirut on the eastern Mediterranean coast and Alexandria in Egypt, with relatively easy immigration regulations and assistance along the way. The voyage to the Americas was also relatively affordable and, for the most part, safe. At the beginning of the twentieth century, ticket fares ranged between 200 and 250 francs, one way, to South America, and 190 francs to New York.[34] Many often borrowed money or received help from various family members who would have considered their contributions as investments in the family's collective economic profit. Khalil Sakakini, for example, a Jerusalemite of modest means and with financial troubles, borrowed money from his fiancée, Sultana, and from a childhood friend, Dawood al-Saidawi, to make the voyage from Jaffa to New York in 1907.

Unlike in the interwar period, the only requirement for travel before 1919 was to purchase the ticket either at the port of departure or from travel agents who visited towns and villages advertising travel deals. Pastor explains that Syrian travelers often selected their destination at emigration offices based on the "first port of call of the next available ship."[35] These emigration offices, she continues, serviced different ship companies: the Compagnie des

Messageries Maritimes, the Compagnie Générale Transatlantique, the Société Générale des Transports Maritimes, or the Compagnie Cyprien. After the migrants had set sail aboard a ship on the eastern Mediterranean coast, they disembarked at European ports into the arms of more agents selling tickets to the Americas. These agents were themselves often Middle Eastern migrants who had taken up residence in European port cities, often in boardinghouses, and operated as middlemen on the long journey.[36] The network of middlemen grew so popular that fraud was pervasive. The result for migrants was to occasionally be "misrouted to unknown destinations," such as some Latin American port rather than New York, for example.[37]

But the experiences of some migrants with unreliable or dishonest agents led to another kind of transnational communication between migrants whereby seasoned migrants and honest agents would alert new migrants to potential fraud or restrictive immigration policies.[38] This included recommendations on which ships to choose for the long journey; as a result, ship companies started competing in advertising. For example, *Filastin* newspaper ran the following advertisement across the bottom of the front page of each issue starting in 1911, the year the newspaper was launched: "To travel to destinations in the direction of America through Marseilles in the fastest time and on the biggest boats of the French Messageries, consult the company's office in Jerusalem outside the Jaffa Gate."[39] The location of the French company's office, at Jaffa Gate, is one of Jerusalem's central locations.

But while the Messageries ship company was one of the most successful, the voyage it promised was certainly not easy. As Jadue's journey indicates, it was considered the workingman's burden to undergo such a long trip for the family's sake. Entries from Khalil Sakakini's diary and excerpts from his letters to his sister, Milia, and his fiancée, Sultana, offer an account of what the journey from Jaffa to New York in 1907 would have been like for thousands of less affluent migrants from the Mashriq. Sakakini, who at twenty-nine was unusually old for a first-time migrant, traveled third class on a French Messageries boat from Marseille to New York. The voyage lasted approximately two weeks and was evidently exhausting. In a poem to his sister in a letter on 14 November 1907, he wrote:

After a trip which makes you old, I arrived to the land of gold
On board, the ship was shaking

Making me regret ever departing
Not a soul with whom to commiserate
And food that leaves you with a terrible aftertaste.[40]

Then, in a letter he composed to Sultana on 22 August 1908 while in London, en route back to Jerusalem, Sakakini complained: "Third-class travel is unbelievably tiring. For nine days, I could hardly sleep. I ate very little and did not change my clothes or wash my face once. When I arrived in England I was spent from hunger, exhaustion, and lack of sleep. I was thoroughly disgusted with myself."[41]

Sakakini's story, however, was rather unusual. Although he had contacts in New York who helped him secure employment upon arrival, his experience in the mahjar was altogether lonely, as he lamented to Sultana in several letters. Most migrants, on the other hand, seemed to have arrived to larger networks of kinsfolk before venturing into the North and South American interiors. As Pastor explains, "while the initial destination was often chosen because kinsfolk were already there, once migrants found their footing, they remained extraordinarily mobile across American geographies." As for the reason, she points out that if North America was considered to be "a land of plenty, Latin America . . . was narrated as a place to discover and conquer."[42]

Notwithstanding this adventurous, arguably colonialist approach to settlement, many Syrian migrants intended to return to their town or village in Greater Syria after accumulating wealth abroad and after circumstances improved back home. Charles Issawi estimates that of the total number of migrants from Greater Syria to the Americas prior to the war, about a third or half would have returned "as soon as they [had] saved enough money in America."[43] "Seldom," says Najib Saliba, "did an emigrant indicate he had left his homeland permanently."[44] In the United States, Syrian migrants would save between 10,000 and 20,000 francs during a five- to ten-year stay, return home, and then decide whether or not to emigrate again based on economic and personal necessity.[45] Assaf's frequent voyages between Lebanon and Uruguay around the turn of the twentieth century reflect this trend, as does the practice of Palestinian migrants in Honduras. Palestinians would often take up residence in Honduras for a few years, turn relatively large profits for themselves and the Honduran government by spurring trade and manufacturing, especially along the northern coast of the country, and return home to their families and properties.[46] Thanks to easier immigration laws before the war, as well as economic opportunities abroad, Palestinian migrants across the Americas managed to establish themselves as a viable commercial class that was in no position to relocate permanently and thus, to assimilate.[47] In fact, Palestinians in Central America remained fairly exclusive socially and linguistically, choosing commerce over settlement, even rejecting land grants offered by the Honduran government.[48]

The option to return was central to the process of migration. To that end, migrants often awaited news of improvements back home in the hope that they could be reunited with their loved ones and return to familiar settings. As an example, the reinstitution of the Ottoman constitution in 1908 and, in effect, the limitation of the sultan's power following the coup in Istanbul initially contributed to the return of many migrants—at least those who would not have joined anti-Ottoman nationalist movements in Syria.[49] The hope of reclaiming their social and political freedoms back home encouraged many Syrian migrants to return from the mahjar and discouraged many more from leaving the watan. Statistics on rates of emigration following the coup illustrate this preference for remaining at home among inhabitants of the Mashriq. In 1908, records indicate that 5,520 Syrian migrants entered the United States, whereas in 1909, only 3,668 did.[50]

Sakakini is perhaps the most famed of returnees due to the detail with which he described in his diary his feelings about returning to Jerusalem from New York.[51] On 7 June 1908, after only seven months in New York and Maine, Sakakini wrote to Sultana that he longed to return to Jerusalem, though he was concerned about what people would say since he had been away such a short time:

> I still spend all day thinking about returning, but how will I pay for my return and what will [people at home] think of me? Will they accept my excuse or accuse me of weakness, cowardice, laziness, and immaturity? What will Sultana say? Will she keep her faith in me and will she still accept me, or will she feel disappointment and regret? And I swear to you, Sultana, if there were gain in my stay here, I would not return this fast. But what do I do if I am not given any hope?[52]

The diary entry conveys the stresses associated with returning home after a short and unsuccessful attempt at economic gain abroad. Then, in another letter to Sultana dated 27 July 1908, Sakakini intimated that he was disillusioned with America and wished to try his luck back home after the 1908 revolution:

> The truth, my love, is that America is worth seeing, but is not fit to be a homeland for us, for it is a nation of toil, and there is no joy in it. I have one hope left, and that is to go back and try my luck back home. I trust conditions are better now that the Sultan has ratified the constitution.[53]

The 1908 coup was therefore a harbinger of change for many migrants for whom economic hardship and the sultan's authoritarian rule were causes to leave and, consequently, for whom return was a preferred option after the coup. Sakakini returned to Jerusalem on 10 September 1908, grew increasingly involved in local politics and education in Palestine, and started a family and a successful school. Though he often reminisced on his sojourn in America in diary entries and letters to his son in the 1930s, he never again migrated westward.

Fundamentally, then, the return of migrants from the mahjar to the watan was a mainstay of Syrians' social lives on both sides of the Atlantic. This was due to the relative success of migrant communities in the mahjar, the remittances they secured for their relatives and communities back home, and the profitable social arrangements that ensued. Though literature on the topic of return migration among migrants from Greater Syria is scarce, Akram Khater offers a compelling example of the importance of return migration for the creation of a "modern" Lebanon. Khater recounts the stories of peasant migrants returning to Lebanon and posits that they were active participants in the various developments in class, family, and gender dynamics in early twentieth-century Lebanon. For Khater, returning peasants have not been given their due consideration in historical narratives about the creation of a "modern" Lebanese middle class with liberal family values and less "traditional" gender roles, a historiography that is in need of revision. As he puts it, "Through these large physical [migrations] a new matrix of social relations was woven around multiple axes," including class, gender, sect, and family.[54] Return migration, he says, was the key factor in creating these productive social intersections among the Lebanese in Lebanon and the diaspora.

The importance of return migration to class, gender, sect, and family was not exclusive to Lebanese society. Cecilia Baeza offers an example of the importance of return migration for Palestinians within Palestine and in the diaspora.[55] She explores the practice of endogamy as a key feature of Palestinian socialization in Latin America during the first waves of migration to the continent. Through a comparison between migrants in Honduras, Brazil, and Chile, Baeza demonstrates that continuous migration and return served to secure not only the flow of wealth to Palestine from the Americas but also communal and familial bonds through marriage. As explained earlier, young men would often return to Palestine after accumulating some wealth in the Americas to bring different members of their families back with them. If unmarried, young men would also choose a spouse from within their original community, marry her in a traditional wedding in Palestine, and then bring her back with him to the Americas. Katrina and Jamil, however, did not have their traditional Palestinian wedding in 1914 owing to the impending war. That said, the practice of endogamy was seen as a highly effective means of social cohesiveness both at home and abroad.[56]

While Palestinian diaspora communities across Latin America were prospering economically and expanding socially, Palestinians in Palestine were also reaping benefits. On the one hand, families would prime their daughters for the possibility of marriage to a returning migrant, thus ensuring the family's gains from future remittances, as well as alleviating their financial burdens by being relieved of a family member. Alternatively, remittances were used as investments in Palestinian towns and villages to contribute to their economic and even aesthetic growth. New neighborhoods in the village of Beitin, near Ramallah, were built with remittances sent back by Beitini migrants. One of these neighborhoods was even named *hayy al-Amrikan,* or "the Americans' neighborhood," since much of it had been built with migrants' remittances.[57] These sorts of investments contributed to the development in Palestine of modern sensibilities and to the association of the migrant lifestyle with "material richness and modernity."[58]

The fact that Palestinian migrants continually returned to Palestine, either temporarily or permanently, before the dissolution of the Ottoman Empire "shows that despite long periods of absence, immigrants did not lose the connections to their original social space."[59] The continual bidirectional flow, furthermore, suggests the awareness among Palestinians of the importance of transferring Palestinian communal practices and structures from the homeland to the diaspora for collective economic and social success.[60] Re-creating the *hamula* (tribe) and the *haara* (neighborhood) in the diaspora through marriage within the extended family or religious community meant that patrimonial ties expanded and persisted and that for these migrants, maintaining and preserving communal structures and traditions was as important as economic gain for the jaaliya. Indeed, 92.5 percent of Palestinian marriages in Honduras between 1900 and 1929 were endogamous.[61]

Matrimonial processes were so intricate and deliberate for Palestinian diaspora communities that even marriage across denominations within the same religion was limited. Families went to great lengths to ensure that their Catholic sons chose Catholic wives, and likewise in Greek Orthodox families.[62] Unfortunately, and with the outpouring of Christians from the Mashriq in the first decades of the twentieth century, this meant that the selection pool grew smaller over the years. Several patrimonial family structures were even discontinued in Bethlehem's registers and reconstructed in Latin America.[63] Migration and return were thus significant to the expansion and maintenance of Palestinian family and community structures throughout the world.

THE MAHJAR AS A SECOND HOME

The history of Syrian migrant communities in Mexico and Chile, both hubs of Palestinian settlement, offers perspectives on how and why these migrants were so successful in the American mahjar. As seasoned merchants, they established profitable networks throughout Latin America as purveyors of "Holy Land" wares; they remained relatively removed from local politics and endogamous in their practices; and they printed Arabic periodicals that connected Arabic-speaking diaspora communities throughout the Americas with one another and with the watan. In time, they amassed enough economic clout that they gradually assumed prominent positions in industry, banking, commerce, and government.

Straddling the Border: The Arab-Mexican Experience

In 1916, Katrina's husband Emilio was killed in a train explosion near Saltillo, in northeast Mexico, in the midst of the ten-year Mexican Revolution, which had begun in 1910. Six months later, she lost one of her two daughters, Elena, to the flu. Katrina and her other daughter, Julia, remained with the Kabandes until 1919, when they moved to Long Beach, California, to live with Katrina's sister and brother-in-law, who had recently settled there. In 1921, Katrina married another Palestinian migrant, Suleiman Farhat, who had immigrated to California from Ramallah (figure 2). Katrina and Suleiman had three more

FIGURE 2. Katrina, Suleiman, and their children, California, 1922. On the left is Julia Kabande, Katrina's daughter with her late husband Emilio. On the right, George Farhat sits in his father's lap. Source: Personal collection of Kathy Kenny.

children, and the family moved back and forth between Mexico and the United States as Katrina and Suleiman opened small businesses together. They eventually settled in South San Francisco during the Great Depression, but their lives—and the lives of their children and grandchildren—in the mahjar were invariably defined by their mobile lives straddling the US-Mexico border.[64]

The choice to immigrate to Mexico was less complicated than the choice to leave to begin with.[65] Mexico's proximity to the United States was central to Syrian migrants' choice to stay there. As Theresa Alfaro-Velcamp argues, most migrants "probably preferred the United States as their final destination," but many were denied entry at Ellis Island due to "illiteracy and/or trachoma" and other illnesses.[66] And due to the risk of being sent home and thus needing to purchase a return ticket, Mexico became a "much more desirable alternative."[67] Close to the United States and relatively lax with immigration policies around the turn of the century, Mexico offered migrants the opportunity to enter North America successfully at the port city of Veracruz. Moreover, once disembarked, migrants could link up with relatives or other contacts through the existing network of Arabic-speaking peddlers, receive a credit line, and then venture into the interior of the country to sell goods.[68] With time, many could hope to find a way across the border into the United States, usually at El Paso, Texas. This route became so popular that the United States government worked to restrict it, though migrants continued to find their way into the country. Many Syrian migrants who settled on the Pacific coast of the United States first came through Mexico, where they had lived for several years, earning considerable wealth and learning Spanish.[69] As Katrina's story indicates, many families also Latinized their names; she left Palestine for Mexico to marry Emilio, no longer Jamil, Kabande.

But not all migrants from Greater Syria continued on to the United States. Many chose to remain in Mexico, filling economically profitable positions as experts of border trade. The hubs of Syrian settlement in Mexico were in the north of the country, in the states of Nuevo Leone, Coahuila, and Chihuahua, all bordering the United States. Maintaining a presence in Mexico was also considered a good decision as it ensured that migrants' relatives and friends back home were guaranteed a similarly successful experience if they chose to emigrate. Travel to Mexico first was considered a sure means of longer-term success in the diaspora for migrants who did not make it into the United

States or who did not wish to travel farther to South America, and migrants hoping for eventual settlement in the United States became aware of this migratory trend. Between 1878 and 1910, the thirty-two-year period known as the Porfiriato, 2,277 documented migrants arrived in Mexico from Greater Syria, though over 2,000 more migrants would have entered illegally during this period as well.[70] The Porfiriato was named after President Porfirio Diaz, whose dictatorial rule over the country directly contributed to the dramatic ten-year Mexican Revolution that began in 1910. However, due to Diaz's vast modernization initiatives and economic policies that expanded the agricultural, mining, and railroad sectors in Mexico, the government also encouraged the in-migration of large numbers of migrant workers and farmers during this period.[71] Notwithstanding these developments, however, most Syrian migrants continued to work independently as peddlers.

This was possible due to the existence of the credit-based peddling micro-economy that was dominated by Arabic-speaking migrants. Indeed, these migrants arrived in Latin America at an opportune moment: liberal Latin American regimes were willing to invest in infrastructure as part of their efforts to join the "global industrial order." And as merchants who had been exposed to the new global economic order back in Ottoman Greater Syria, "Mashriqis contributed to the creation of regional markets through their itinerant credit economies and transnational business networks."[72] This arrangement ensured that the jaaliya would withstand the economic consequences of the Mexican Revolution that ended the Porfiriato, and it also ensured that Syrian trading elites could espouse dual loyalties in their host country. They could connect with the modernizing elite and even the revolutionary movement, even though they preferred a significant degree of separation from the general population and avoided full assimilation.

This dual lifestyle, so to speak, was both a blessing and a curse to the burgeoning jaaliya. During the Mexican Revolution, Syrian migrants managed to make use of their peddling networks to transport food and arms to different revolutionary groups, especially along the border with the United States. As Alfaro-Velcamp argues, "The ability to cross into the United States enabled some Middle Easterners to amass large profits while Mexicans found their country in turmoil."[73] With many of Mexico's railroads destroyed during the violence, it was peddlers who managed to navigate the arid northern Mexican terrain with the most success, bringing them in direct contact with members of the different revolutionary factions as well as the elite. In this way, Syrians were able to profit from selling goods and bartering during the revolution, in addition to taking advantage of wealthy merchants' and officials' "unseemly activities such as looting, bribery, or extortion."[74]

The end of the Mexican Revolution in 1920 came two years after the end of World War I in the Middle East and Europe. And with the long economic and political recovery of various former Ottoman territories underway, many residents in the Mashriq sought economic betterment abroad. As earlier in the century, Mexico was again a popular destination thanks to the thriving economic networks the existing jaaliya had forged before and during the revolution and also thanks to the now very active lines of communication and financial remittance between the Middle East and Mexico. Since many of these migrants could speak Arabic, Spanish, and English, they could hope to tap into the United States border markets that many of their Spanish-speaking counterparts could not.[75] In the aftermath of the revolution, therefore, "Middle Eastern migration to Mexico quadrupled," and many of these migrants succeeded.[76]

The subsequent disproportionate prosperity of Middle Eastern migrants in Mexico incited resentment from many Mexicans. This "xenophobic attitude" continued into the 1920s and was further buttressed by skepticism at the governmental level.[77] Moreover, United States border officials began monitoring these Syrian migrant networks, thus spurring concern in Mexican and other Latin American government offices regarding the legality or desirability of Middle Eastern migrant trade in the Americas. Starting in 1921, Mexican ports were required to present passenger lists to United States authorities in order to prevent undocumented migrant entries into the United States.[78] Health inspections were also now being conducted at these ports, and steamship companies were tasked with transmitting this information to consular offices in North America and Europe. Consequently, and with more and more migrants from the Middle East making the journey westward, European, Mexican, and US steamship and border control agents were busy monitoring migrants' activities.[79] In this context, and with the Mexican economy suffering from a depression following the revolution, anti–Middle Eastern sentiment was on the rise in Mexico.

Mexicans began distrusting Syrian migrants, who seemed far less affected by the economic downturn and who were not even naturalized Mexican citizens. As foreigners who were dominating local jobs, Syrian migrants were deemed undesirable and Mexicans were quick to express their disapproval of this minority population in their midst. As a first step, in 1926, a Mexican immigration law was passed with an expanded list of "medical reasons for which immigrants could be refused entry."[80] Migrants also needed to have 10,000 pesos in their possession upon arrival at Mexican ports. And though this did not specifically target Middle Easterners, a new piece of legislation enacted in July 1927 was more explicit, giving a firm timeline for suspending immigration from the Middle East:

> Whereas the immigration of persons of Syrian, Lebanese, Palestinian, Arabic and Turkish origin has reached a limit that makes itself felt in the national economy in an unfavorable manner, . . . the Secretariat of the Interior . . . orders:
>
> FIRST—Commencing the last four-monthly period of the present year and during the years of 1928 and 1929 the admission of laboring immigrants of Syrian, Lebanese, Palestinian, Arabic and Turkish origin is suspended.[81]

To be sure, the legislation applied to all laborers not possessing 10,000 pesos upon arrival, and although spouses, children, and descendants were exempted, it is noteworthy that these nationalities were singled out and that Mexican legislators listed them specifically. That Lebanese, Syrian, and Palestinian migrants were listed separately in this legislation and that Arabic and Turkish were also included—presumably as ethnic groups falling outside the first three—suggest the transnational impact of the interwar mandates in the Middle East, as well as the migrants' shared reputation within the mahjar.

The Syrian population in Mexico had amassed considerable economic clout and concomitantly, to an extent, politically as well. As a result, the immigration legislation was not easy to enforce; migrant networks had grown so successful that bypassing Mexican authorities at arrival ports with direct bribes was not uncommon.[82] As Alfaro-Velcamp puts it, "it appears that Mexican policy makers were caught between responding to their constituents and appreciating the cheaper goods and services provided by the Middle Eastern merchants."[83] These services had reached virtually every part of Mexico thanks to the jaaliya's ceaseless and expansive peddling. Syrian migrants were effectively there to stay, whether legally or otherwise and whether Mexicans liked it or not.

Palestine West of the Andes: The Case of Chile

At the turn of the twentieth century, arriving in Chile was no small feat. Upon arrival in Buenos Aires after a six-week journey, migrants would have had to take a train west to the Andes in order to trek across the steep mountain range by mule before getting on a train on the Chilean side of the mountains to access the Chilean interior. Specifically, after disembarking at Buenos Aires, migrants would have taken a train westward to the town of Mendoza at the edge of the Argentine Andes. There,

> the adventurers had to wait for the weather to settle down before crossing the mountains. Then they undertook the journey on mules, challenging for about four days dangerous cliffs and the cold Andean mountain range in order to reach the city of Los Andes on Chilean soil. Only in 1908 did the railroad come to the mountain range of Puente del Inca and in 1912, to the station of Las Cuevas, and down to the Chilean station, Caracoles. From there, the passengers continued on mules to Juncal, where they boarded the Chilean Trans-Andean train.[84]

But if the journey was so long and dangerous, why did so many Palestinians choose Chile as a destination?

Emilio Dabed, a Chilean of Palestinian origin, has reflected on this question. In the preface to his doctoral dissertation, he wonders what would have motivated his great-grandfather, a merchant from Beit Jala, to choose Illapel, Chile, as a final destination for settlement and ultimately, permanent residence. The town of Illapel is home to approximately thirty thousand residents and is nestled in a valley where the western foothills of the Andes meet the coastal range, three hundred kilometers north of Chile's capital. The trip by car to Illapel from Santiago is strenuous even today; the hills rise dramatically a few kilometers inland from the flatter coastal terrain, and the single road that leads into the mountains narrows and snakes upwards for another forty kilometers before briefly plateauing and plummeting toward Illapel.

Following his doctoral fieldwork in Beit Jala, Dabed believes he managed to solve the mystery of why his ancestors chose Illapel. The landscape and climate they arrived to in Illapel would have reminded them of the Palestine they had left behind, as Dabed describes:

> I remember that from the age of twelve onward I started speculating about the reasons that brought my family from Beit Jala, Palestine, to my village, in Chile. They went from Beit Jala to Haifa; from Haifa on boat to Marseille and then to Le Havre in France; from Le Havre on boat again to Buenos Aires; and from Argentina, on donkey backs through the Andes mountain chain, to Chile, and

> subsequently, to Illapel. At the time, I advanced all kinds of metaphysical and material reasons for this journey and I am sure that all of them are part of the final explanation. Yet, I had to wait to know Beit Jala in order to understand that immigrants, wherever they go, try in one way or another and more often than not to reproduce the world that they know. I was in awe to discover that Beit Jala and Illapel were in many ways—geographically, topographically, climatically, economically and socially—almost one and the same place.[85]

Indeed, the hills that surround Illapel bear a striking resemblance to those of Beit Jala and its hinterlands. Frequent droughts, mild winters, and sunny, dry summers also characterize this mountainous enclave, much like most of Palestine's towns and villages inland from its humid coastline. Consequently, following weeks traveling by ship, foot, train, and mule, there is little wonder that these early migrants chose a destination that reminded them of home. Furthermore, Illapel's geographic isolation within the foothills of the towering Andes (figure 3) would have appealed to early migrants seeking less competitive markets to sell their goods. Buenos Aires and São Paulo were already flooded with migrants and merchants, and Santiago and Valparaiso (Chile's main cities) were but a few hundred kilometers away. The chances of economic success were thus promising.

On 8 October 1927, the Santiago-based *al-Watan* newspaper published a story in its "migrants' news" column that offers an interesting example of the relationship between Chile's landscape and its Palestinian migrants. In the story, two fictionalized Palestinian characters, Abu Azar and Abu Elias, sit and chat upon the latter's arrival in Santiago:

> ABU AZAR: Where have you been all these long years and why haven't I gotten news from you?
>
> ABU ELIAS: . . . I went back to the homeland and I was thinking about living out the rest of this life there, but after staying there seven months, I was shocked seventy times over! So, I traveled to Brazil, and two years later I moved to Argentina, and today I came to Chile because they told me that its climate and lifestyle are like our homeland. . . .
>
> ABU AZAR: You did well coming here. Chile is stunning in its values, rich in its nature, attractive in its lifestyle, and healthy in its regions.[86]

Chile appealed to Palestinian migrants of all ages. In the story, Abu Elias's wife had just died and his children had all married. Living out the remainder

FIGURE 3. The hills surrounding the town of Illapel, a hub for Palestinian settlement in Chile where the Andes meet the coastal range, bear a striking resemblance to the hills of many Palestinian cities, including Bethlehem, Beit Jala, Beit Sahour, Jerusalem, and Ramallah. Source: Franciscopf, CC BY-SA 3.0.

of his years in politically and economically volatile Palestine was far less appealing than the more relaxed lifestyle he could enjoy in Chile, a country that reminded him of home.

Though information is limited, a handful of scholars have explored the experiences of the first Palestinian migrants in Chile. Saffie and Agar show that, in 1941, 2,994 Arab families were registered in Chile. This included approximately fifteen thousand people, "of whom 85 percent were immigrants and 15 percent were their first offspring born on Chilean soil. Half of them were of Palestinian origin."[87] Specifically, Palestinians from the predominantly Christian townships of Beit Jala and Bethlehem were the most likely to emigrate and settle in Chile. Olguin and Peña estimate that between 1900 and 1930, 36 percent of Palestinians who arrived in Chile came from Beit Jala and 35 percent from Bethlehem.[88] The remainder would have come from Jerusalem, Ramallah, Beit Safafa, Beit Sahour, and other neighboring towns and villages. Beit Sahouris, for example, accounted for nearly 6 percent of Chile's Palestinian migrant community between 1900 and 1930.[89] Furthermore, it has been estimated that 18 percent of all Arab migrants in Chile came from Beit Jala and that 17 percent were from Bethlehem.[90] The continuous flow of migrants from Bethlehem and Beit Jala to Chile was due to the stories of success that migrants from those towns would have brought back to Palestine in the first years of migration in the latter half of the nineteenth century. Moreover, as evidenced by the Abu Azar and Abu Elias account, the attraction was the topographic and climatic similarity between Palestine and Chile. In other words, the proven promise of success in a diaspora that resembled home compelled many Palestinians in Bethlehem and Beit Jala to make the arduous journey to Chile.

In addition to its geographic and climatic resemblance to Palestine, Chile was in many ways the most promising economically for aspiring peddlers and merchants in the southern portion of South America. The prevalence of Syrian and Lebanese migrants in the richest commercial zones of Latin America—namely, São Paulo, Buenos Aires, and the Mexico-US border region—motivated many Palestinians to invest in "intermediary economical development zones like Chile, Peru, Bolivia, and Central America."[91] As in Chile, most of the migrants were Bethlehemites and Bajjaalis, with 90 percent of Palestinians in Central American countries coming from Bethlehem; Peru, however, received mostly Bajjaalis.[92] The choice to settle in less competitive markets was a way for these Palestinians to avoid what Baeza terms "suicidal concurrence" with their Syrian and Lebanese neighbors. For the benefit of the greater Syrian jaaliya, Palestinians chose less economically developed destinations to avoid competition with other Syrian migrants, or *paisanos* (countrymen), as they were wont to call each other.

Migrants in Chile were, in many ways, mimicking the entrepreneurial practices of their successful compatriots in neighboring countries. Jaaliyaat in Buenos Aires and São Paulo, for example, were considered role models in their businesses, as well as for their cultural, social, and political initiatives.[93] By the time Palestinian communities were forming in Chile, Syrian migrants in Brazil and Argentina had already established the first sports clubs, colleges, and schools as early as 1912 in São Paulo and Buenos Aires.[94] These communities also established many political organizations devoted to nationalist causes that concerned the homeland and the diaspora. Syrian and Lebanese migrants across the Americas played important roles in supporting and subverting homeland politics during the 1908 Young Turk Revolution, World War I, and the French mandate.[95] Chile, as a later stopping point for migrants, would see similar developments starting in the 1920s and 1930s. For example, Palestinian migrants in Santiago established the Club Deportivo Palestino in 1920, and to this day, it remains one of Chile's most loved soccer clubs.[96] Similarly, in 1924, they established La Sociedad Juventud Palestina, which worked to protect the rights of Palestinian migrants within Chile, including keeping them abreast of developments back home. Settlement in Chile, therefore, was beneficial not only for the large number of Palestinians there but also for the larger jaaliya in the mahjar.

As for settlement patterns within Chile, most Palestinians chose smaller towns and villages over the bigger cities. In Chile, these villages and towns included Illapel, La Calera, and Ovalle to the north of Santiago, and Concepcion, Chillan, and Los Angeles to the south. This type of "chain migration" was common to Syrian migrants, and by 1940, 62 percent of the total Arabic-speaking population of Chile was settled in towns and villages outside the major urban centers. Likewise, only 36 percent of Palestinian families chose Santiago as their place of work and residence.[97] Notwithstanding, Santiago and Valparaiso remained the hubs of the Chilean Arabic press, the jaaliya's associations and clubs, and European consulates to which migrants needed to go for permits to travel back home.

Although Palestinians in Chile would come to dominate large sectors of Chile's economy, including banking, manufacturing, and textiles, throughout the latter half of the twentieth century, they had humbler beginnings upon arrival to Chile. Like many Syrian migrants across the Americas, Palestinians in Chile first took to peddling Holy Land goods including olive wood, oils, and other Christian souvenirs they carried with them from Palestine. Within a few years of arriving, however, most would have found a means to travel less and to sell a variety of daily necessities locally, door to door. These vendors, Saffie and Agar point out, were known as *falte* due to the phrase they would yell repeatedly in broken Spanish while roaming the streets: "*¿Hay algo que le falte?*" ("Is there something missing?") as if to ask if anyone needed anything. These items included "scarves, socks, mirrors, pins, spools of thread, soap, buttons and combs." By the time the first Syrian peddlers set up shop in Santiago in 1910, they had visited virtually every settled part of Chile.[98] In fact, some have pointed out that Arabic-speaking peddlers exposed many remote regions of Chile to modern and urban sensibilities through their travels across the country.[99]

These accomplishments earned Syrian migrants relative economic success within Chile, though discrimination was not absent either, most of which was linked to their commercial habits. Various Chilean Arabic newspapers in the 1920s urged Syrian shop owners to reduce corruption in their trades. Specifically, these merchants were known to swindle customers and compete with shop owners in other neighborhoods. Moreover, the merchants were notorious for staying open until late in the evenings and on Sundays and holidays, which left neighboring merchants disgruntled and complaining to the Chilean authorities. Arabic newspapers thus frequently urged their readers to be more respectful of local custom by closing their shops before dinnertime and always on Sundays and holidays. In the exchange between Abu Azar and Abu Elias, for example, *al-Watan* newspaper reported a conversation in which the characters complain of the impropriety of members of their jaaliya who refuse to abide by local customs:

> ABU AZAR: I have begun thinking about an issue that has surprised me often when it comes to our community in Santiago. They keep their stores open until 9 p.m., while in Brazil they close up at 6 p.m. and go have dinner with their families. . . .
>
> ABU ELIAS: Until 9 p.m. only? [They stay open] until 10! Until midnight! They stay open on Sundays and on holidays, and if they could connect the night with the day, they wouldn't say no. Frankly, if they stopped work on church holidays, the scourge of the country would be relieved. But they do not abide by the sanctity of the national holidays to such an extent that they are not aware of the indignation of the Chilean countrymen. They have started openly holding [Arabs] in contempt. What would you say if you knew that many of our community's merchants stay working until 11 at night, and on Sundays and holidays until 1 and 2 in the afternoon?
>
> ABU AZAR: Jeez! Stop, stop! You've torn up my heart.[100]

But since many of these workers would have lived in dwellings attached to their stores, either in the back or upstairs, it is small wonder that many Syrian migrants lived modestly and worked around the clock to make ends meet.[101]

FIGURE 4. The Club Palestino, the main social, intellectual, and political venue for Santiago's Palestinian community, is located in the upscale neighborhood of Las Condes in Santiago de Chile. Source: Personal collection of Constantino Marzuqa Giacaman.

From simple street vendors to modest shop owners, Syrian migrants in Chile managed to enter virtually every sector of the country's economy fairly quickly. Within fifteen years, businessmen of Middle Eastern origin owned 80 percent of Chile's textile and spinning mills. In 1937, the Palestinian Yarur family, which today is one of the wealthiest in the country, built the country's most advanced spinning mill, introducing Chile's textile exports to regional markets. Other business ventures started by Palestinians in Chile include ones in the agriculture, livestock, mining, and pharmaceutical sectors, and by 1941, Middle Eastern–owned industries employed between nine thousand and ten thousand workers at a time of high unemployment and an economic crisis that had depressed the economy since the 1930s.[102] As Marco Allel put it in 1937, "members of Arab families, from their arrival to Chile, played an important role in business development; and in this country, it was in need of a strong push."[103]

TRANSNATIONAL MOBILITY AFTER THE WAR

World War I altered Syrians' decades-old migratory trends. In the years leading up to the war, figures suggest a surge in emigration attributed to preemptive behavior by many across Greater Syria who were escaping Ottoman conscription policies and imminent war. Indeed, the largest recorded difference in the number of Syrian migrants entering the United States was between 1912 (5,525) and 1913 (9,210), with a similar figure in 1914 (9,023).[104] However, during the war, there was a sharp decline: from 9,023 migrants registered in 1914, the number fell to 1,767 in 1915, 676 in 1916, 976 in 1917, 210 in 1918, and 231 in 1919.[105] This was in large part due to the blockade imposed by the Allies on the port cities of the Ottoman Empire starting in 1915.[106]

The end of the war and the lifting of the blockade were critical turning points for residents of the former Ottoman Arab provinces. Following the war, there was a resurgence in westward migration among residents of Greater Syria. In the Cairo-based *al-Basir* newspaper, for example, a correspondent writing from Beirut on 4 April 1920 described the unstoppable outpouring of residents from the region:

> The stream of emigration to lands beyond the seas and the New World is continuous and unchecked. Every ship carries its full quota. The local government is contemplating plans for checking the tide by persuasion, but there seems to be little hope unless the means of livelihood through commerce, industry and agriculture are rendered abundant and unless public safety is assured. Otherwise, and at this rate, emigration shall prove a general disaster extinguishing the little that is left in the life of this country.[107]

Yet once abroad, the option of return was no longer matter-of-fact. Beyond the economic and political instability in the watan that would have discouraged migrants from returning, the mandates system directly impacted Syrians' ability to move. The new interwar world legal order rendered Ottoman travel documents obsolete and introduced new ones issued by mandate authorities that included new restrictions and requirements for nationality and citizenship.[108]

The desire to return was most palpable among the increasing number of Syrians in the mahjar who were thrilled by the ouster of the Ottomans and who longed to be home, at least temporarily. In 1924, Hitti described the mood among Syrian migrants in the United States. He explained that as word of the Allies' victory in 1918 reached them in the diaspora and as "the lure of freedom [from Ottoman rule] and self-determination began to loom high in the sight of the submerged nationalities of the Old World," many Syrians started to consider returning.[109] But the unfortunate reality, Hitti continued, soon struck: returning to a homeland that was newly divided politically and that was recovering economically was not a wise choice for migrants or their families back home. He went on: "Many of the Syrian Americans who had planned to return home have since changed their mind, and the few who did return are already coming back. Some are going to Syria, but only to settle their business there, sell their property and bring the rest of their families."[110]

But by 1924, the option to return to settle businesses and collect family members was increasingly difficult for Palestinians. The new mandates in the newly divided Mashriq were governed differently, and the experiences of mandated communities with mobility varied. The ability to travel as a recognized national of a mandate—and the right to return home either permanently or for a visit—varied depending on the restrictions imposed on these populations by mandate governments. While the French in Syria and Lebanon and the British in Iraq and Transjordan encouraged the extension of French and British citizenship, respectively, to residents of and migrants from these regions, British authorities in Palestine prioritized naturalizing Jewish migrants above all others, effectively denying it to thousands of Palestinian migrants. How did these Palestinian migrants react to this new reality? How did this new reality impact the ways in which Palestinians addressed one another and how they identified with Palestine or within the larger jaaliya? In short, how did they grapple with their new ambiguous international standing that rendered them stateless and without international representation?

The experiences of Palestinian migrant communities with exclusion from Palestinian citizenship must be considered in tandem with the realities they were facing as a distinct community with its own desires, priorities, and concerns. These realities were fundamentally linked to a way of life to which they had grown attached, including bidirectional travel, open channels of financial remittance, as well as endogamous social arrangements. In other words, securing their ability to remain legally connected to Palestine while also living and working in the diaspora was crucial, both to migrants demanding their rights to Palestinian citizenship as well as to their families back home. To leave successful businesses and tightly knit communities in the diaspora and return to a newly mandated Palestine in order to qualify for citizenship was not an obvious or desirable choice, nor was it an economically responsible one. Palestinian migrants who protested the denial of their applications for citizenship were effectively fighting to preserve a way of life that meant a great deal to them, to their families, and to Palestine.

CHAPTER 2

THE TRADITION OF TRANSNATIONAL "PRO-PALESTINA" ACTIVISM

WORLD WAR I LED to the political and legal isolation of Palestine and Palestinian migrants in ways that inspired a generation of transnational Palestinian activism in the interwar period. But unlike the interwar years when Palestinian migrants' citizenship applications were denied, during and immediately after the war, Syrian migrants were largely calling for the defense of the territorial integrity of Greater Syria, with Palestine as its southern province. This was echoed by Syrian migrants throughout the mahjar, and by the time the victorious Allies met in Versailles in January 1919 for the start of the postwar negotiations, they were fully aware of the extent of transnational Syrians' objection to the plans to give Palestine to the Zionists.

On 18 February 1919, a copy of an article from a New York–based newspaper was enclosed in a dispatch to the Foreign Office in London under the translated title "Palestine Is Part of Syria; Will Palestine Awake from Its Deep Sleep?" The chief officer of the Egyptian Expeditionary Force in Palestine, Gilbert Clayton, included the following excerpt in the dispatch with the recommendation that "anti-Zionist articles" be forwarded to Emir Faisal—soon to be crowned King of Syria—for his information.[1] The excerpt from Clayton's dispatch, which he titled "Palestinians in America," reads as follows:

> We know quite well that our country is the object of Zionists. They intend to build up their glory, cost what may be, in the land of our Ancestors, and yet we do not take this matter into consideration.

> It is needless to explain to you the Zionist peril, as everybody knows it. You have to bear in mind that every Palestinian or rather every Syrian in the World, participated from afar in the patriotic demonstration. . . .
>
> When will Syrians give a helping hand to their brethren, the Palestinians, to defend their rights.
>
> Time is ripe, O brethren, let us give up every individual or religious interest and join together to strike the iron while it is hot.
>
> The whole of Syria is for Syrians, and every care must be taken to attain this end.[2]

Syrian migrants across the diaspora were aware of British and Zionist machinations to create a Jewish national home in Palestine. And while the Palestinian experience was distinct in the context of interwar European colonialism, mahjar press editors worked to bring it under the umbrella of Syrian anti-colonial nationalism, calling on all Syrians in the mahjar to set aside their differences and unite in the face of the Zionist threat.

By November 1917, when the Balfour Declaration was announced and made public, mahjar presses were championing a type of collective solidarity among their readers that was also expressed by nationalists in the Mashriq. To defend Palestine from the Zionists was also to defend Syria; Palestine was the southern part of Syria after all. How did this transnational solidarity around Palestine come to be, especially when, a year before, Palestine—and all of Greater Syria—had been Ottoman? If anti-Ottoman sentiment had been on the rise during the war, how did it spread to the diaspora? Who in the diaspora added their voices to the struggle for independence from the Ottomans? Who added their voices to the anti-colonial nationalist fervor that swept throughout the Mashriq when European powers severed the southern region of Greater Syria between the Jordan River and Mediterranean Sea and promised it to the Zionists?

THE SECRETS OF THE GREAT WAR

By the time British forces entered Jerusalem in December 1917, they and their allies had already laid the foundations for a radically transformed Greater Syria through a series of secret agreements. The most significant of these with regard to Palestine were the 1915 Constantinople Agreement, the 1916 Sykes-Picot Agreement, and the 1917 Balfour Declaration. Though the war was far from over by the time they began negotiating secretly in March 1915, the Triple Entente proceeded under the premise that they would defeat the Ottomans and carved up Ottoman territorial holdings between them. Their first agreement, the Constantinople Agreement, laid the groundwork for the subsequent two. Between March and April 1915, the Triple Entente determined that, in the event of victory, Russia would be granted Constantinople and the Dardanelles, Britain would maintain a "sphere of influence" in Persia, and France would annex all of Syria, including Palestine. They agreed to leave the governance of the Hijaz and its holy sites to Muslim rulers.

Then, in January 1916, British and French diplomats, Mark Sykes and François Georges-Picot, respectively, and with the assent of their Russian and Italian allies, met in secret to demarcate their territorial gains more concretely. During their meeting, Sykes and Picot determined that they would effectively divide the Ottoman provinces north of the Arabian Peninsula into British and French "spheres of influence." Britain was allocated the southern portion of geographic Palestine as well as the ports of Haifa and Acre and the vast desert territory east of the Jordan River as far as southern Iraq. France would take control of southeastern Anatolia, northern Iraq, Syria, and Lebanon. For their part, Russia would receive western Armenia, Constantinople, and the Turkish Straits, and Italy would take southern Anatolia. The remainder of Palestine, including the northern half of the Mutasarrifate of Jerusalem, as well as the Sanjaks of Nablus and Acre, would fall under "international administration." The Sykes-Picot Agreement was fully ratified by the British and French governments on 16 May 1916.

But the fate of Palestine was not yet sealed. A year and half later, on 2 November 1917, British foreign secretary Lord Balfour made his promise to Walter Rothschild. As with the previous agreements, the Balfour Declaration was premised on the assumption the Ottomans would lose the war. And weeks later, on 11 December, British forces made their formal entry into Jerusalem, effectively terminating four hundred years of Ottoman rule in Palestine. But unlike previous agreements, the Balfour Declaration was made public when Balfour's letter to Rothschild was published in London-based *The Times* a week later on 9 November.[3]

Britain's military occupation of Palestine continued until the newly formed League of Nations officially granted the territory to Britain as a mandate during the San Remo conference in April 1920. The conference was attended by the prime ministers of Britain, France, and Italy, though no representatives from former Ottoman territories were present.[4] The prime ministers of the victorious Allies divided Greater Syria and Iraq into mandates administered by Britain and France: Syria and Lebanon would be split into separate mandates, both governed by France, and Britain would split the southern portion of Greater Syria into the mandates of Transjordan and Palestine and to the east, the mandate of Iraq.[5] By December 1920, the League of Nations established the Permanent Mandates Commission (PMC) to oversee the operation of these mandates, including ensuring the fulfillment of Britain's 1917 promise to the Zionists.[6]

Residents of former Ottoman provinces immediately protested what they saw as the theft, division, and sale of their lands. Most significantly, the Syrian National Congress convened in Damascus beginning in May 1919 to draft a list of grievances and demands to submit to the Allies, who were weeks away from signing the Treaty of Versailles, effectively sealing the fates of former subjects of the Ottoman Empire. Representatives from all parts of Greater Syria, including Palestine and Lebanon, attended the congress in Damascus, and although disagreements arose, in their final report, members of the congress declared that they "reject the claims of Zionists for the establishment of a Jewish commonwealth in that part of southern Syria which is known as Palestine." They elaborated: "We desire that there should be no dismemberment of Syria and no separation of Palestine or the coastal region in the west or the Lebanon from the mother country."[7] The congress called for a united Arab Kingdom of Syria that included Syria, Palestine, Lebanon, and portions of northern Mesopotamia, and that would be governed by Emir Faisal.[8] These demands were ignored by European powers.

Throughout the diaspora, Syrian migrants also reacted immediately. In addition to the division of Greater Syria into mandates, the issue of Palestine received considerable attention. At once, Palestinian migrants formed committees throughout the Latin American mahjar, members of which sent petitions and letters to European authorities protesting, above all, the Balfour Declaration. This transnational "pro-Palestina" activism between 1918 and 1920, when the League of Nations established the PMC, laid the foundations for a tradition of communication between Palestinian migrants and British authorities that continued throughout the interwar years. That is to say, by the time Palestinian migrants were protesting the rejection of their applications for Palestinian citizenship starting in 1926, they had been partaking in a tradition of communication with their distant occupiers that had begun nearly a decade prior. Their demands in 1918, to be sure, were not for citizenship but that Palestine, rightfully belonging to them, not be given to the Zionists. Letters, petitions, and pleas between 1918 and 1920 from Palestinian migrants throughout the mahjar who identified with Palestine or as Palestinians signal their continuous and meaningful interest in their homeland and in preserving their multilayered connections to it. They also demonstrate the extent to which collective national Palestinian consciousness was a transnational development in the immediate aftermath of the war.

TRANSNATIONAL SYRIAN ACTIVISM AROUND THE WAR

The prewar years were significant for residents of the Mashriq and their counterparts in the mahjar. Much was at stake for them politically, especially as the Ottomans were appealing to them worldwide for their loyalty. What they said, what they did, and how they identified as a collective with transnational economic significance as subjects of the Ottoman Empire mattered, and they were aware of it. Searching for transnational Palestinian political activism before the interwar period would therefore be anachronistic. As migrants from Ottoman Greater Syria, their voices had not yet been parsed nationally, so to speak, into Syrian, Lebanese, and Palestinian in the historical record. For their part, the Ottomans also considered migrants from Greater Syria as one category. While provincial and confessional distinctions were recognized throughout the Ottoman Middle East, largely for taxation and legal purposes, these were not reflected in migrant registries. It would therefore be more accurate to speak of transnational Palestinian activism before 1918 as transnational Syrian, Syrian Ottoman, or Arab activism.

Nevertheless, different groups within the Syrian mahjar were taking shape in the years before the war, and they coalesced into multinational political collectives immediately after. Discussions about identification among Syrian migrants appeared as early as 1912. Nadi Abusaada's research indicates that Ottoman Palestinians in the mahjar discussed how they should identify before the fall of the empire. In an interesting interplay between homeland and diaspora periodicals, Abusaada shows how Palestinians debated the most suitable identifier that would answer the existential question used as the title of the newspaper article: "Who are we and what are we called?" The article appeared in the 12 October 1912 issue of Jaffa-based *Filastin* newspaper in Palestine, but it had first appeared in *al-Zaman*, an Arabic periodical based in Argentina. The article described an incident that occurred in Chile regarding the community's preferred mode of identification. Abusaada summarizes the incident: "Some, especially Palestinians, insisted to call themselves 'Ottomans' while others wanted to be called 'Syrian Ottomans.' . . . Both groups [were angered] when a committee had decided to call them 'Turks.'"[9] He reports that the author of the article that appeared in *al-Zaman* posed the question to his readers, emphasizing the community's resistance to many identifiers:

> Answer me, dear Palestinians, what are we called and what is our name? . . . If we called ourselves Syrians, you will refuse; if we called ourselves Turks, you will object; if we called ourselves Syrian Ottomans, you would turn your back to us; if we were Arabs, you would say that we are civilized and not Bedouin; and if you called yourselves Ottomans, we would also object. . . . The time for addressing what we are called and who we are is long overdue.

In response, the editors of *Filastin* had the following to say: "We see that the right decision was made by the immigrants of this district [Palestine] because they requested to be addressed as Ottomans, no more and no less, and not as Turkish, Syrian, or Palestinian, which separates the hearts rather than unifying them."

While the transnational debate described by Abusaada suggests the difficulty residents of Greater Syria experienced in selecting an identifier that would honor the historic, cultural, and political realities of a diverse population, it also indicates the fluidity of these categories of identification and the relative ease with which the debaters were willing to adopt one over the other before 1918. At the outset of the war in 1914, Arabic periodicals in the mahjar were quite diverse; each "was organized around the politics of its masthead and, sometimes, around distinct confessional communities." But, while confessionally based press in the mahjar might indicate the absence of secular forms of socialization and organization among Syrian migrants, it should also signal the growth of a "political community struggling for control over the terms of its civic nationalism and the responsibilities of the mahjar toward its homeland."[10] In other words, if prewar mahjar press nomenclature represented a community whose political character was in process, it is clear that mahjar Syrians' struggle to define themselves persisted with the continued frustration and denial of their nationalist aspirations after the war.

Syrian jaaliyaat throughout the Americas were never disconnected from one another or from the transformative events taking place in the Mashriq. Throughout the rapidly changing years surrounding World War I, migrants in New York, Buenos Aires, and São Paulo—the hubs of settlement and of mahjar presses—were invested in developments taking place back home—indeed, so much so that the Ottomans, Entente powers, and mandate authorities recognized the importance of these migrants for their own political gains. In the years surrounding the 1908 Young Turk Revolution, for example, the Ottomans took advantage of Syrian migrants' financial and economic networks. Publicizing their revolution as being aimed at constitutional reform and liberty, the Young Turks, represented by the new Committee of Union and Progress (CUP), promised freedom of expression, the lifting of press censorship, and pluralistic parliamentary representation. They made sure this campaign reached Syrians in the mahjar who had been agitating for these reforms. "Between 1903 and 1912," Stacy Fahrenthold explains, the CUP built consulates in Argentina, Brazil, and the United States and established "pro-CUP Syrian clubs" in each place. Thanks to migrants' wealth, these clubs "incentivized émigré investment in the homeland, promoted commercial links with foreign powers, and encouraged guest-work programs as well as permanent migrant repatriation." For the Ottomans, satisfied Syrian migrants would benefit an empire seeking "transhemispheric diplomacy." And certainly, Syrian migrants benefited from helping the Young Turks through enhancing their rights "as transnational citizens of the Ottoman Empire."[11]

Syrian migrants' loyalty to the Ottomans before the war was therefore mutually beneficial. The fact that *Filastin* newspaper's editors recommended Palestinians in Chile identify as Ottomans in 1912 despite internal disagreements is significant. Syrian migrants did not discuss seceding from the Ottoman Empire before the war:

> In 1912, no one in the mahjar envisioned a Syrian future outside the framework of the Ottoman Empire. Although the politics of Arabism, decentralism, and reformist criticism of the CUP were mainstream among Syrian migrants, there is little evidence to support assertions about Arab separatism in this diaspora before the First World War.[12]

But loyalty to the Ottomans was short-lived. Once Istanbul declared its alliance with Berlin in 1914, it effectively transformed its relationship to its Syrian migrant subjects in the Americas, many of whom looked to the United States as a beacon of reform and progress. What is more, and as discussed in chapter 1, Istanbul's censorship laws intensified throughout the provinces such that "Syria's newspaper industry sputtered in an environment defined by press closures and extra-judicial harassment of journalists."[13] Istanbul's heavy-handedness in Syria impacted the Syrian mahjar, especially since Ottoman consuls across the Americas were tasked with spying on Syrian jaaliyaat. Syrian migrants thus began calling for armed resistance against the Ottomans, even if it meant collaborating with the Entente. During the war, Syrians across the Americas contributed to humanitarian relief efforts that benefited the Allied forces. They also translated pro-Entente propaganda into Arabic, recruited for the American Army, and enlisted in Entente armies, including the French, British, American, and Canadian ones.[14] The Syrian mahjar press from New York to Santiago became the staging ground for anti-Ottoman propaganda. What all periodicals shared, to be sure, was a call for a liberated Syria.

The end of the war and defeat of the Ottomans was cause for celebration across much of the Syrian mahjar. Not only had they chosen the side of the victors, they had also contributed to the liberation of their homeland through their various efforts, especially through fighting in Entente armies. Syrian migrants thus shared their counterparts' expectations in the homeland that European forces would reward them, if not with immediate independence, then with fulfillment of geopolitical aspirations. In the immediate aftermath of the war, Syrian migrants expected that the demands of their compatriots in the Syrian National Congress would be met when European powers convened in Versailles in 1919. Similar congresses formed throughout the Americas, most notably the Syrian Congress of Buenos Aires and the New Syria National League (NSNL) of New York City, of which Philip Hitti was a member. The NSNL's slogan "Syria for the Syrians, independent and undivided under American guardianship" represented the organization's platform: "Greater Syria's unity (including Mount Lebanon and Palestine) and independence under an Arab government and a limited American Mandate."[15] These demands mirrored those of the Syrian National Congress in Damascus, as well as those of pro-Palestina collectives in Latin America. Preserving the territorial integrity of Greater Syria, restoring its administration to its peoples with the help of the United States, and keeping European hands off it were demands heard from Syrians across the world.

For their part, British and French authorities attending the 1919 Paris Peace Conference went to great lengths to keep the plethora of petitions from Syrians in the Mashriq and the mahjar out of the conference meeting halls. Indeed, the NSNL's representative was denied entry at the 1919 Paris Peace Conference. With the majority of their voices thus silenced at the conference, Syrians were largely unrepresented during the negotiations that determined their fates. Instead, British and French authorities at the conference "constructed a significant legal fiction: that the Arab Middle East lacked a viable means to independence and required foreign tutelage, and that Syrians and Lebanese—especially those living in diaspora—supported the Mandate principle."[16] And so, while most Syrians throughout the diaspora fervently protested French and British rule, through a strategic transnational propaganda campaign, France and Britain managed to present the idea that newly liberated former Ottoman subjects desired European rule. This tactic was exposed early on, and migrants took to their periodicals to warn their readers of British and French schemes to silence and misrepresent them. As a result, British and French authorities faced a two-pronged task: to colonize the Mashriq and domesticate the mahjar.[17]

Notwithstanding the shared goals of the Syrian National Congress and the NSNL, among others, the mahjar in the immediate postwar years remained home to an array of nationalist sentiments that were represented by a spectrum of political organizations and publications. Across the mahjar, ambitious nationalists of all creeds took the postwar moment as an opportunity to organize into new collectives representing different political interests back home. The years between 1918 and 1920, when the League of Nations effectively dealt a decisive blow to nationalists calling for an undivided Syria by establishing the mandates system, thus witnessed the proliferation of nationalisms in the mahjar. Migrants began organizing into Syrian, Lebanese, and Palestinian collectives that would apply pressure on British and French authorities in new ways. The efforts of these groups "papered the Syrian colonies of the Atlantic from Canada to Chile," and their activism certainly inconvenienced their distant overlords.[18] By occupying their homelands, French and British mandate authorities were "forced to contend with the political demands of a half million emigrants who began gathering outside French [and British] consulates across the Americas."[19] As Palestinian, Syrian, and Lebanese subjects of the new mandates, migrants demanded rights to voting, transnational representation and protection, and repatriation. These demands were heard around the world in multiple languages and in different written mediums.

Postwar Transnational Pro-Palestina Activism

With the news that Britain promised Palestine to the Zionists in late 1917 reaching North and South American shores, Syrian communities across the mahjar spoke out vehemently against the separation of Palestine from Syria and the consequent disenfranchisement of Palestinians. With its promise to the Zionists, Britain made its goals in Palestine clear, and it was wholly committed to fulfilling them. The creation of a Jewish "national home" in Palestine would thus become the most cited cause for protest among Palestinians worldwide. Hundreds of petitions authored by self-identified Palestinian committees across Latin America protested British policies in Palestine. Collectively, these documents indicate the preponderance of what was termed "pro-Palestina" activism at a transnational level among Palestinian migrants and their allies in the immediate postwar context.

Certainly, Palestinian migrants were not alone in their transnational outcry following the war. Lebanese and Syrian migrants also had much to protest with France's takeover of Lebanon and Syria. Yet beyond partitioning lands and imposing foreign rule, Palestinian migrants stood to lose all connections to Palestine. As a result, they seized the moment to organize into Palestinian political committees and demand national rights from British authorities across the Americas. The most salient themes in these demands were that Palestine not be split from Syria, that it not be given to the Zionists, and that it be delivered to its rightful heirs, the Palestinians. Most of these petitions, to be sure, included a confessional element. Palestinian migrants were largely Greek Orthodox, and they had been anticipating the liberation of Palestine from Ottoman Muslims. Britain's choice to give it to the Jews was therefore a cause for concern among the depleting minority of Christian Palestinians who wished to secure their presence in Palestine. Altogether, the petitions signify the first transnational protests among Palestinian migrants about the future of Palestine as the southern region of Greater Syria and the place of its dispersed peoples in relation to it.

As the 1919 excerpt Clayton sent to the Foreign Office suggests, Palestinians in the mahjar frequently expressed their steadfastness in the struggle for Palestinian self-determination in terms of greater Syrian nationalism. This call to protect the integrity of Greater Syria with Palestine as its southern province was also voiced inside Europe. On 28 March 1919, the Paris-based Fédération Palestinienne submitted a petition to Eric Drummond, member of the British delegation to the Paris Peace Conference—and a month later, the first appointed secretary-general of the League of Nations—that outlined the "claims which we have the keen desire to present to the Peace Conference." Namely, the petitioners wanted it to be known that they considered that "Palestine is an integral part of Syria" despite recent attempts to separate the two. But "in the case that Palestine is to form an independent state, its inhabitants demand that they be considered within the principle of 'the right of the people to self-determination,'" therefore refuting other religious claims to sovereignty over Palestine. The petitioners explained: "The only proprietors of this country are and must remain its inhabitants: the Palestinians. For the peace and tranquility of the entire world, and to avoid conflicts from which this country has cruelly suffered, no privilege should be given to any nationality or to any religion."[20] Yet even the demands of political Palestinian collectives within Europe were ignored.

The precarious relationship of Palestine to Syria and vice versa after the war was a point of contention between Palestinian migrants and the British vice consul in Bolivia. On 28 November 1918, the Committee for the Liberty of Palestine in Oruro, Bolivia, declared in a petition to the British consular offices in La Paz that the members, "representing more than four thousand Palestinians and Syrians resident in the Republic of Bolivia, desire to express to the Allied Powers the feelings that agitate our hearts." These petitioners considered themselves to be both Palestinians and Syrians, and the distinction they drew between the two identifiers was meant to forestall the possibility that the consular office would distinguish between them legally, which it was wont to do. These Syrians, many of whom also identified as Palestinians in Bolivia, were Christians and felt concerned that the oppressive rule of the Ottomans would be replaced by the more serious "Israelitish [*sic*] danger." For them, the "evil that threatens our people" was embodied in the moral and racial distinctions that characterized the Christian-Jewish divide. If the Jews were to maintain power in Palestine, they believed that "the exodus of Christians would be its inevitable consequence." To prevent this inevitability, members of this committee, "which represent the sincere and unanimous wish of all the Palestinians scattered throughout the world, and the common feeling of our race," asked for a free and sovereign nation to be governed by the Allied powers and not by "the Israelites."[21]

When reviewed by the Foreign Office on 20 February 1919, it was determined, however, that the petitioners' concern "does not seem to be very important" and that it was "merely fear." Then, the vice consul at Oruro notified the Foreign Office that the Committee for the Liberty of Palestine was "really representative of the Syrian Colony . . . of Bolivia" and therefore not exclusively Palestinians.[22] Although Palestinian migrants considered themselves to be Syrians, the vice consul believed otherwise. In early 1919, therefore, a little more than a year after British forces entered Jerusalem and began their military occupation of Palestine, British authorities were already treating Palestine as a distinct territory. While members of the Committee for the Liberty of Palestine considered Palestine to be the southern region of a contiguous Greater Syria and thus saw its defense from a Zionist takeover as a Syrian and a Palestinian struggle, a British consular officer in Oruro believed Palestine was altogether separate from Syria. Its administration as a territory would be distinct from any other part of Syria and, as the 1925 citizenship ordinance would make clear a few years later, only those who could satisfy the British mandate's criteria for proving Palestinian citizenship would receive it.

The fear of a Jewish takeover of Palestine reverberated across the predominantly Christian Palestinian diaspora. On 17 December 1918, the British legation in Santiago, Chile, sent a dispatch to the British foreign minister, James Balfour, in London in which were enclosed two letters written by "the Syrian Pro Palestine Committee urging the national claims of Syria and protesting against the establishment of a Jewish State in Palestine."[23] One of the signatories of the letters, the first of which was written on 19 November and the second on 3 December, was the Orthodox bishop of Tyre and Sidon, Elie Dib, who at the time was residing in Santiago de Chile. Mr. Stronge of the British legation in Santiago added that the diverse Syrian population in Chile was quite successful, having established itself through its modest yet reliable and efficient commerce. In the first letter, the bishop started by defining himself as "Palestinian by birth and Syrian by diocese," and he quickly explained that he had taken up temporary residence in Santiago. Dib therefore considered himself to be both Palestinian and Syrian: Palestinian because he was born in geographic Palestine, and Syrian because he had joined the Syrian Orthodox diocese, which had a long association with historic Syria. Next, he expressed his "sincere congratulations" to the victorious Allies for their heroic triumph over the Ottomans, which ensured "universal peace." These sentiments, he added, were also those of his "Syro-Palestinian Christian brothers," whom he identified as Arabs by race. For Dib, while it was important to highlight the political component of Palestine in the context of British colonialism, there was no ethnic, linguistic, religious, or cultural distinction between Palestinians and Syrians. They were both Arabs, and the two modes of identification were not mutually exclusive.

In the second letter, Dib wrote the British foreign minister on behalf of "Palestinians resident in Chile," who addressed themselves "respectfully" to the Allies. He then elaborated on Palestinians' rightful claims to Palestine: "Few people have as many titles to the recognition of their nationality as the Palestinians." He explained why by highlighting Palestine's Arab past:

> Ethnologically, we are Arabs since the seventh century; the Arab conquest smothered the extant races and idioms and replaced them: our language is actually Arabic, and despite the Turkish constraint, the Turkish language, which was imposed on us, it remains the official language, and nothing else. . . .
>
> The Palestinians . . . have made contact with the outside world; they know how to employ themselves with success in all branches of human activity; they have learned the benefits of democratic governments and are assimilated with the modern forms of the political state.
>
> Reassured about the legitimacy of their claims to autonomy, the Palestinians are moved by the same movement that tends to give the Jews their property rights, in the heart of their country.[24]

The racialization of the Palestinians' right to an autonomous state reminded London of its promises to the Arabs following the surrender of the Ottomans and the various agreements and treaties signed between British and Arab forces.[25] If Palestinians were also Arabs, and certainly not Turks, then they, too, were due their independence. To be sure, Dib's reiteration of the legitimacy of Palestinians' claims to national autonomy within the context of a greater Arab past was commensurate with the rising tide of Arab nationalism in the early twentieth century that called for collective national self-determination as Arabs. Palestinians, like Jews, were fully informed of the benefits of democratic, representative state structures; they were therefore also entitled to their own nationality on their own land.

Dib then explained the injustice being committed against Palestinians with the impending Jewish takeover of Palestine, and he linked this to nationality: "The principle of nationalities is the basis of the ultimate goals pursued by the Entente. It is therefore in the name of this principle that the Israelites could pretend to create a state. But is it also in the name of this principle that our nation should be used to give them satisfaction?" Dib left no doubt that he considered Palestine to be the site of a self-determined national home for Palestinians. Following a schematic historical account of the claims of the Jews to Palestine, which portrayed them as easily dismissed, Dib declared: "The Palestinian Arabs, Christians and Muslims, live in a state of perfect accord, and the difference of faith does not prevent this harmony."[26] He signed the letter as honorary president on behalf of the Pro-Palestine Committee in Chile. And though "no action [was] taken in this matter" by the Foreign Office, it is noteworthy that in this early phase of transnational solidarity with Palestine, leaders among diaspora Arabic speakers strategically employed categories of identification including Palestinians, Arabs, and Christians, when making transnational political claims relating to Palestine. In referring to Christianity within the struggle for Palestinian self-determination, Dib effectively pandered to what he believed he and Palestinians, unlike Jews, shared with Britain.

This perception that Palestinian migrants shared their Christianity with British authorities was salient in activism among the jaaliya in Mexico. On 14 December 1918, the British vice consul in Monterrey, Mexico, conveyed a petition from the Sociedad Patriotica de Palestinos of Linares, a small town to the south of Monterrey, to King George V of England, French president Raymond Poincaré, and the pope. Another copy of the petition was evidently sent to the president of the United States, Woodrow Wilson. The document, though relatively short, started with the petitioners' conclusive declaration that Palestine belongs to them, the natives of Palestine, and not the Jews:

> We the undersigned, natives of Palestine . . . , formerly under the domination of the Ottoman Empire, the territory of which we have always regarded as the soil of our ancestors and for which we feel the sacred love and respect which every native should feel for the country of his birth, submit to Your Majesty . . . that it has come to our knowledge . . . that the forthcoming Peace Conference

> between the Allied Nations and the Central Powers will discuss the question of the delivery of our beloved country to the Jews, and considering, both we and the great majority of our compatriots, that this action not only is not desirable, but is an encroachment of our rights and contrary to all humanitarian sentiments, and feeling most profoundly that it is our duty to cooperate in finding a better solution of the problem . . . all the children of Palestine who live in this small town in the Republic of Mexico have joined together to raise our voices, filled with emotion and moved by the modest ardent patriotic feelings TO PROTEST IN THE MOST ENERGETIC AND SOLEMN MANNER AGAINST THE DELIVERY OF OUR MOST BELOVED PALESTINE TO THE JEWS.[27]

For the members of the Sociedad Patriotica de Palestinos, who represented the "children of Palestine" in Linares, Palestine had always belonged to its native population, the Palestinians.

They then enumerated reasons for why Palestine, for them a historically Christian homeland for both European and Arab Christians, would not be a good location for a Jewish state. Specifically, they conveyed why they believed Britain giving their beloved Palestine to the Jews would pose a grave threat to Christian Palestine and its Christian inhabitants:

1. Jews do not like us and their lack of sympathy towards us is traditional.
2. The result of this traditional lack of affection would be ill treatment, which would breed hate.
3. The Palestinians would suffer from oppression, which is unworthy of modern civilization.
4. The Jews do not profess the religion of love instituted by Jesus Christ, whom they crucified and ridiculed.
5. The germs of mutiny and revolution would be sown on each occasion when distinctions were made in the application of the laws of justice.
6. The Jews do not speak the same language and perhaps are ignorant of the Palestinian tongue.
7. It would be difficult for the Jew, who does not love the inhabitants of Palestine, to govern, and if this were by misfortune to happen, our poor people would suffer the same fate as in the time of the Turks.

The president of the society, Juan Buchaar, reflected the concerns and fears of a population of mostly Christian Palestinian migrants who believed that the replacement of Ottoman Muslim rule with Jewish rule would spell the end of Christian hopes for Christian protection in their homeland. Buchaar and the petitioners hoped their appeal would resonate with their Christian European occupiers. The petition signaled a pervasive attitude among the diaspora community—namely, that patriotism and longing for the homeland were still linked to confessional attachments. The Foreign Office pointed this out in its internal notes on 4 February 1919, in which it dismissed the Linares petitioners' concerns:

> This is evidently the petition of more Syrian Christians now resident in Mexico, against the establishment of Jewish rule in Palestine. Their principal objection is religious. If a reply is considered necessary, it might be well to point out that in the declaration the civil and religious rights of non-Jews are fully ascertained while nothing is said about the establishment of a Jewish government.[28]

Not all calls for the rights of Palestine and Palestinians from the diaspora were driven by religion, however. In fact, most did not mention it and, instead, employed Arab indigeneity as cause to honor Palestinians' national self-determination. On 26 December 1918, Abdullah George Abu Ghattas of the Club Arabe Palestina in Arequipa, Peru, submitted a petition on behalf of "the Palestinians and Syrians residing in Peru" to the British foreign minister in London, requesting his support "to obtain independence" for Palestine. Speaking on behalf of this collective, Abu Ghattas expressed his "confidence in the sincerity of the declarations made by Mr. President Wilson" regarding self-determination. "It is the Arab race," he affirmed, "that populates Palestine and Syria," and as for the Jews, they were "not the indigenous." For Abu Ghattas, national self-determination was determined by race, which he linked to indigeneity, not religion. Like Dib, Abu Ghattas believed that Arabs, and not Christians, Muslims, or Jews specifically, were entitled to self-determination. Abu Ghattas concluded: "Convinced of our rights and encouraged by the principles proclaimed by Justice, we hope for the support of His Majesty and His government."[29]

Other pro-Palestina groups were less indignant about Jewish self-determination, but they agreed that Palestinians' native connection to Palestine outweighed any other. On 28 December 1918, days after Abu Ghattas's petition, Palestinians in San Pedro Sula, Honduras, submitted a petition to the Paris Peace Conference, which would begin in January 1919, protesting the establishment of a national home for the Jews in Palestine.[30] In the document, the petitioners referred to themselves as "citizens of Palestine." They also explained that they had no objection to the creation of a nation for the Jews: "Such intentions are worthy of the noble ideals which the Allies have pursued in the tremendous struggle which has come to an end." Their objection, rather, came as a subtle reminder of the proper and just conduct of "the law of life." They explained further that their rights to be citizens of Palestine were indisputable:

> We have been citizens of Palestine, by descent and birth, for more than two thousand years. . . . We Palestinians, decimated and persecuted by the cruel Ottoman despotism, live today in hospitable foreign lands. . . . In the formation of a nationality in our native lands, the racial ties and the possession of the country for twenty centuries give us the most legal right to be citizens of the newly born country.[31]

These petitioners used the language of citizenship, determined by descent, birth, race, and shared experience in the land of Palestine, to lay claim to nationality. Accordingly, they believed that Jews should be able to do the same, but elsewhere.

What is more, for this group of Palestinians in Honduras, nationality and citizenship were co-constitutive. As citizens of Palestine, they were entitled to be nationals of a self-determined Palestine, and as nationals of Palestine, they were entitled to Palestinian citizenship. Though the 1925 Palestinian Citizenship Order-in-Council would not be enacted for another six years, for these petitioners, the threat of losing nationality was tantamount to losing their lands to a Jewish nation. They explained that the loss of nationality would leave them exiled, wandering the world without the protection of a flag:

> The principal conditions of nationality are the possession of territory and the community of interests, beliefs and ideals of a race. . . . We have complete faith that this Supreme Conference will not take away from us the country which saw our birth; that it will not consent, with its just judgment, to leave us exiled and wandering through the world, without the consolation of being able to protect ourselves beneath a flag; and that it will not deprive us of the lands in which for twenty centuries our forefathers have dwelt, and where we ourselves have lived, consecrating it with the love of our life. No! That will never happen!

In their impassioned declaration, the petitioners held European leadership accountable for securing the transnational status of Palestinians. They were certain the leaders would not compromise their rights, but they subtly warned them nonetheless:

> But if unfortunately, through the bias of the actual historical moment, this Honourable Conference should forget its noble mission of justice, . . . we would energetically protest, with the firmness which right and reason give us, in defense of noble and just causes, and would appeal in the future, before the world's conscience, in the supreme tribunal of History.

As early as December 1918, a year after the British forces entered Jerusalem, Palestinian migrants in Honduras were vehemently protesting imperial schemes on the basis of national and citizen rights that they believed were owed them as Palestinians still significantly connected to the land and history of Palestine.

That Palestinians transnationally were entitled to national self-determination in Palestine based on a history of shared experiences that were inextricable from the land was a critical component of Palestinian migrants' protests against giving Palestine to the Zionists. Where else would Palestinians form a self-determined nation if not in Palestine? On 27 January 1919, Palestinians in Managua, Nicaragua, sent a petition to the chairman of the Paris Peace Conference protesting "energetically against any idea of being under an Israelite Government."[32] The petitioners, speaking on behalf of the "Palestine Colony" in Nicaragua, added: "We aspire to have our age-old dreams of autonomy realised, in support of which we invoke our ethnical and geographical characteristics, our history and our customs."[33] Their desire was for autonomy as a people with a common ethnicity and geography, two characteristics that the Zionists did not share with them. Much like the appeals of the members of the Syrian National Congress in Damascus, the migrants' protests from Honduras and Nicaragua were ignored. But they suggest that in 1918, an effort to demand national rights along religious, racial, geographic, historical, and communal lines existed among Palestinians transnationally. These Palestinians considered themselves to constitute a community that was connected to the land of Palestine in southern Syria and that was awaiting a new form of legal sovereignty after the war.

The surge in petitions and protests surrounding the 1917 Balfour Declaration and the Paris Peace Conference from across the world point to the transnational networks of political and historical identification with Greater Syria as a homeland among migrants as early as 1918. Palestinians in Palestine, the

United States, Nicaragua, Peru, Chile, Honduras, and elsewhere who identified themselves as Palestinians, Syrians, Christians, Muslims, and Arabs were active in voicing anger and disbelief at a range of British policies that affected the Palestine of southern Syria. These petitions, along with tense and increasingly untenable realities in Palestine, compelled London's high-ranking officials to action. In an urgent letter submitted to the Foreign Office in London on 26 March 1919, Clayton explained the risk of anti-Zionist activity to British authorities in Palestine. These concerns, he explained, were compounded by news emanating from the Americas that Palestinian migrants were also agitating for Britain to revoke the promises made to the Zionists. Writing from Cairo, he immediately clarified that the recent increase in "anti Zionist propaganda" among Palestinians signaled that Muslims and Christians were unsettled by the "fear that political and economic advantages may be given to Jews in [the] peace settlement." The fear, he continued, "is increased by the rash actions and words of the Jews themselves. . . . There are considerable grounds for belief that anti Jewish riots are being prepared in Jerusalem, Jaffa and elsewhere."[34]

Clayton's alarm at the tense situation in Palestine was shared by Palestinians transnationally who were also voicing concern at the increasing religious fanaticism in Palestine. Unlike Clayton, however, Palestinian migrants were concerned with the repercussions of disenfranchising Palestinians from their rights to national self-determination. On 22 February 1919, members of the Central Committee of the Pro-Palestine Society in Central America submitted a petition to the Paris Peace Conference. Written in Guatemala, the petition called for members of the Peace Conference to delay making their decision regarding the future of Palestine so that in the interim, one or several of the Allied forces could govern it instead of the "fanaticism par excellence" that characterized Zionists and their opponents in Palestine. "This is the most prudent solution," the petitioners declared. In an internal memorandum, however, the Foreign Office overlooked the committee's concerns:

> These anti-Zionist petitions from Palestinians at home and abroad are becoming onerous.
>
> But [the Zionists] are expecting a Jewish commonwealth, and will, it is to be hoped, be reassured when the constitution we contemplate is accepted by the Conference and promulgated.[35]

The Foreign Office therefore dismissed the suggestion of the Central Committee of the Pro-Palestine Society in Central America for an interim government composed of Allied forces—and not fanatics among Jews and Arabs—as anti-Zionist. Britain was steadfast in its promises to the Zionists.

In the aftermath of World War I and the instatement of European rule in the Mashriq, Palestinian activists throughout the mahjar formed collectives that staked claims to transnational rights as Palestinians. In doing so, they strategically singled out Palestine as the site of their nationalist aspirations based on a long history of indigenous and racial attachment to the land. This logic was due, in great part, to Britain's plan to separate Palestine from Syria and to give it to the Zionists. Palestinian migrants thus came together and petitioned European leaders in collectives that identified as Palestinian, much to the chagrin of British consuls. Yet these groups also considered themselves to constitute a larger collective of Syrians aspiring for national self-determination from European rule. That British and other European officials did not agree that they were at once Syrians *and* Palestinians indicates the fundamental inconsistencies between European laws and policies on the one hand and multinational Syrian activists' claims and desires worldwide on the other. Petitions and other written protests submitted by self-identified pro-Palestina collectives throughout the mahjar reflect this deadlock and the uphill battle Palestinians would continue to fight as Britain's partisan rule became more entrenched in the watan throughout the interwar years.

THE NEW MEANING OF NATIONALITY

The establishment of European mandates in Greater Syria affixed new meanings to modes of identification that migrants now had to deliberate legally and politically. With the term *Ottoman* no longer applicable or desirable as an identifier and with the term *Syrian* no longer sufficient, formerly Ottoman migrants in the mahjar now had to affiliate with new legal and political configurations known as Lebanon, Syria, and Palestine in order to be heard. As Eric Hooglund puts it, in the interwar period, "the development of local identities . . . was encouraged" both within the Middle East and abroad. He explains that migrants began questioning their origins after the war: "Were the Syrians who had immigrated from villages in Lebanon and Palestine still Syrian? Or were they Arabs . . . ? The tendency was to identify according to the new lines of nationality, that is, as Lebanese, Syrians, and Palestinians."[36]

Ottoman + Syrian no longer used – names as a form of identity – striped

Additionally, the failure of the Syrian nationalists to secure a desired outcome for Syrians after the war unleashed a maelstrom of activism that lacked the unanimity presented by Syria's representatives at the peace conference. While the instatement of the mandates activated migrant communities politically throughout the Americas, it also uncovered the reality that migrants did not, in fact, agree on a plan for life in Greater Syria after the Ottomans. As Philip Hitti explained in 1924, the interwar mandate order amplified confessional cleavages in the Syrian mahjar: Christian Syrians often preferred foreign intervention after the war, ideally American over British or French, whereas Muslim and Druze Syrians championed Arab rule under Emir Faisal.[37] Distance from the homeland was therefore not the only impediment to nationalist mobilization among these diaspora communities. Coalescing into a political collective with a shared vision for a social and political future despite the scope and diverse makeup of the diaspora from Santiago to New York often proved to be half the battle. However, notwithstanding the variations in migrants' political visions about the homeland, mahjar periodicals substantiated an expanding and unifying discourse of solidarity and identification with the Greater Syria watan, including Palestine, Syria, and Lebanon, among migrants throughout the diaspora.

The call to political and nationalist activism in mahjar publications impelled a readership of confessionally and ethnically diverse and conflicted Syrian migrants to remain connected to—and to care for—the homeland. It is therefore ironic that the promise of national self-determination nominally offered by French and British mandate authorities was in many ways the main shared political platform across these diaspora communities whose homeland was being divided with borders. Nevertheless, given the complex and conflicting range of voices in the mahjar, the documents indicate that the surge in nationalist rhetoric in diaspora periodicals was more a call for migrants to put into practice the liberal principles of collective social and political activism than a call for return to the homeland to engage in organized anti-colonial resistance. Syrian migrants' demands in periodicals for independence and national self-determination should therefore be considered a sort of collective release for migrants who felt frustrated with the way things turned out after the war back home and who were engaging with a new world order defined by political self-determination for transnationally diverse groups.

Challenging the Mandates Transnationally

The mandates transformed Syrian migrants' daily lives in fundamental ways. Not only would they need to decide how they identified nationally, they would also need to be able to prove to French and British consuls throughout the mahjar why they qualified for whichever identifier they chose. As Camila Pastor puts it, "The recognition of Mahjaris as simultaneously imperial subjects (Ottoman, French) and postcolonial subjects (Lebanese, Syrian, Mexican) alerts us to the fact that they navigated geographies framed by distinct and unequal projects."[38] French and British officials were the sole authorities to confirm these identifiers with a stamp in a new travel document: the passport. The passport system would become the surest way for mandate authorities to regulate their new subjects' ability to move, reside, or seek legal representation and recourse transnationally.[39] Throughout mandate rule, French and British authorities increasingly used citizenship as a means of demographic control in their territories, keeping those they wanted in, and those they did not want out.[40] This transition from Ottoman to European rule "was vital, establishing new boundaries within Mahjar networks and communities, organizing institutions, aligning categories of subjects. It was essential to migrant social mobility."[41]

Mandates forced migrants from former Ottoman territories throughout the diaspora to make a decision about who they were nationally and thus, how they would be identified and represented legally. The literal and figurative social spaces of mahjar Syrians' worlds were radically restricted with the instatement of mandates. Prior to the interwar period, these migrants enjoyed the mahjar as "a multifaceted transregional formation" that they inhabited "as the floating world of *elsewhere*," worlds away from the watan but invariably still connected to it. The new world order ushered in by the League of Nations in the aftermath of the war fragmented transnational lives with "the legalities of national and imperial constructions. Migrants were subject to distinct administrative practices that operated simultaneously, constituting overlapping frames to migrant trajectories."[42]

To be sure, many of these migrants questioned the desirability of national identifiers altogether. As Akram Khater describes, Lebanese migrants in the Americas were ambivalent toward the idea of a modern national identity around the turn of the twentieth century. He argues that their experiences in the mahjar would "quickly reveal that there was no such thing as 'Lebanon.' Conversations, debates, and arguments which took place in New York and Buenos Aires manifested the ambiguity and irrelevance—in many ways—of a 'national' identity."[43] New political nationalisms therefore did not represent the default, or most desirable, mode of identification for migrants from Greater Syria throughout the mandate period; rather, they adopted political nationalisms as identifiers as a means to an end. To continue being able to travel, remit money, carry out business, seek legal and political representation transnationally, and maintain property and inheritance rights in the homeland, migrants needed to qualify for the citizenship of one of the new mandates.

Identifying according to political nationalities was also the most effective mode of collective mobilization in the face of Europe's mandates. In order to understand the relationship between the diaspora and the practices of European mandate authorities, it is therefore important to examine the ways in which formerly Ottoman diaspora communities articulated their political desires vis-à-vis the discourses of the new interwar legal world order. For Reem Bailony as well as Khater, the range of responses to these new national identifiers among Syrian migrants "reveals an ambiguity toward the national project as laid out by the League of Nations." In this way, the debates about nationalism and independence that filled the pages of mahjar periodicals throughout the Americas evinced migrants' "multiple interpretations of the self-determination logics of Wilsonian principles," and they took advantage of this ambiguity.[44] Geneva and London could speak of new geopolitical configurations in Greater Syria in concrete and legal terms, and they could use them to limit the mobility and livelihoods of Syrian travelers worldwide. But Syrian migrants could now also use the same legal language and national categories to stake transnational political claims, especially when they were used to deny their demands. And behind the scenes, they could continue to identify as they wished.

Now, the most effective way for migrants from geographic Palestine to protest the Zionist takeover of Palestine, for example, was to submit written grievances as Palestinians, a new identifier with legal and political implications recognized in the new legal world order. Palestinians, who also considered themselves Syrians, were therefore also strategically employing nationality to impose a form of control on mandate authorities through their periodicals and petitions. Even if they ignored them, mandate and League of Nations authorities would need to receive and read these documents authored by pro-Palestina organizations representing self-identifying Palestinians transnationally. The process of nation-state formation and the development of nationalist modes of identification in the postwar moment was therefore never uniformly European or localized. Rather, it played out transnationally and with forms of authority and legitimacy that were not exclusively dictated by Britain, France, or the League of Nations. Migrants were invariably involved in the formation of these new legal and political configurations, and Palestinians, too, chose when, how, and why they were Palestinians. The new passport system was therefore inconsequential in terms of self and group identification to Palestinian migrants; even permanent exile could not strip them of their sense of being Palestinian.

The Birth of Transnational Palestinian Consciousness

Between 1918 and 1920, Palestinians throughout the world routinely voiced collective expressions of transnational identification with their homeland. These expressions came in a variety of political forms—historical, cultural, ethnic, racial, linguistic, and religious—and in protest against European machinations to divide Syria and give its southern province, Palestine, to the Zionists. Therefore, by the official establishment of the British Mandate for Palestine in 1923 and by the legislation of Palestinian citizenship in 1925, European officials in Europe and the Middle East were fully aware of the scope of the grievances of former Ottoman subjects across the world. They were also aware that a large number of migrants from what was Ottoman Syria now considered themselves Palestinians—and Syrians, for that matter. And while the British Foreign and Colonial Offices, the League of Nations' Permanent Mandates Commission in Geneva, and the Government of Palestine in Jerusalem could disregard the petitions and protests, they could not silence them.

The continued dismissal of petitions from groups and committees that identified politically as Syrian, Palestinian, and Arab only served to strengthen and consolidate a form of pro-Palestine activism in an expanding network of Arabic speakers transnationally. This network of individuals and communities who believed they had good reason to demand Palestinian citizenship fueled the petitions and appeals that flooded European offices throughout the interwar period. Nevertheless, the petitions that emerged after 1925 were different from their predecessors. The new ones demanded citizenship using the legal jargon that appeared in the citizenship and nationality legislation emanating from Jerusalem, Geneva, and London. That is, in their new petitions, Palestinians throughout the mahjar adopted the liberal interwar language of national, racial, and birth rights that appeared in 1920s European citizenship legislation to reinforce their claims to belong racially, legally, and permanently to a now bordered Palestine as Palestinian citizens.

The thousands of petitions that were sent to British colonial authorities from across the mahjar after the first citizenship rejections were doled out to Palestinian migrants in 1926 thus had their origins in a tradition that stretched back eight years and that validated transnational pro-Palestine collectives. Palestinian political activism after the defeat of the Ottomans thoroughly involved Palestinians across the world whose subsequent distance from Palestine has persisted to this day. As Khater put it, "colonial and nationalist discourses have constructed landlocked histories of the Middle East," leaving little room for discussions of the historical interplay between the national and the transnational.[45] In speaking of early twentieth-century Palestinian nationalism, we must therefore continue to expand the historical lens from the national to the transnational to account for diaspora voices.

CHAPTER 3

THE 1925 PALESTINIAN CITIZENSHIP ORDER-IN-COUNCIL

ON 24 JULY 1923, the victorious Allied forces and the government of the newly formed Turkish republic signed the Treaty of Lausanne.[1] The treaty officially delineated the borders of the Turkish Republic, and in exchange for the Allies' recognition of Turkish sovereignty, the new republic relinquished all its claims to its former territories, including the Arab provinces, now under European mandates. Consequently, former Arabic-speaking subjects of the Ottoman Empire ceased to be Ottomans, and unless they opted for Turkish nationality, they were officially considered subjects of either British or French trusteeship.[2] How did this impact newly mandated subjects? And more to the point, how did this impact migrants from these formerly Ottoman territories who resided abroad and who held only Ottoman travel documents?

This is where the story of Palestine and Palestinians diverges from the interwar experiences of transnational Syrian communities. The years that followed the ratification of the British Mandate for Palestine in 1923 saw sweeping governmental, infrastructural, economic, and legal changes across Palestine.[3] These transformations included new policies on citizenship and immigration that privileged incoming Jewish migrants at the expense of Palestinian migrants applying for the same citizenship. Between 1925 and 1929, out of a total 20,168 applications for Palestinian citizenship, 15,551 were approved, with non-Jewish naturalization accounting for only 1 percent of this total.[4] This lopsidedness continued throughout the period of Britain's occupation of Palestine between 1917 and 1948, such that, by 1937, about 9,000 applications for citizenship had been submitted by Palestinians residing in Latin America, "and of these not more than 100 were accepted."[5] Over the course of the 1920s and 1930s, therefore, Palestinian migrants came to occupy unique positions in a new world order defined by borders, citizenship, and nation-states. That is, while they had been considered Ottoman subjects prior to 1923, they effectively became stateless following the Treaty of Lausanne and Britain's refusal to offer them transnational recognition and representation as Palestinian citizens. Without British consular representation and protection, they lost their international standing.

THE LOGIC OF THE 1925 PALESTINIAN CITIZENSHIP ORDER-IN-COUNCIL

British officials handled matters surrounding immigration to Palestine diligently. Starting in 1922, under the tutelage of the attorney general of Mandate Palestine, Norman Bentwich, British policy makers drafted several versions of the Palestinian Citizenship Order-in-Council.[6] Following three years of deliberations, amendments, and draft revisions, the Palestinian Citizenship Order-in-Council was officially promulgated in July 1925. The ordinance provided the legal framework for regulating Palestinian citizenship during the British mandate. It determined the criteria governing the ability of immigrants to Palestine, Jewish and otherwise, to secure the status of British subjects. This status entailed international legal protection and representation, rights to residency and employment in Palestine, and assurance of Palestinian citizenship to children and spouses.[7] The legislation was also unique to Palestine. As Mutaz Qafisheh explains, the ordinance was the "only nationality law enacted by Britain, in all the territories assigned to it as a Mandatory."[8] Subjects in other mandated territories, including the Cameroons, Togo, and Tanganyika, were assigned British protected persons status. Moreover, in Iraq and Transjordan, local authorities, not His Majesty's Government itself, were tasked with enacting nationality laws in 1924 and 1928, respectively.[9]

In theory, the ordinance was equitable. In practice, however, it would prove difficult to implement equitably since citizenship was significantly linked to the mandate's built-in mission of creating a Jewish "national home" in Palestine with a population of Jewish citizens who would contribute to Britain's modernizing global empire.[10] In July 1922, as negotiations were underway in London as to the desired effect of immigration legislation relating to Palestine, the following memorandum was circulated in the Colonial Office: "One of the most essential parts of the programme for establishing a Jewish National Home in Palestine [is] necessarily a system of organized Jewish Immigration into that country." Subsequently, legislation pertaining to this matter would need to ensure the organized settlement of Jews in Palestine in a legal fashion; in other words, through granting citizenship that was "proportioned to the necessities of the country and its ability to absorb and support immigrants."[11] The logic of citizenship legislation for British officials, therefore, was that it fulfilled the promises made to the Zionist Organization by securing a Jewish population in Palestine, and it ensured the economic viability of a modernizing and developing Palestine as a British mandated territory.

The native population of Palestine, whether inside or outside Palestine, was ultimately not a major concern to British authorities in designing the 1925 Palestinian Citizenship Order-in-Council. What is more, the extent to which British authorities denied citizenship to Palestinians was unique to British rule in Palestine. While French authorities also burdened Lebanese and Syrian migrants with cumbersome and impractical requirements for acquiring Lebanese and Syrian citizenship during the French mandate, their policy was to generally award it, though more readily to the former. The high commissioner for Beirut even included Lebanese migrants in the country's 1921 census, and consequently, they could claim Lebanese citizenship based on the census four years later when the citizenship law was enacted in Lebanon.[12] Syrians, on the other hand, were largely seen as rabble-rousers whose nationalist aspirations would inconvenience French mandate authorities. Applicants for Syrian citizenship were thus subjected to harsh vetting to ensure their compliance with French rule. Notwithstanding the vetting process or stringent requirements, French authorities encouraged migrants from what would become the French mandates of Lebanon and Syria after 1923 to apply for Lebanese and Syrian citizenship at French consulates abroad. On the one hand, French authorities were interested in populating their mandates with wealthier, westernized, and mostly Christian citizens. On the other, extending citizenship to migrants originally from the mandated territories would indicate that there were Lebanese and Syrians in the mahjar who wanted French rule, dealing a blow to Lebanese and Syrian nationalists. In Palestine, British mandate authorities' policies simply favored

Jewish over Palestinian migrants, naturalizing the former at the expense of the latter.

British authorities facilitated the travel and international representation of Jewish immigrants even before the mandate was ratified, and certainly before the 1925 Palestinian Citizenship Order-in-Council was promulgated. In a telling example, Secretary of the Home Office John Pedder sent a dispatch on 7 June 1920 to the Foreign Office expressing concern at the "considerable embarrassment" being caused to the Home and Immigration Offices in London when Palestinian immigrants, Arab and Jewish, arrived by ship at English ports holding British passports awarded as "emergency certificates" in addition to Turkish passports. These certificates were granted as travel documents since Ottoman representation had vanished after the war and residents of Palestine could not obtain permits to travel from any other authority. Evidently, Pedder explained, there had not yet been clear protocol regarding a person carrying certificates in which "he is described . . . as a British subject who must in law . . . be regarded as a former enemy alien." He requested that this situation be remedied immediately as these cases were not infrequent. In response, the Foreign Office on 2 July gave orders to "authorize the issue of emergency certificates only to Palestinian Jews."[13]

How did this unequal practice become codified following the promulgation of the ordinance? How did British authorities negotiate and determine the exclusion of tens of thousands of Palestinian migrants from Palestinian citizenship throughout the interwar period despite their eligibility and despite their ongoing appeals? How did this practice change over the course of mandate rule, if at all? And importantly, how did the ordinance become so significant for the development of transnational Palestinian national consciousness and for the formation of Palestinian diaspora communities?

LEGISLATING THE EXILE OF PALESTINIAN MIGRANTS

The 1925 Palestinian Citizenship Order-in-Council had dramatic implications for the lives of Palestinians worldwide during the interwar period, but it also presented challenges to British mandate rule. While the ordinance fulfilled Britain's promise to the Zionists by populating Palestine with naturalized Jewish immigrants, it also introduced an inescapable complication that British authorities had not anticipated but that persisted throughout the entirety of their rule in Palestine: the legal status of Palestinians residing abroad. Throughout British rule in Palestine, Jewish naturalization thus invariably occurred alongside the denial of citizenship to Palestinian migrants, and the deliberations during the 1920s in and between British offices in London, Jerusalem, and several consulates throughout Latin America indicate this asymmetry in Britain's governance of Palestine.

The deliberations also indicate that Palestinian migrants persevered in demanding their rights to Palestinian citizenship throughout the mandate period. And although they were ultimately unable to effect change in British policy, they were able to create enough noise, as it were, to instigate correspondence between British authorities transnationally throughout the mandate regarding what to do about this expanding migrant population. Like their predecessors had done a few years earlier, mahjar Palestinians responded immediately and continuously to the Government of Palestine's denial of their applications for Palestinian citizenship. In petitions and periodicals, letters and fundraising campaigns, Palestinians and their allies spoke out worldwide against what they perceived to be a grave injustice. Through these efforts, they began speaking about themselves more deliberately and exclusively as Palestinians, a rising transnational political collective that would oppose Zionist claims to Palestine and also call for Palestinian national self-determination. The 1925 citizenship ordinance contributed in significant ways to the formation of a Palestinian diaspora and to the development of Palestinian national consciousness transnationally.[14]

The 1925 ordinance was divided into four parts with twenty-seven articles. The first article began by defining residents of Palestine as Turkish subjects: "Turkish subjects habitually resident in the territory of Palestine upon the 1st day of August, 1925, shall become Palestinian citizens." As far as Britain was concerned, it introduced and awarded Palestinian citizenship to the residents of its new mandate. This was contested by Palestinians worldwide who always considered themselves to be Palestinians from the southern region of Syria know as Palestine. But it was the following article that presented Jerusalem and London with the most complications legislating citizenship throughout the mandate. Interestingly, Britain recognized Turkish subjects who were born in Palestine but who were "habitually resident abroad" in the second article of the ordinance, but they did not anticipate how many applicants would qualify for citizenship under this article:

> 2—Persons of over eighteen years of age who were born within Palestine and acquired on birth or subsequently and still possess Turkish nationality and on

> the 1st day of August, 1925, are habitually resident abroad, may acquire Palestinian citizenship by opting in such a manner as may be prescribed by Regulation under this Order, subject to the consent of the Government of Palestine which may be granted or withheld in its absolute discretion:
>
> Provided that without prejudice to the foregoing provisions the consent of the Government of Palestine may be refused unless an agreement on the subject has been concluded between the said Government and the Government of the country where the person concerned is resident and shall be refused if the person desiring to opt possesses another nationality in addition to Turkish nationality. This right of option must be exercised within two years of the coming into force of this Order.

This article was pivotal. It acknowledged the existence of communities of individuals who were born in Palestine but who were residing outside of it, and it laid out key requirements in the application process including the age of the applicant, the time frame for applying, and the position of the Government of Palestine vis-à-vis the applicant's right of option for Palestinian citizenship. Regarding the latter, it made clear that the Government of Palestine would be the ultimate decider in issues relating to naturalization.

Articles 4, 5, and 7 provided further guidelines on the limited circumstances under which applications for Palestinian citizenship would be considered:

> 4—(1) Any person over 18 years of age, who, within two years from the date at which this Order comes into force, by declaration made as hereinafter provided states his desire to become a Palestinian citizen and satisfies the authority before whom the declaration is made that he fulfils the following conditions, namely:
>
> (a) That the declarant was born within Palestine and acquired on birth or subsequently and still possesses Turkish nationality; and
> (b) That the declarant shall have been resident within Palestine for not less than six months immediately prior to the date of making such declaration; and
> (c) That the declarant has not, while resident in any country other than Palestine acquired any foreign nationality
>
> may, subject to the approval of the High Commissioner, acquire Palestinian citizenship, and the High Commissioner may grant to such a person a certificate of Palestinian citizenship.

The condition of six-month residence in Palestine as a prerequisite for citizenship presented many Palestinian migrants with difficulties. How could they leave their profitable businesses abroad and reside in Palestine for six months in order to qualify for the only citizenship for which they were eligible? Was their birth in Palestine and the fact that they had not acquired any other nationality not sufficient? The architects of the ordinance did not anticipate these questions. After all, it was the high commissioner for Palestine who determined who would be granted a certificate of citizenship. This was made clear in article 5:

> 5—(1) Persons who have made a declaration of their intention to opt for Palestinian citizenship in accordance with Article 2 of the Palestinian Legislative Council Election Order, 1922, and have received provisional certificates of Palestinian citizenship and have, since declaring their intention to opt for Palestinian citizenship, been ordinarily resident in Palestine shall be deemed to have made a declaration under Article 4 of this Order and shall, subject to the approval of the High Commissioner, be deemed to be entitled to acquire Palestinian citizenship under that Article, and the High Commissioner may grant to such persons certificates of Palestinian citizenship.

Applicants could qualify under articles 2 and 4, but the acquisition of Palestinian citizenship was ultimately at the discretion of the high commissioner and no one else. This was affirmed in article 7, along with new requirements, the first and third of which would prove unworkable for thousands of migrants—namely, residence in Palestine for at least two years prior to the application date and proof of intention to reside permanently in Palestine:

> 7—(1) The High Commissioner may grant a certificate of naturalisation as a Palestinian citizen to any person who makes application therefor and who satisfies him:
>
> (a) That he has resided in Palestine for not less than two years out of the three years immediately preceding the date of his application.
> (b) That he is of good character and has an adequate knowledge of either the English, the Arabic or the Hebrew language.
> (c) That he intends, if his application is granted, to reside in Palestine.[15]

Beyond acknowledging the presence of Turkish nationals abroad who were born in Palestine and their right to opt for Palestinian citizenship, British officials remained rather unrealistic in their requirements and vague about any nuances or unique circumstances pertaining to applicants who applied under article 2 of the 1925 ordinance. Many of these circumstances would become clearer to British authorities as Palestinian migrants began petitioning the Government of Palestine and the League of Nations, and appealing the rejection of their applications for citizenship at British consulates throughout the Americas starting in late 1926. Nonetheless, London, Jerusalem, and Geneva would continue the policy of denying their applications with increasing ease.

How did the ordinance come to signify such an obstacle to Palestinian migrants? The most immediate challenge to Palestinian migrants was the impractical and rather confusing time frame for them to apply for citizenship and fulfill the residency requirements needed to receive it. In fact, British authorities deliberately overlooked this error before the promulgation of the ordinance in July because they did not expect many applicants would be impacted. They were mistaken. It concerned the last line of article 2 of the ordinance, which stated: "This right of option" afforded to Palestinians residing abroad who were born in Ottoman Palestine "must be exercised within two years of the coming into force of this Order" in August 1925. This conflicted with the time frame given to former Ottomans residing abroad to apply for the citizenship of their new state under article 34 of the Treaty of Lausanne. Effectively, "the Lausanne Treaty gave these former Ottomans until August 1926 to return to Palestine and take on citizenship, while the citizenship order-in-council gave the same individuals until August 1927 to do so."[16]

In addition, articles 4 and 7 indicated that, to qualify for Palestinian citizenship, applicants were required to return to Palestine six months before applying for citizenship with an intention to do so permanently. Otherwise, they received Turkish nationality. But Herbert Plumer, who took up the post of high commissioner for Palestine in August 1925, amended article 2 on 6 November 1925 in order to match article 34 of the Treaty of Lausanne. This decision shortened the time given to Palestinians residing abroad to opt for Palestinian citizenship to less than a year, and with the six-month residency requirement, it effectively gave them three months to close down their profitable businesses in the mahjar, pack their belongings, and return to Palestine permanently by February 1926. This was an unrealistic and unrealizable requirement for migrants whose livelihoods relied on their continued residence and work abroad. What is more, Plumer's amendment was not widely publicized, and so thousands of migrants would already have been unable to fulfill the requirements for acquiring Palestinian citizenship by the time they began applying for it in 1926.

In addition to impractical logistics in application requirements, British officials agreed on a set of rather arbitrary requirements for approving citizenship applications, the most important of which were ascertaining the motivation behind applicants' decisions to apply and their intention to remain permanently in Palestine. On 2 December 1923, a representative of the Government of Palestine sent a letter to John Shuckburgh, head of the Middle East Department of the Colonial Office, with suggestions for adding a clause to the ordinance that would assess the applicants' intentions to reside permanently in Palestine. This clause, he stressed, "would check the application for Palestinian citizenship by immigrants who have not established any permanent home in Palestine but who may be birds of passage and desire to obtain that citizenship in order to enjoy British protection."[17] Including this clause was urgent, he added, as "over 20,000 persons" had declared themselves to qualify for Palestinian citizenship in 1922. The notion of intention of permanent residence thus acquired significance in the citizenship application process and subsequently, in handpicking the would-be citizens of Palestine. As for how to determine applicants' intentions, British consuls were told to use their discretion, and with the large number of requests for citizenship pouring into British consulates worldwide, failure to provide sufficient proof of intention for permanent residence in Palestine became a frequently cited pretext for rejecting non-Jewish applicants throughout British rule in Palestine. It was sufficiently prescriptive and strategically vague.

The requirement of proof of intention to return permanently, British officials argued, was based on Britain's reluctance to create a "large class" of individuals who would receive British protection abroad. This reason was so central to British citizenship policy that it acquired an irrefutable logic of its own among British policy makers in Jerusalem and London. For example, the Report of the Commission on the Palestine Disturbances of August 1929 that was prepared for members of the British Parliament in March 1930 included the following subsection, titled "Minor Arab Grievances:"

> 2) Position of Ottoman subjects born in Palestine and now resident abroad.
>
> The refusal to grant the status of Palestinian citizenship in the cases to which this complaint relates is based on the general principle that it is

> undesirable to create a large class of persons who, though permanently resident in foreign countries, are entitled to British protection. We see no ground to dissent from that principle. . . . In the circumstances we are satisfied that this complaint is not well founded.[18]

While most Palestinian migrants did declare their intentions to return permanently to Palestine after amassing sufficient wealth abroad, London and Jerusalem considered this insufficient in the interim and saw no reason to reconsider. What is more, the report included the issue of Palestinian migrant citizenship under "Minor Arab Grievances." Despite nearly three years of uninterrupted petitions and appeals from Palestinian migrants throughout the mahjar and from within Palestine regarding the gravity of losing their international standing without citizenship, the 1929 report prepared for members of Britain's Parliament reduced them to negligible grievances. Britain was selective in the ethnic and racial demographic of those it wished to include in its domain, and Palestinian migrants quite simply did not fit the bill, even though they constituted a sizable collective of economically successful merchants who, as British subjects, could be a boon for Britain's expanding transnational influence in the interwar period.

The practice of excluding native Palestinian migrants from Palestinian citizenship had its origins in the early deliberations that defined the British mandate's commitment to settling and naturalizing Jews in Palestine. British authorities were so committed to the in-migration of Jews to Palestine and to the facilitation of their naturalization as Palestinian citizens that they set the required years of residency in Palestine for applicants for Palestinian citizenship to only two years, which, some argued, was far too short. Edward Keith-Roach, British colonial administrator in Palestine and later governor of Jerusalem between 1926 and 1945, brought this reality to Jerusalem's attention in 1924. In a memorandum submitted to the Government of Palestine on 24 November 1924, Keith-Roach suggested that the Government of Palestine take a closer look at the means by which naturalizing Jewish immigrants would feature in the governance of Palestine. Specifically, he was concerned that the two-year residency requirement in Palestine for citizenship applicants was too short and would cause Jerusalem and London more problems in the long run. He pointed out that the two-year residency requirement had been implemented because of the misconception that "the Palestine problem presents a set of circumstances unparalleled in the history not only of

Great Britain, but of the world, and therefore Palestine required treatment different from any other country in the world."[19] The notion of Palestine's uniqueness, he added, was based on the declaration, in 1921, that Jews should receive full citizenship in accordance with article 7 of the mandate. London and Jerusalem, he reminded his recipients, were in agreement about this. But he suggested that in order to acquire a passport that afforded the person British protection abroad, the person "should go through a pretty hard school," as in many other countries. As examples, he mentioned that the United States, Great Britain, and Italy all had five-year residency requirements. He also pointed out that Belgium, Switzerland, and France required lengthier stays, and that Australia and New Zealand required immigrants to prove "first they are 'squatters' and not 'drifters'" before granting them passports. Two years were not enough, and there was no need for Palestine to differ from other countries.

The concern was valid from a political and legal standpoint. In order to avoid Palestine becoming a "transit station" for people like Russian Jews fleeing Bolshevik rule, Keith-Roach added, there needed to be stricter and more universally recognized practices put in place in Palestine. Jewish applicants, he said, could easily fulfill the existing two-year requirement and subsequently move back to Europe carrying with them British passports. He added that the Zionist Organization had even tried to reduce the requisite years to one rather than two, and this, he believed, was absurd. Interestingly, Keith-Roach also pointed out the perspective of the existing Arab population: "I am certain in Palestine the Arabs will let up a tremendous howl when they learn that a man from a ghetto in Poland can qualify in two years for citizenship of Palestine. And I think [they are] right." Keith-Roach subsequently advised that the required length of stay in Palestine before acquiring a passport should be increased to five years, in keeping with the global trend. Responding on 4 December 1924, the Government of Palestine claimed it was too late to make the amendment, but it also added that Palestine was exceptional because "a naturalized Palestinian can be denaturalized after 2 years' absence from Palestine."[20] Replying once more the following day, Keith-Roach wrote: "From a legal aspect 2 years is a very short period for this purpose, but the question is, in Palestine as elsewhere, mainly one of policy," and the Government of Palestine was ultimately free to decide on whichever policies it desired, including extending citizenship selectively.

The decisions to approve Jews' applications for citizenship and to reject Palestinian migrants' were invariably intertwined. This is to say, while Palestinian immigrants were having their applications for citizenship denied, Jews continued to enter Palestine "virtually without check of any kind," as Shuckburgh relayed to the office of the Zionist Organization in London on 25 May 1925.[21] Palestinians across the world were protesting this practice before the citizenship ordinance was officially promulgated. For example, in February 1925, Palestinians in Port-au-Prince, Haiti, petitioned London for redress regarding their inability to leave Haiti due to the absence of travel documents. London had refused to issue travel documents to Palestinians in Haiti seeking to travel for business purposes since they had not officially applied for Palestinian citizenship. Though the citizenship ordinance would not be enacted until July of that year, provisional certificates of Palestinian nationality were regularly issued to Jewish immigrants entering Palestine. The immigrants in Haiti pointed this out in their petition, and on 11 March 1925, the British consul in Port-au-Prince, Mr. Carvell, conveyed to the Home Office in London his concern that the requirements for obtaining provisional certificates did "constitute a hardship for Palestinians resident abroad." These immigrants, he assured the Home Office, were "nearly all Christians" who felt that they were "being victimised by the Jewish element in the Palestine Government." Carvell requested to be allowed to issue travel certificates to these Palestinian merchants for travel to the United States and Britain if London did not wish to modify the existing requirements. Travel was central to these migrants' economic viability as textile merchants since, according to the petitioners, "the citizen of Palestine who emigrated to America did not come for pleasure. He came for work and to make a certain fortune to render him capable of living well and contributing to the prosperity and progress of his country."[22]

The petitioners also pointed out that the requirement of providing proof of an intention to remain permanently in Palestine was absurd. "It is ridiculous," they protested, "that the government of Palestine requires of the citizen who requests a Palestine passport a formal declaration of wanting to live in Palestine in a permanent manner." In fact, they proceeded, "isn't the simple fact of requesting a Palestinian passport already evident proof that we want to safeguard our nationality?" The requirement signaled to them the Government of Palestine's "perfect ignorance of what is patriotism and the human heart." Or, they continued, it signaled "the cruel and unmentionable desire to oblige us to adopt another nationality to get rid of us and deprive our nation of the good that our commerce renders us capable of doing it." Entreating the British minister further to guarantee their voices were heard in Jerusalem, the petitioners added that they were speaking "on behalf of all the citizens of Palestine residing in America."[23] While Carvell did not relay this portion of the petition to the Home Office, it is noteworthy that these complaints were voiced before the enactment of the citizenship ordinance. Palestinian migrants were concerned about existing and forthcoming British policies when it came to their ability to travel and return to Palestine.

In response to Carvell's dispatch, on 16 April 1925, George Mounsey of the Foreign Office granted Carvell the authority to issue provisional certificates to Palestinian merchants in Haiti seeking to travel to the United States and Britain. Mounsey added that Carvell should warn applicants for certificates that "no further protection can be accorded to them unless they can eventually establish a claim to Palestinian citizenship," thus rendering obsolete their existing claims to nationality. A few days later on 27 April, Hubert Young of the Colonial Office confirmed Mounsey's decision and added that the certificates should be marked "'valid for six months only' and that they will in any case cease to be valid as and when the Palestinian Citizenship Order-in-Council comes into force."[24] The migrants' claims to eligibility for Palestinian citizenship were ignored. But while inconsequential at the time of Mounsey and Young's responses, the Haitian petition suggests that the byproduct of arbitrary citizenship application requirements and exclusion tactics elicited significant responses from a community that was experiencing a new reality as a Palestinian diaspora.

As another example of this lopsidedness in the treatment of Jewish and non-Jewish migrants to Palestine before the official promulgation of the citizenship ordinance, Arthur King, British consul in Tegucigalpa, Honduras, sent a letter on 11 May 1925 to the Home Office requesting permission to grant Palestinian migrants there provisional certificates to return to Palestine in order to gain British protection. The applicants were evidently experiencing hardship with the Honduran government and had in their possession proof of birth in Palestine, intention to apply for "Palestinian nationality" as soon as the citizenship ordinance was enacted, and proof of future permanent residence in Palestine.[25] King was specifically asking whether he could approve their applications if they did not specify the exact date of return to Palestine. On 30 June, the director of the Department of Immigration and Travel in Jerusalem replied to King that unless all conditions for return migration and residence in Palestine were met, laissez-passers were not issuable without exception. The applicants, he added, could visit Palestine with no objection and pending the issuance of emergency travel certificates, but taking up residence would not be considered since the ordinance had not been enacted. Two weeks later, on 17 July, Colonial Secretary Hubert Young replied to King that nothing could be done for the applicants seeking British protection until the ordinance was passed. The applicants' existing documentation and testimonies were evidently insufficient.

But these Palestinian merchants in Honduras were also considered valuable assets to businessmen in England whose exports to the South American country were being delayed due to the absence of protection for their goods within Honduras. Three spokesmen on behalf of Robert Francis Brown & Co., a British export company with business in Honduras, submitted a letter to the Foreign Office on 9 June 1925 asking whether His Majesty's Government would extend British protection to the merchants in Honduras in order that "the export trade to Honduras may be resumed with some measure of safety." Responding on 7 August 1925, a week after the citizenship ordinance came into effect, the Foreign Office told the businessmen that they had been misinformed of the circumstances. Specifically, these merchants, the Foreign Office clarified, "are mostly of Palestinian birth or descent, but pending the issue of an Order-in-Council respecting Palestinian nationality, it will not be possible to define their status." But, it was added, "it is not anticipated that many of these persons will in any case qualify under the terms of the order when issued as entitled to British protection."[26] Foreign Secretary Chamberlain would therefore not be making any arrangements to extend British protection to these merchants or to facilitate trade with Honduras. Days later, on 12 August, Young relayed to Chamberlain's office that it needed to modify the letter it sent to the businessmen since the ordinance had in fact already been issued and come into force on 1 August 1925. There is no archival evidence that Chamberlain's office modified its response.

Jerusalem continued to seek approval from London to populate Palestine as it pleased even after the citizenship ordinance was enacted. On 15 October 1925, Plumer asked the Home Office to be relieved of restrictions placed on his ability to admit incoming Jewish immigrants that fit into certain predetermined classes of migrants. Jewish immigrants applying for Palestinian citizenship were required to present valid identification documents, including passports or other documents establishing nationality, upon entry to Palestine. The high commissioner, however, had been authorized to use discretion in admitting individual immigrants who were "bona fide" unable to produce such documents. In the letter to the Home Office, Plumer requested that the provision of allowing only individual cases be reconsidered since, as it stood, the legislation could result in the "rejection of many hundreds of Yemenite [Jewish] applicants" who were "regarded as valuable recruits to the Jewish agriculture and general labour service."[27] Instead, Plumer wished to revert to the original legislation whereby he had been authorized to waive the immigration requirement to incoming Jews who fell into those classes as he pleased. In addition to Yemeni Jews, Plumer listed Russian, German, Romanian, and Polish Jewish immigrants, as well as foreign residents holding British laissez-passers in Egypt, and he requested exemptions for Yemeni Jews and foreign residents arriving from Egypt and Germany. There was no mention of incoming non-Jewish immigrants.

The issue was brought to London in November 1925 following deliberations with the Zionist Organization as well as with British authorities in Yemen. Colonial Secretary Leopold Amery sent a dispatch from Aden acknowledging the urgency of addressing Plumer's request. He agreed that delaying the arrival of these valuable Yemeni Jews would be counterproductive, but he wished to ensure Jerusalem's right to deport any migrant who proved to be "undesirable" following entry to Palestine. On 13 November 1925, and with the blessing of Chaim Weizmann of the Zionist Organization, Amery authorized the admission of Yemeni Jews to Palestine without the passport requirement while their applications were under review. The issue of deportation evidently fell outside of the purview of these officials. Moreover, if any immigrant possessed real estate in Yemen, "he need not dispose of that property in order to qualify for admission to Palestine as a person of independent means."[28] In other words, while Palestinian migrants in the diaspora were petitioning for travel facilities so as not to close down their businesses and relinquish their valuable assets abroad, Plumer was receiving authorization to permit Yemeni Jews with property in Yemen and no documentation to enter Palestine and apply for citizenship.

Despite the ongoing imbalance in the treatment of Jewish and non-Jewish migrants, British authorities were obliged to address certain issues that fell through the various legal loopholes of the 1925 Palestinian Citizenship Order-in-Council. For example, what were the British to do with the children of migrants born abroad whose parents were applying for citizenship and could show evidence of a plan to return permanently? According to the ordinance, nationality was to be awarded jus sanguinis, which dictated that children, by law, acquired their parents' citizenship at birth. But given the unique circumstances of populating Palestine and naturalizing its residents, British authorities sought to distance themselves from this practice. On 17 December 1926, an official from the Colonial Office, under instruction from British Foreign Secretary Austen Chamberlain, forwarded a dispatch from the consul-general in Mexico City to Plumer in Jerusalem that declared that "it is not the practice of His Majesty's Consular offices to notify the births of British Protected Persons to the Government of the Protectorate concerned." The birth of children born to Palestinians residing abroad, therefore, was not Jerusalem's concern. But the dispatch also added that since Palestinian citizens abroad are "not British subjects," the birth of their children "cannot be registered at His Majesty's Consulates" unless it was proven that they had a valid claim to Palestinian citizenship under the 1925 Citizenship Order-in-Council.[29] On 5 January 1927, Amery sent a letter to Plumer confirming the decision to refrain from involving Jerusalem in these deliberations.

In another instance, Mr. Graham of the British Consulate in Valparaiso, Chile, sent a dispatch on 25 May 1926 to the Home Office requesting advisement on issuing Palestinian passports to applicants in Chile. Specifically, he was concerned that the requirements outlined in paragraph 6 of the Foreign Office circular of 21 December 1925 appeared vague and thus may not have been met by the applicants. Evidently, Graham found it sufficient if the applicants indicated a desire to return to Palestine, but, wary of Jerusalem's reaction, he added that he would furnish further "particularizing grounds on which recommendation is being made (e.g., race, property, intending residence in Palestine)" if the existing information did not suffice.[30] London received the dispatch and was also concerned that most of the applications from Chile failed to provide the qualifications of the applicant, or they contained "such scanty particulars as to be useless for the purpose contemplated by paragraph 6 of the Foreign Office circular" of 21 December 1925.

To be sure, the sixth paragraph of the circular was quite vague. It explained that the Government of Palestine would not grant citizenship "as a matter of course" and that consular officers were asked to help Jerusalem in ascertaining whether it would be "reasonable and proper" for an applicant to receive "British rather than Turkish protection":

> You should bear in mind that the consent of the Government of Palestine to such options [to acquire citizenship] will not be given as a matter of course. It is not intended to accept options from persons who desire to obtain Palestinian citizenship merely as a means of obtaining British protection, and in general it is not intended to accept them except in cases where the applicant can show that it would be reasonable and proper for him to be under British rather than Turkish protection. In forwarding each application you should, therefore, in addition to seeing that the particulars required under the regulations are fully and properly given, add any observations as to the application which, in your opinion, would assist the Government of Palestine in forming a decision as to whether or not to accept it.

London was apparently slow in replying. Graham submitted another dispatch on 29 May 1926 asking again for a reply "as application covering many hundreds of persons depends on settlement of question raised therein and time is pressing." Finally, on 7 June, John Shuckburgh at the Middle East Department of the Colonial Office replied that Chamberlain reiterated paragraph 6 of the circular, providing little in the way of clarity. Shuckburgh declared:

> In cases . . . in which it is patently undesirable that the applicant should be accorded British protection, or it appears that the applicant has no real intention of returning to or maintaining connection with Palestine, attention should be drawn to these facts when the applications are forwarded.[31]

How applicants' patent undesirability or intention of returning permanently could be determined was not explained, but the ambiguity of London's response suggests that the implementation of exclusionary policies based on abstract qualifications was bound to be abstruse itself. By 1926, therefore, Palestinian migrants appealing the Government of Palestine to reconsider the rejection of their application for citizenship were responding to a longstanding logic for excluding them that was built into the practices of British citizenship legislation in Palestine.

But if by 1927, Palestinian migrants in Latin America were not legally British protected persons or non-Jewish citizens of Palestine, and if they were no longer Ottomans and never Bolivians, for example, what were they? Briefly, they were all without legal nationality. Some in the British Colonial, Home, and Foreign Offices agreed that this was an untenable situation. An interesting case offers insight into this predicament. On 8 April 1927, R. C. Michell at the British legation in La Paz, Bolivia, relayed to the Home Office the case of Sari Mohammed Ismael, a Palestinian who had been given a laissez passer by the Egyptian Expeditionary Force in Jerusalem in May 1920 to travel to Bolivia but subsequently had his Palestinian citizenship application denied in 1927. Ismael had apparently conveyed to Michell that he was "anxious to return to Palestine to resubmit his application" but he was now concerned that with the high commissioner's amendment to the application deadline, effectively shortening the window for citizenship applications to a few months, he would not have enough time to reapply, even if he could prove intention to remain permanently in Palestine.[32]

Michell was concerned that the Government of Palestine would contravene international law meant to protect the rights of the native population of Palestine and deny Ismael's citizenship request even though he had not "severed ties" with his homeland or been absent for longer than twelve years—the maximum number of years the Government of Palestine had allotted applicants to have been abroad. Mentioning several other cases like Ismael's, Michell stated that if an extension of time for the application were awarded, "there will doubtless be no objection to granting these persons, without further reference to the Government of Palestine, a travel document to enable them to return to Palestine."[33] Michell wanted this issue resolved, and he was aware Jerusalem was unlikely to weigh in, given its recent reticence. The pressure would have to come from London.

Ismael's precarious legal status was further complicated by the ambiguity of the new connection between nationality and international law by the time of the 1925 Citizenship Order-in-Council. In the same dispatch, Michell mentioned that the Bolivian government considered Ismael and others in his situation as British protected persons since "there is no Ottoman representative in Bolivia to whom they can apply for passports and the Spanish Consul, who is in charge of Ottoman interests, . . . has no authority to grant them passports as nationals of Turkey." He then suggested that it would be in the interest of the Government of Palestine, whose policy was presumably "not to exclude these persons from Palestine altogether," to grant them travel documents to return to Palestine and apply for citizenship so that they would cease to benefit from default British protected personhood if they were in fact ineligible for it.[34]

London acted on 28 July 1927. Secretary of the Home Office John Pedder, on behalf of Austen Chamberlain's office, sent a dispatch to be presented to Colonial Secretary Amery in which he declared that the Government of Palestine should grant Ismael "some form of laissez passer," but only if it saw fit:

> While this matter appears to be one primarily for the Colonial Office . . . , [Chamberlain] is of the opinion that the proper solution of the difficulty would be afforded by the provision of some form of laissez passer or other document by the Government of Palestine, if they are willing after further inquiry that Mr. Ismael should return to Palestine for the purpose of resubmitting an application for Palestinian citizenship.

High Commissioner Plumer finally replied on 12 September 1927 indicating his agreement that "some general procedure is required for dealing with cases of this kind. In its absence embarrassing incidents such as that to which your dispatch . . . refers, are bound to arise." Evidently, there had been concern that Ismael's case was suspect since other applicants in his situation had obtained travel visas for Palestine under the pretext of traveling to Syria thereafter but then remained in Palestine illegally. However, Plumer added, "permission to settle in Palestine is invariably granted to a person born in Palestine and still possessing Turkish citizenship, provided that there is no political or medical objection or objection on account of character."[35] Unfortunately for Ismael, this was not the case. There were ultimately no effective measures put in place to hold the British mandatory government accountable for its policies, not even through the League of Nations, although Palestinians frequently turned to it.

On 10 June 1927, the Sociedad Fraternidad Palestina of Salvador petitioned the League of Nations expressing frustration with the "futile pretexts" put forth to reject Palestinian migrants' citizenship applications. They explained that they had applied for Palestinian citizenship according to the stipulations of the Treaty of Lausanne and that Britain's refusal to grant them citizenship on "unheard-of" grounds was unacceptable:

> We Palestinians resident in this Republic applied to the British Legation for registration as Palestinian nationals, and submitted documents in proof of our

> origin and nationality but in vain; on various futile pretexts registration was refused to the majority of the applicants.
>
> What, then was the use of the notices published by the British Legation calling on Palestinian nationals to register, since when the moment came, our lawful aspirations were refused on the unheard-of ground that ten years or more of absence from his native country deprives an applicant of the right to be registered as a national of that country?
>
> How is it possible to allow in the domain of public law that mere absence can break the natural and indissoluble tie to the mother country?
>
> Would Great Britain, France, Germany and the other Powers uphold such theories in the case of their own subjects or citizens?[36]

The Sociedad Fraternidad Palestina was composed of "more than a thousand persons of Palestinian origin," and its members felt certain that they could not be "indifferent to the manner in which the Mandatory Power is treating us," especially considering that "Jewish immigration is most favourably received." As they explained it, soliciting the League of Nations for help was a way for them to safeguard the rights afforded them by the victorious Allies in the aftermath of World War I.

But the Permanent Mandates Commission (PMC) allowed the office of the high commissioner for Palestine complete autonomy in policy making. During a meeting of the PMC in Geneva between 24 October and 11 November 1927, delegate Anna Wicksell expressed her opinion regarding the rejection of Palestinian petitions for citizenship from various Latin American locations: "The legal right of the British Government to refuse the application of the petitioners cannot be contested," and this reflected article 2 of the citizenship ordinance.[37] As Susan Pedersen argues, "the League [of Nations] almost invariably supported the imperial powers, reiterating the system's paternalistic and not emancipatory intent."[38] Ismael and the members of the Sociedad Fraternidad Palestina were out of luck.

The case of Ismael was one of many, as Michell pointed out, and the correspondence transmitted between the various British offices from La Paz to London and to Jerusalem suggests that the legislation of nationality in 1927 was complicated and often contentious. In another instance, on 30 July 1927, members of the Comité Hijos de Palestina in Saltillo, Mexico, submitted a petition to the British consulate in Mexico City requesting travel facilities for one of its members, Carlos Andonio. Apparently, Andonio had applied for a visa to return to Honduras, where he had been prior to Mexico, but had been denied departure by the Mexican government. Andonio, married and father of four, had left Palestine in 1920, had settled in Honduras, and had subsequently traveled to Mexico for business purposes. Now, he was stuck in Mexico and could not return to his wife and children because he lacked the necessary travel documents that the Mexican government insisted needed to be issued by British authorities. "We make this petition," the document read, "because if a pass or passport is not given to him by British Consular Officers there is no one else to whom we can apply."[39] Receiving this petition, the British legation in Mexico City relayed to London its concern over Andonio's situation. On 10 August 1927, the British Legation declared that if the petitioners were correct in their description of Andonio's difficulties acquiring travel permits,

> the inability of persons of Palestinian origin to obtain any kind of travel document . . . must presumably inflict serious hardships upon them, while their situation is rendered more difficult by the absence of any form of Turkish diplomatic or consular representation in this country.[40]

On 28 October 1927, London replied that "British Consular Officers should not issue travel documents to natives of Palestine not possessing Palestinian nationality in order to enable them to travel to countries other than Palestine."[41] It is unknown what happened to Andonio.

In the years surrounding the promulgation of the 1925 Palestinian Citizenship Order-in-Council, British authorities in London and Jerusalem prioritized the naturalization of Jewish migrants over any other group, including Palestinian migrants across the Americas who were born in Palestine, had family in Palestine, owned property in Palestine, and sought to one day return to it permanently. Palestinian migrants were thus denied citizenship based on what they considered to be arbitrary stipulations, including inadequate proof of intention to return permanently, insufficient claims to substantive connections to Palestine, and lengthy stays outside of Palestine. These stipulations became significant means of permanently distancing Palestinian migrants from Palestine in an effort to populate it with Jews, and this practice persisted throughout Britain's thirty-year occupation of Palestine.

THE LONG-TERM NORMALIZATION OF EXCLUSION

The practice of excluding Palestinian migrants from citizenship was not aberrant in the great scheme of history. After all, the British mandate was in every way part of an entrenched imperial tradition where the management of difference, as Jane Burbank and Frederick Cooper have termed it, was central to maintaining power.[42] And in an age of expanding political, economic, and legal networks, the disenfranchisement of a relatively small number of migrants was not a pressing issue, especially since Britain's stated priority, which it was practicing efficiently, was ensuring the uninterrupted immigration of Jews to Palestine and their naturalization as Palestinians. And while British authorities did occasionally tend to Palestinian migrants' demands for redress, especially when British consuls intervened and spoke on their behalf, London and Jerusalem's official position was to dismiss their demands as unfounded, erroneous, and nonessential.

The extent of the Government of Palestine's deliberate practice of excluding Palestinian migrants from citizenship is apparent with a closer look at the ways in which British officials dealt with the issue in the longer term. Several documents throughout the 1930s suggest that the official British position on rejecting the citizenship applications of Palestinian migrants remained mostly unchanged. The sources point to an ongoing practice of rejecting applications for Palestinian citizenship that varied little if at all in language and application by 1940, fifteen years after the promulgation of the Palestinian Citizenship Order-in-Council. Throughout the interwar period, various British officials in different offices in London, Jerusalem, Geneva, and across Latin America normalized the exclusion of Palestinian migrants from citizenship and thus from long-term settlement and employment in Palestine over the course of British rule in Palestine.

In some instances, London, Jerusalem, and Geneva even colluded in providing reasons for dismissing Palestinians' demands for redress when it came to citizenship and immigration legislation. As an example, on 19 May 1934, Ihsan al-Jabiri, a prominent Arab nationalist who at the time was residing in Geneva, sent a petition on behalf of the Cairo-based Syro-Palestinian Delegation to two recipients: the president of the Council of the League of Nations and the president of the PMC.[43] The petition was an expression of frustration. To the president of the PMC, al-Jabiri wrote that, after fourteen years of reaching out to the League of Nations, he was again asking for justice regarding Britain's inequitable governance of Palestine and specifically, their plan to populate it with Jews:

> Mr. President,
>
> Here is the fourteenth year in which we address ourselves to the League of Nations, hoping still that it will see to imparting justice to our grievances. We have not ceased to remind it that the method of application of the Mandate over Palestine is diametrically opposed to the spirit and the text of the Pact of the League of Nations. We permit ourselves again to attract your serious attention to the irreparable evils which the Mandate has caused. . . .
>
> We desire simply to signal that it is impossible to find any concordance between the charge of transforming Palestine into a Jewish "home"—against the volition of its inhabitants—and the established sense of the term Mandate . . . to educate and develop the community under the Mandate and not to oust or dislodge it to replace it with another people.[44]

Al-Jabiri explained that British mandate authorities in Palestine had overstepped their jurisdiction as ordained by the League of Nations and the PMC: the "anomaly" of "introducing, arming, and protecting, to the detriment of the autochthonous, Jewish immigrants, is an operation entirely outside of the established principle of the Pact of the League of Nations." Calling it a "violation," al-Jabiri proceeded to analyze the text of the mandate itself, pointing out the British authorities' clear negligence of Arab rights—namely, through the transformation of Palestine into a "totally British administration"; the continued in-migration of Jews and, thus, the contravention of the "absorptive capacity" policy that was meant to limit the overextension of Palestine's territorial and economic abilities; the unequal distribution of wealth and professional opportunities between Jews and non-Jews, as well as biased taxation; and the absence of Muslim and Christian Arab representation in government. Al-Jabiri was assertive and thorough.

On the issue of immigration, al-Jabiri elaborated at the end of the petition that there was an "unjustifiable, and even paradoxical, difference between the Arab and Jewish immigrants; a fact which can account for the noise heard concerning the intentions of the English to eliminate the Arab race in Palestine."[45] For him, the continued influx of Jews into Palestine was leading to

Arab unemployment, and further, the disparity in opportunities and profits was linked to citizenship acquisition. To portray the difference, al-Jabiri offered a hypothetical scenario where a Jewish immigrant from Russia was naturalized while a Palestinian inhabitant of Syria, which he explained included Palestine, was denied:

> An inhabitant of Syria, a country whose extensive geographic and historical space includes Palestine until Aqaba, cannot be considered a Palestinian subject, even if he has been an inhabitant of the country for many years; whereas a Jew, arriving from a Bolshevik Russian background, is naturalized as soon as he sets foot in Palestine. And thus the impassable obstacles are created to prevent the establishment of some, while others are favored in all ways.

In the margins of the document, the British official who received and reviewed the petition exclaimed "NO!" at the assumption that Jews were naturalized "as soon as" they arrived in Palestine.[46] The topic of immigration was certainly sensitive for all parties involved.

How did London and Geneva react to al-Jabiri's allegations that British authorities in Palestine contradicted the League of Nations' mission in their administration of Palestine? On 31 October 1934, Mr. Hall of the office of the high commissioner in Jerusalem sent a dispatch to the office of the colonial secretary in London expressing his view that it was "not considered necessary to comment in detail on the petition" sent by al-Jabiri. Hall was echoing London's position on the matter, which it had announced in August of that year, that His Majesty's Government, acting as sole arbiter of legislation regarding Palestine, need not consider a petition "addressed to the League of Nations by a body which does not apparently consist of Palestinian nationals and has no direct concern with Palestine."[47]

Al-Jabiri's petition was dismissed because he was not considered a Palestinian national and further, because he represented "a body which . . . calls itself 'The Syro-Palestinian Delegation' and, to judge from the contents of the petition, is a Syrian rather than a Palestinian organisation." London continued: "Would [His Majesty's Government] be expected to defend itself against allegations made to the League of Nations by, e.g. an association of Brazilians or Japanese?" As discussed in chapter 2, the practice of denying Palestinian migrants' claims to being Palestinian by arguing that they were, in fact, Syrians, was common among British authorities. This logic belied all evidence to the contrary—namely, the historical contiguity of Greater Syria with Palestine as its southern region, as well as more than a decade worth of political organizing among residents of former Greater Syria and their counterparts across the mahjar into groups and committees whose names and platforms treated Syria and Palestine as one and the same. To dismiss the committee as not Palestinian because it was based in Cairo and because its name and members included Syrian nationals thus indicates that policy makers in London and Geneva conceived of geopolitical Palestine much differently than did Arab petitioners worldwide for whom the historical category of Greater Syria was still significant, especially when it came to legislation in the interwar period. Furthermore, London's response that the petition may as well have been from Brazil or Japan signals its readiness to disregard documents that brought to light failures or discrepancies in its governance of Palestine.

Nevertheless, in a dispatch dated 2 August 1934, His Majesty's Government addressed the matter of naturalization as presented in al-Jabiri's petition with the PMC in Geneva. The author of the dispatch stated that the hypothetical scenario al-Jabiri described in his petition regarding the biased way Jews were naturalized was inaccurate:

> We might add that as a typical example of the inaccuracies which the petition contains, reference is invited to para. 8 of the petition, where an account is given of the conditions under which Syrians and Jews respectively can obtain naturalisation as Palestinian citizens, which, as the [Permanent Mandates] Commission are no doubt aware, is entirely inconsistent with the provision of the Palestine Citizenship Order-in-Councils-in-Council of 1925 and 1931.
>
> (But I think it would be preferable to offer no comment on details.)[48]

London disregarded any allegation that it was not following its own legislation. It was not obliged to address further any claims that it mishandled its policies or the League of Nations' charter since the allegation was evidently typically inaccurate. His Majesty's Government's recommendation was to therefore offer no comment to al-Jabiri. This behavior was quintessential, and Geneva condoned it, though the PMC weighed in months later, after it received copies of al-Jabiri's petitions along with London's observations from His Majesty's Government. On 7 December 1934, the PMC announced that it would not be making any recommendation to the Council of the League of Nations regarding the petitions:

> The Commission,
>
> Having examined the petitions dated May nineteenth, 1934, from Mr. Ihsan el Djabri [*sic*] and the mandatory Power's observations thereon:
>
> Considers that there is no call for any particular recommendation to the Council on the subject.

Furthermore, the PMC explained that it had already been determined following Hall's dispatch of 31 October that the naturalization issue was being carried out equitably between Jews and non-Jews. Jerusalem declared that "there is no preference given to Jews in the matter of naturalization."[49]

As for why no recommendations or further observations were made regarding al-Jabiri's petitions, the PMC agreed with London that they lacked substance. Evidently, al-Jabiri had a history of submitting petitions that did little more than irk London. On 27 February 1934, three months before al-Jabiri petitioned the presidents of the PMC and the Council, London announced that the petitions al-Jabiri had evidently sent to Geneva from Cairo in 1933 "are concerned with protesting in a general manner against the way in which the mandate is administered by the Mandatory Power. But the protest appears to deal with nothing sufficiently specific to enable detailed observations to be offered."[50] Geneva was glad to concede that al-Jabiri was a troublemaker bent on rousing suspicions about British governance in Palestine. And if London and Jerusalem felt confident they could dismiss his claims by simply stating otherwise, Geneva found no reason to disagree.

Between 1927 and 1934, therefore, London, Jerusalem, and Geneva remained unwilling to address or examine Palestinians' demands for redress regarding immigration and citizenship policies as they pertained to Palestine. Indeed, British authorities often avoided dealing with new cases throughout the 1930s by instead rehashing former decisions from London or Jerusalem. On 28 May 1937, Mr. Martin of the Treasury in London sent an "immediate and confidential" dispatch to Mr. Jones of the Foreign Office in which he proposed that Palestinian migrant requests for citizenship in 1937 should be denied. As for why, Martin included an excerpt from a dispatch from the colonial secretary to Plumer dated 7 October 1927, a copy of which was sent to the Foreign Office on the same date. Specifically, the excerpt enumerated three reasons why the applications should be denied, including the migrants' lengthy stays abroad, their dubious intentions for applying, and the undesirability of extending British protection to subjects residing abroad:

> (1) It is undesirable to grant Palestinian citizenship to persons who have been absent from Palestine for several years and who have no intention of returning to Palestine within a reasonable period and of residing there permanently. (2) It is considered that in many cases the principal object of applicants in such cases is to obtain British protection for the purpose of pressing claims against the Governments of the countries in which they reside. (3) Further, it is undesirable on general grounds to create a class of persons permanently resident abroad who would be entitled to British protection.[51]

Martin then asked Jones if there would be any objection from the Foreign Office to using the same reasons to reject the 1937 applications, explaining that the Colonial Office had none. A few days later, on 4 June, Jones replied that he and the Foreign Office also had no objection. This indolent behavior suggests that London did not ascertain the exact circumstances of Palestinian migrants' citizenship applications in 1937, over a decade after they rejected the first wave of applicants.

But London was fully aware of the extent of the problem by 1937. In May of that year, members of the Peel Commission, formally known as the Palestine Royal Commission, were suggesting that revisions needed to be made regarding the status of Palestinians residing abroad who were seeking citizenship. The Peel Commission was sent to Palestine on 11 November 1936 to investigate the unrest among Arabs of Palestine that had started that year with a six-month general strike. The situation had gotten so dire in Palestine that London decided to intervene, and members of the commission published a report on 7 July 1937 in which they outlined the causes of the unrest and possible solutions to it; chief among them was a plan to partition the land of Palestine between Jews and Arabs. One of the main causes for the unrest among Arabs mentioned in the report was the continued influx of Jewish migrants into Palestine. As the authors of the report described it: "The continued impact of a highly intelligent and enterprising race, backed by large financial resources, on a comparatively poor indigenous community, on a different cultural level, may produce in time serious reactions." Moreover, they continued, "though the Arabs have benefited by the development of the country owing to Jewish immigration, this has had no conciliatory effect. On the contrary, improvement in the economic situation in Palestine has meant the deterioration of the political situation."[52] The solution to the conflict, British authorities were wise to concede, would need to include revisions to the policies that angered the Arabs.

Earlier that year, on 21 May 1937, Harold Morris, a barrister and judge who was appointed to the Peel Commission, submitted a draft revision to a section of the upcoming Peel Report entitled "Nationality Law and Acquisition of Palestinian Citizenship" in which he suggested amendments to the 1925 Palestinian Citizenship Order-in-Council. Namely, Morris explained, article 2 of the ordinance dealing with "the question of the position of Turkish subjects born in Palestine who were and are habitually resident abroad" needed to be clarified since "an Arab witness put before us the case of Arabs who had left Palestine before the War intending eventually to return but had been unable to obtain Palestinian citizenship." This Arab had explained to Morris that approximately forty thousand migrants, most of whom were resident in South America, were experiencing the same predicament. Morris was baffled by this oversight and proceeded with details about this population: "They were loyal to the Ottoman Government until King Hussein proclaimed the revolution and then they threw in their lot with the Allies. They intend ultimately to return to Palestine where many of them have relations and some of them have property."[53]

Morris then pointed out the difficult situation these migrants faced due to the impractical time frame for applying for citizenship as it was laid out in the citizenship legislation. He elaborated that Palestinians residing abroad had originally been given two years from 1 August 1925 to opt for Palestinian citizenship under article 2 of the Citizenship Order-in-Council, but that time had subsequently been shortened on 6 November 1925 to two years from the date the Treaty of Lausanne came into force, 6 August 1924. By 6 November 1925, therefore, "Turkish nationals born in Palestine but resident abroad only had nine months instead of two years within which to exercise their option" to opt for citizenship. The Arab witness, Morris explained further, had added that the Citizenship Order-in-Council "was not fully advertised and the wording of the application form was not clear," leaving many migrants frustrated and unable to apply within a reasonable time frame. One of the unclear questions in the application form that the migrants had trouble answering was "Where do you intend to reside?" which most migrants evidently misinterpreted as meaning "Where do you intend to reside at the present time?" and thus provided their current country of residence.[54]

Morris also presented the migrants' current untenable situations. These individuals, he wrote, "are people in a foreign country who, owing to the Great War, through no fault of theirs, have practically ceased to have a country of their own." "It is an undoubted fact," he continued, that neither Turkey nor Britain offer them protection,

> nor can they obtain such protection, except by giving up their business and proceeding to Palestine, a course of action which many of them, doubtless, are in no position to afford and which in any case is not required of a national residing abroad who seeks his country's protection.[55]

Morris's insight into the difficulty of the migrants' situation was notable considering that, days later, the Peel Commission used the same reasons for denying citizenship that the Foreign Office had used in 1927. Morris subsequently explained that he was aware of these policies and the commission's existing stance on naturalizing Palestinians residing abroad, but he pointed out that "though the grievance is felt by all the individuals concerned, it is a greater hardship for those who have not severed their connexion with the land of their birth and intend to return there in their later years."[56]

Although Morris was sympathetic to the plight of many Palestinian migrants, he also pointed out a reality that he resolved was significant enough to warrant limited revision of the nationality law. In his report, he elaborated: "There is no genuine enthusiasm to be observed in Palestine for Palestinian citizenship. It is only the Arabs in South America who are really anxious for it. And under present conditions this does not surprise us." Morris was referring to the 1936 Arab Revolt and the general anger among Arabs in Palestine at the continued influx of Jews to Palestine who were then being naturalized as Palestinians. As for the "educated Palestinian Arab," he continued, "who has always resented the separation of Palestine from Syria, the very idea of Palestinian citizenship is obnoxious as being associated with the mandate and all it involves."[57] Morris concluded with his recommendation to the commission: "We suggest that at least those who are prepared to give a definite formal assurance of their intention to return to Palestine should be admitted to Palestinian citizenship."[58] Despite a decade of appeals and protests from migrants throughout the diaspora, and despite his acknowledgment of the difficulties the strict application requirements presented Palestinian migrants, Morris recommended in the report that the arbitrary stipulation of proving an intention to return permanently to Palestine should remain part of the citizenship application and rejection process.

Days later on 28 May 1937, another member of the Peel Commission, Morris Carter, submitted a more strongly worded amendment to the nationality law in which he elaborated on the unacceptable precariousness of these Palestinians' legal standing. In addition to inserting direct excerpts from the various policy documents drawn up in the 1920s, including the Treaty of Lausanne, he laid out the precise difficulty in determining the national status of Palestinians abroad as a result of the unreasonable time frame given to them to opt for citizenship. Yet he continued to deny their original claims to Palestinian nationality. "These persons," he explained, "technically remained Turkish subjects but the Turkish consuls abroad were and are not prepared to give them any assistance. They, therefore, are not given Turkish passports and they may not be given Palestinian passports." The next sentence began a new paragraph in which Carter explained that "they are people" who are connected to Palestine and wish to return to it after securing profit abroad:

> They are people who do not wish to be regarded as Turkish citizens; they feel that they owe no allegiance to Turkey and that Turkey does not wish for their allegiance. They regard Palestine as their country where their relatives still live; on the whole, they maintain a substantial connexion with their families and their hope is to return to Palestine after earning a competence on which to retire.

Carter continued by describing the challenges these migrants faced even after some were awarded travel facilities to enter Palestine on temporary visas: "Once they are in Palestine difficulties occur with regard to their national status, particularly when they wish to travel." Carter concluded by reiterating that the circumstances he had described "outweighed" the reasons given to deny their applications and that it was "reasonable and proper that protection should be extended to these people by the power which now governs the country of their origins." Finally, he proclaimed, "every effort should be made to restore to these Arabs a right ordinarily enjoyed by the nationals of civilized peoples."[59] Carter's recommendations were never implemented. Nevertheless, his report shows that by 1937, officials in London and Jerusalem were still debating whether migrants who had left Palestine while it was under Ottoman rule were considered Turkish citizens, a legal designation promulgated as a result of the 1923 Treaty of Lausanne and the creation of the Turkish Republic.

The deliberations that took place in London in May and June of 1937 indicate that officials in London were conflicted, as Michell in La Paz, Bolivia, had been a decade earlier, regarding what to do with migrants claiming rights to Palestinian citizenship. They also indicate that legislating citizenship over the course of the 1920s and 1930s was characterized by indolent, capricious, and obstinate behavior on the part of London and Jerusalem. Confidential dispatches and internal disagreements continually circled back to erstwhile policies, but considering British officials' priorities when it came to the governance of Palestine, London and Jerusalem were not impelled to make progress legislating Palestinian citizenship when it came to non-Jews. In March 1937, the Peel Commission asked the Government of Palestine to supply information regarding the naturalization of Jews during the 1930s. In response, it was reported on 8 March that more than 28,000 Jews had been naturalized in Palestine between 1931 and 1936, and that out of a total of 4,941 certificates of citizenship granted in 1936, the Government of Palestine reported that 4,847 were for Jews.[60] It is therefore unsurprising that in May 1937, authorities in London were linking Palestinian migrants to Turkish nationality and that in early June, Mr. Martin of the Treasury and Mr. Jones of the Foreign Office found no reason to amend the policy on denying citizenship applications to Palestinians residing abroad.

But the Arab Revolt, which by the time it ended in September 1939 had left approximately 5,000 Arabs, 300 Jews, and 260 Britons dead and which subsequently alerted Britain to the importance of reconsidering its approach to the opposing inhabitants of its mandated territory, did bring change to the governance of Palestine. On 6 November 1939, two months after the revolt ended, article 2 of the 1925 Palestinian Citizenship Order-in-Council was officially amended to clearly state the stipulations that applicants needed to have "maintained an unbroken personal connection to Palestine" and that they intended to reside there permanently:

> Persons over eighteen years of age at the 6th of August, 1924, who were born within Palestine and acquired on birth or subsequently and still possess Turkish nationality and on the first day of August, 1925, were habitually resident

> abroad and have since maintained an unbroken personal connection with Palestine and intend to resume permanent residence in Palestine, may acquire Palestinian citizenship by opting in such a manner as may be prescribed by Regulation under this Order, subject to the consent of the Government of Palestine which may be granted or withheld in its absolute discretion.[61]

On the one hand, the addition of these two requirements might indicate that the Government of Palestine revised the amendment to be more transparent about its policies so as to appease the Arabs of Palestine, whose three-year revolt was significantly connected to the continued influx of Jewish migrants to Palestine. On the other hand, it upheld that these applicants were considered Turkish nationals, despite their claims to the contrary, and reiterated its absolute discretion in granting or withholding Palestinian citizenship so as to assert its power over an insurgent population. In an ironic way, then, British policy makers' commitment throughout Britain's rule in Palestine to distancing thousands of Palestinian migrants legally and permanently from Palestine by continually and for the same reasons refusing to acknowledge their claims to Palestinian citizenship substantiated an expanding diaspora of people who could only identify—and be defined—as Palestinians.

PALESTINIAN MIGRANTS AND THE INTERWAR WORLD ORDER

The long-term collaboration between London, Jerusalem, and Geneva in designing and applying citizenship legislation that at once ensured the naturalization of Jews and the disenfranchisement of Palestinian migrants serves as an example of the colonial foundations that underlay the practices of British rule and international law in the interwar period. Antony Anghie has argued that the history of international law since the nineteenth century is one in which "international law continuously disempowers the non-European world" since "colonialism was central to [its] constitution."[62] In other words, if it were not for the colonial encounter, European sovereignty, whether in the form of mandates, nation-states, or the League of Nations, would not have reached its fullest global potential. The "dynamic of difference" between the center and periphery, the civilized and uncivilized, or the European and non-European propelled international law "in its necessarily endless drive towards universality."[63]

The Government of Palestine functioned as the sole authority in Palestine during the interwar period, and accordingly, it established categories of legal belonging and non-belonging to the territory of Palestine that were confirmable with passports, new documents that accorded eligible applicants benefits associated with citizenship. As Rogers Brubaker and Frederick Cooper put it, the state is "a powerful 'identifier' . . . because it has the material and symbolic resources to impose the categories, classificatory schemes, and modes of social counting and accounting . . . to which non-state actors must refer."[64] Yet while the state is a powerful identifier, so too are various social collectives like "families, firms, schools, social movements, and bureaucracies of all kinds" that can challenge the state in different ways, for "even the most powerful state does not monopolize the production and diffusion of identifications and categories; and those that it does produce may be contested."[65] In the history of the emergence of Palestinian national consciousness as a mode of collective political identification in the first half of the twentieth century, Palestinian migrants were central. The thousands of Palestinian migrants who protested the rejection of their applications for Palestinian citizenship contributed to the circulation of modes of identification among Palestinians worldwide that defined them as Palestinians, thus posing a direct challenge to colonial authorities who denied them that very identifier. These modes of self and group understanding had already existed among this population of southern Syrians, and they grew in significance and potency with the persistence of inequitable European policies in the Middle East.

The historical processes of constructing self or group modes of identification, whether through the mediation of the state or social groups, are therefore "fundamentally situational and contextual."[66] In effect, identifying with a nation or a nationalist movement must be understood as a historical process that is always marked by "hard work and long struggles" for state actors and individuals alike.[67] If early twentieth-century British rule in Palestine can be characterized by the creation of opposing categories between the citizen and the non-citizen that fixed identification in a new way, then the reactions of Palestinian migrants in petitions, newspapers, and appeals throughout the 1920s and 1930s should be seen as constituting durable and meaningful strategies for self and group identification that emerged alongside, sometimes in response to, and at times irrespective of the practices of colonial control emanating from London, Geneva, or Jerusalem.[68] This transnational "stage" of colonialism, as Timothy Mitchell has termed it, was filled with a range of actors reacting to and producing a variety of legal, political, and social categories of practice.[69]

The imperial nature of Britain's "civilizing mission" in Palestine is the backdrop to the subsequent chapters' exploration of transnational Palestinians' reactions to their exclusion from Palestinian citizenship in petitions, letters, and newspapers. Even though petitions and protests from communities across the world were routinely ignored and even though the "Mandates Commission did its best to discredit and silence many of these voices—to bar them from their meetings, to reject their petitions, to impugn their motives—they could never quite shut them up."[70] The noise these voices created was loud, and it was foundational to the formation of Palestinian jaaliyaat worldwide.

CHAPTER 4

MEXICO'S PALESTINIANS TAKE ON BRITAIN'S INTERWAR EMPIRE

FOLLOWING THE REJECTION of their applications for Palestinian citizenship, mahjar Palestinians immediately drafted protests and appeals in carefully worded petitions addressed to different British and European officials. Between December 1926 and May 1927, Palestinian migrants in Mexico, centered largely in the northern towns of Linares, Monterrey, Saltillo, San Pedro, and Torreon, organized into several committees and drafted lengthy petitions, signed by hundreds of Palestinians, that were submitted to British consular offices in Saltillo and Monterrey. One petition in particular, authored by members of the Centro Social Palestino de Monterrey, was substantive in length and content. The six-page petition conveyed the attachment of Mexico's Palestinians to Palestine—as Palestinians—and their concerns following Jerusalem's denial of their applications for citizenship in November 1926. The petition also challenged British mandate policy and pointed out Jerusalem's contravention of international law as laid out by the League of Nations.

On 5 February 1927, the Centro's president and secretary signed the petition, addressed to the high commissioner for Palestine, Herbert Plumer, and submitted it to the British consul in Monterrey. President Salamon Canavati[1] and Secretary B. J. Kawas, speaking on behalf of "at least nine tenths" of other Palestinian migrants in Mexico, declared their rights to Palestinian nationality:

> We firmly believe we have a right to [Palestinian] nationality and to be held as citizens of Palestine, forming an integral part of our Common Country to which we are tied by all bonds of our birth, our customs, our traditions, our language and all the other ethnic and social elements which contribute to make what we call Fatherland.[2]

Like their predecessors throughout the Americas who had protested the Zionist takeover of their homeland a decade prior, Palestinian migrants in 1927 Mexico demanded their rights as a disenfranchised collective. In other words, while London and Jerusalem were deliberating and implementing the policies that would ensure the long-term exclusion of Palestinian migrants from Palestine—and, for that matter, while the Mexican government was legislating restrictions on migration from the Middle East—these communities were also circulating petitions that defined them, unequivocally, as Palestinians.

READING THE PETITIONS

What, exactly, was the petitioning process, and why did it emerge to begin with? The right of subjects of mandates to petition their European trustees emerged as an unintended consequence of the 1919 Paris Peace Conference. During the conference, representatives of the victorious Allies negotiated the fates of the defeated Central Powers, including laying the groundwork for the mandates system as a way to manage their former territorial holdings. They also formed the League of Nations to act as the first international, intergovernmental organization devoted to maintaining world order and to supervising the administration of the new mandates. Throughout this process, neither the Covenant of the League of Nations, article 22 of which established the PMC to oversee the mandates, nor the texts of the mandates themselves, made provisions for a petition process.[3] In fact, there was great objection to it from both British and French authorities at the conference. Yet petitions persisted for the duration of the European mandates in the Middle East and West Africa in large part due to the ceaseless outpouring of objections to European rule from newly mandated territories. As Susan Pedersen puts it, "On a fundamental level . . . , the emergence of that process [of petitioning] was the achievement of petitioners themselves—of those thousands of men and women who, often at considerable risk, raised their voices against the new dispensation."[4]

By late 1917, word had spread of Britain and France's plans to assume power in the region and of Britain's support for the establishment of a Jewish "national home" in Palestine. As a result, petitions from across the Middle East and the Arabic-speaking diaspora flooded European offices. In West Africa, moreover, inhabitants of British-mandated Togo and Cameroon were outraged when Britain handed over the majority of these territories to France in 1919. They, too, petitioned. Eventually, representatives of the Allies in attendance at the Peace Conference decided that they needed an organized system through which they could manage their noisy spoils of war in the Middle East and West Africa. On 11 October 1921, William Rappard, director of the Mandate Department of the League of Nations, sent a letter to Eric Drummond, first secretary-general of the league, explaining his thoughts regarding the "strong case" being made by Arabs against European rule: "Personally, I cannot bring myself to feel that we are doing our full duty towards the inhabitants of these territories."[5] He added that while Arab protests were "often naïve and badly worded, . . . I do feel that they can make out a strong case against the way in which they have been and are being treated by France and Great Britain."[6]

In London, William Ormsby-Gore of the Colonial Office had also been calling for an organized petition process that would manage the volume of appeals they were receiving. The PMC had received 613 appeals from Syria and Palestine alone by its second meeting in August 1922.[7] Rappard and Ormsby-Gore thus recognized that "inhabitants under mandate must have the right to petition the League,"[8] and they managed to ratify, in August 1922, a proposal for "a petition process, through which populations living under mandatory rule learned to claim that they, too, were nations deserving to be heard."[9]

But given the strict and restrictive guidelines for their content and submission, petitions could not subvert the authority of the mandates or the League of Nations. Those that did simply never made it to their recipients. Consequently, while petitions gave voice to transnational mandated subjects, they often arrived "muted, ventriloquized, and distorted—into the rooms in which their fates were determined."[10] Yet petitions invite a different kind of analysis. The fact that petitioners did not deny the legitimacy and sovereignty of mandate governments even though they did not gain redress regarding their repeated appeals and protests throughout the interwar period suggests that they were aware of what they were doing. Why would they have continued petitioning for as long as they did if they were not, in some ways, benefiting from it?

Petitions should be examined as more complex forms of social practice that instantiated an expanding transnational network of politically active, colonized subjects cleverly navigating the new liberal world order. As Natasha Wheatley puts it, "petitions document the mandate's interpretation and deployment in something we might term a strategic grassroots internationalism" whereby petitioners "still assumed the system possessed some power, and sought to manipulate it as best they could."[11] Working within the system, as it were, petitions and their authors inspire a series of historical queries. Who among these transnational communities knew to come together and draft documents to send to distant colonial powers? Whose signatures did they seek? How did they select and phrase the political and legal jargon that was necessary for these petitions to reach the desks of European authorities? What did petitioners ultimately hope to accomplish by pointing out a mandate government's use or misuse of power? How did they adapt to the changing process of petitioning between the 1920s, 1930s, and 1940s? Concomitantly, how did individuals and communities make sense of the utility of petitioning over these dramatically shifting decades, especially with Britain's continued rejection of their petitions and Geneva's continued silence? Finally, to the extent that petitions can be read as reflections of their authors' voices, what can we conclude about the ways in which migrant petitioners self and group identified in the interwar period?

The conspicuously political language Palestinians across Mexico used in their petitions points to the emergence of the term *Palestinian* as a distinct and legal mode of self and group identification among Palestinians in 1920s Mexico. In other words, treating petitions as windows into the social aspects of interwar Palestinian history, we can ascertain the ways in which members of Mexico's Palestinian jaaliya strategically employed the liberal discourses of the interwar world order to define themselves culturally, historically, politically, and legally, as Palestinians. In their petitions, Palestinians asserted their claims to Palestinian citizenship based on, among other connections, birth, race, ancestry, and property; they conveyed their serious concerns at being denied their rights to Palestinian nationality; and they made clear the urgency with which they hoped British authorities would redress the injustice.

In the aftermath of the 1925 citizenship ordinance, most petitions were addressed to the high commissioner for Palestine, who was responsible for the decisions regarding naturalization emanating from Jerusalem. But petitioners also addressed their missives to the League of Nations in Geneva and the Colonial, Foreign, and Home Offices in London, as well as to the offices of the Arab Executive in Jerusalem. Petitions were first submitted to local British consulates, who then forwarded them to the appropriate recipients, most commonly in London, Geneva, and Jerusalem. For their part, consuls took these petitions rather seriously, expeditiously forwarding them to their intended recipients. In turn, London, Geneva, and Jerusalem responded, normally within weeks, but at times months went by before local consuls were instructed on what to do. Yet rarely did these petitions win their authors redress. Out of thousands of petitions submitted to London, Geneva, and Jerusalem from Middle Eastern migrants throughout the Americas during the interwar period, the majority were rejected.

Notwithstanding, the act of petitioning was not without merit. Petitioners served to keep the mandate's practices in check by consistently reminding mandate authorities that their subjects were not only observing them but also critically evaluating their leadership in written documents that, in theory, could hold them accountable for breaches of power. Moreover, the language petitioners used in their petitions indicates the internationalization of the interwar liberal world order, which promised self-determination and rights to new national collectives. Palestinian migrants across the Americas were demanding their rights to Palestinian nationality and citizenship using the same discourses of justice and rights being produced in London, Geneva, and Jerusalem. Palestinian migrants thus continually put to the test the new world order that promised them national independence, at least nominally. And in the process, they formed into a distinct political and legal collective that was decidedly Palestinian and that was committed to achieving Palestine's self-determination. Palestinian national consciousness thus also has roots in early twentieth-century Mexico.

Joining the "Liberal" Interwar World Trend

Petitions written by Middle Eastern migrants throughout the mahjar indicate that their authors firmly believed that they were entitled to the liberal right of self-determination that was inscribed in the pages of postwar treaties across

Europe. The law was the law, after all. And according to the law, they deserved national rights as liberated subjects of the former Ottoman Empire if not because of their support for the Entente Powers during the war, then certainly because they were promised these rights. Accordingly, they continued to take their claims to the international community, regardless of Geneva, London, or Jerusalem's positions. Interestingly, British consuls throughout the Americas, and even some in Jerusalem and London, recognized that Palestinian migrants did deserve to be afforded recognition as Palestinians or at least to have their demands heard. As an example, on 19 April 1927, the consul general in Mexico City, J. B. Browne, forwarded a petition to the Foreign Office in London that had been submitted to the vice-consul in Saltillo, R. H. Jeffrey, by members of the Comité Hijos de Palestina in Saltillo. The petition was written on 12 April 1927, and evidently, the vice-consul's office in Saltillo considered it to be of sufficient import that it had it translated before sending it to Mexico City.

President Jesus Talamas and Secretary Bishara Andonie of the Comité submitted a petition to Jeffrey protesting the news of Jerusalem's refusal to grant Palestinian citizenship to several members of their community, of which they had been informed on 16 March 1927. They were outraged at the reasons given for refusing their applications—namely, "because they have not shown their desire to return to their country and because they have been for a long time away from Palestine."[12] Talamas and Andonie declared: "We do not consider that the declarations of the Palestinian Government are based on right or justice." They requested from Jeffrey that, since he knew them well, he relay to Jerusalem that the Palestinian community in Saltillo had "always been on your side and on the side of the Cause both morally and by giving cash." They were referring to the assistance they offered the vice-consulate during World War I. They then affirmed every member of their community's intention to return to Palestine and reiterated that "if we do not do it at once," it is on account of economic obligations. In Mexico City, Consul General Browne seemed to agree with Jeffrey that the petition should in the least be considered, and so he forwarded it to London. In his brief dispatch to the Foreign Office to which the petition was attached, Browne stressed that Jeffrey had explained to him that these Palestinians were known to him as "Pro-Allies." Jeffrey had evidently told Browne that, during the war, the Comité "used every effort to assist the Vice-Consulate more particularly in connexion with propaganda work."[13] London did not respond directly to this petition, though it submitted a rather unsympathetic official statement regarding all applicants for Palestinian citizenship under article 2 of the 1925 citizenship ordinance later that year in October.

Notwithstanding London and Jerusalem's tendency to ignore or deny petitioners' requests, petitioners used petitions to continually remind their distant rulers that they were legally accountable for securing their national rights and that they would continue to do so for as long as their citizenship was denied. That is, "petitioners in the 1920s attributed authority and efficacy to the League's law, experimenting with the system's premise that international law constrained British colonialism: that one could 'speak mandate' to power and expect a result."[14] And though the reality throughout the interwar period frequently proved otherwise for Palestinian migrants, the fact that they continued to petition signals their confidence in the validity of their claims to Palestinian citizenship based on international law. Staking claims to Palestinian citizenship through birthright and racial, linguistic, familial, and material connections to Palestine reinforced the diaspora community's international legal and political standing *as* Palestinians.

The frequency and volume of petitions throughout the interwar years indicates that the liberal language of international law promulgated by the League of Nations continually impelled petitioners transnationally to come together into political collectives to demand national rights. Moreover, the longevity of the petitioning process suggests that petitioners knew they needed to continually update their approaches to communicating with the league by employing new "discourses that articulated more foundational rights" as the rhetoric of international law, citizenship, and national rights evolved.[15] Petitioning mandate authorities was thus a strategic and critical component of collective political and legal claims-making among transnational migrant communities over the course of European rule in the Middle East.

But since petitions ultimately reinforced colonial control, the process of petitioning mandate authorities necessarily meant that Palestinian migrants had to endorse the authority and sovereignty of the mandate and Britain's right to be in Palestine. Through this, petitioners tacitly accepted their status as subjects and, as a result, petitions effectively strengthened the league's hegemony, wherever that may have been. Natasha Wheatley argues that "petitioning was an instrumental part of the world of rule: a channel of communication between the governed and those who governed them, but also a practice that summarized and performed the logics of the political order in question."[16] The act of petitioning, which was sanctioned by European authorities, showed how the league's new international legal order "offered particular openings for critique and protest" that served to formalize and escalate a "style of politics" characterized by top-down, unequal distribution of rights and privileges.[17] Simply put, the League of Nations and the PMC could allow petitions in order to project an image of democratic transnational governance where subjects' voices were heard, but they could also easily and conclusively dismiss them, affirming their ultimate sovereignty.

Over the course of mandate rule in the interwar period, laws and amendments were instated that limited the number and restricted the content of petitions received in Geneva, London, and Jerusalem. Not just any petition could be submitted; the guidelines for petitions were quite strict and formulaic:

> A petition needed to satisfy certain conditions to be deemed "receivable." It must be sent first to the mandatory power . . . ; it could not be anonymous, challenge the mandate itself, nor complain of a matter that could achieve legal remedy in the municipal law of the mandate territory. If the petition made it through this procedural obstacle course, a member of the PMC was then tasked with drafting a report to be discussed by the whole commission before it was sent to the council.[18]

This precarious journey ensured the premature death of many petitions, but it also encouraged petitioners to take the process seriously by doing the necessary research and work. This included consulting friendly local consular offices, collecting signatures of support from as many voices in the diaspora as possible, and consequently, meeting as collectives to word cogent, concise, and realistic grievances and demands. These grievances and demands had to abide by the league's guidelines for submitting petitions, yes, but they also had to reflect their authors' confidence and perseverance in engaging in a new world order that promised them and their community rights and privileges so long as they played by the rules. In effect, Palestinian migrants did not demand that the British leave Palestine in their petitions; rather, they acknowledged Britain's right to be in Palestine following its liberation from the Ottomans but pointed out the British mandate's mishandling of international law and its abuse of power as it pertained to migration, land distribution, and citizenship legislation for migrants.

Over time, petitioners grew increasingly aware that petitioning would bring them little more than frustration and disillusionment with the new world order that paid little attention to their rights. This was due to the way in which the League of Nations administered its mandates and the Palestine mandate, more specifically. Although the league offered mandated subjects the right to "talk" to their mandate authorities through petitions, there was no system put in place to guarantee that mandate governments consider the petitions. "Put bluntly," Pedersen begins, "League oversight could not force the mandatory powers to govern mandated territories differently; instead, it obliged them to *say* they were governing them differently."[19] This, to be sure, was built into the logic of interwar international governance. To wit, the interwar liberal "international system" dominated by Europe—and that universally publicized and validated state-centered, self-determined nationalisms—was paradoxically also the justification European states used for the unprecedented forms of power, violence, and injustice they inflicted upon different transnational populations throughout the twentieth century.[20]

And when it came to Britain's administration of Palestine during its mandate, Geneva maintained a more extreme hands-off policy. Petitions that reached Geneva regarding Palestine were directly forwarded to London, so long as they did not question Britain's right to be in Palestine or its promise to the Zionists. As an interesting example, a small group of eleven Palestinians in Trujillo, Honduras, petitioned the League of Nations directly on 23 April 1927 following the high commissioner's rejection of their applications for Palestinian citizenship. The petition, signed by "a part of the many rejected Palestinians," was originally written on 11 April 1927 and submitted to A. H. Tatum, British consul in Trujillo. It reached Geneva on 25 May 1927 with a short letter from its author, Juan Sikaffy, requesting that the league address their concern at the soonest time.[21] Sikaffy and the ten other petitioners were protesting against the "arbitrary and unjust decision of the High Commissioner." They declared that each of them was "of Palestinian birth, . . . and we are actually owners of many thousands of acres of lands valued at several thousand pounds sterling, lands handed down to each of us from generation to generation." Accordingly, they were "decidedly against" the high commissioner's decision, which was based on their prolonged absence from Palestine. They explained that they had not adopted any other nationalities since their time away from Palestine and had no intention of doing so. They promised to continue to fight for their right to Palestinian citizenship and that they would be sending the petition to the British minister in Tegucigalpa, the Home Office in London, and the League of Nations. Intriguingly, they also strategically asked if the high commissioner would advise them of "any Jewish bankers or financiers, who are willing to make a settlement with us for all our holdings" and that they be informed "of the status of citizenship we hold" so they know "to what flag we owe our allegiance" in the event that their applications were denied again.

On 4 June 1927, Secretary-General Drummond, under instruction by the chairman of the PMC, sent Sikaffy's petition to the foreign secretary in London. He indicated that he would transmit to the PMC "any observations on this matter which the British Government may desire to make." The Foreign Office subsequently deliberated with Under-Secretary William Ormsby-Gore at the Colonial Office, who had spoken with his superior at the Colonial Office, Leopold Amery, who had already been in contact with George Symes, chief secretary of the Government of Jerusalem, regarding Sikaffy's petition and several more from Mexico. On 7 October 1927, and with the foreign secretary's consent, Ormsby-Gore submitted a letter to Plumer indicating that London saw no reason to amend the requirements for citizenship for Sikaffy, his fellow petitioners, or others whose applications were rejected since "there can be little doubt" that their "principal object . . . was to obtain British protection for the purpose of pressing claims against the Governments of the countries in which they reside." He reiterated Jerusalem's right to implement citizenship as it saw fit and added that he believed that the current administration of article 2 of the citizenship ordinance "should not be in any way relaxed."[22] Finally, he told Plumer that he would be sending his reply to Drummond and that he would send Plumer a copy of his letter to Drummond in due course.

The demise of Sikaffy's petition reflects the hierarchical chain Geneva established for the administration of its mandates, and especially for the most contested among them: Palestine. Petitions submitted to the League of Nations regarding Palestine were first forwarded to the PMC, which then determined whether to disregard them altogether or forward them to London. To be sure, the PMC did not make decisions on behalf of London when it came to Palestine. If it decided to proceed with the petition, it would send it back to the secretary-general to forward to London's Foreign Office. Members of the Foreign Office would consult with the Colonial Office and the Government of Jerusalem, which was routinely assured that it need not amend its policies. Britain effectively administered its mandate over Palestine outside the law, and Geneva endorsed this. The League of Nations and its mandates were therefore "mechanisms for generating talk" about self-determination, independence, and governance while putting little pressure on the actual mandate powers to put this rhetoric into practice.[23] Ultimately, there was no legal precedent for the protection of the rights of would-be nationals in the early years of international law; there was only colonialism.[24]

Over the course of mandate rule in the interwar period, "more than 3,000 appeals, charges, or communications of some kind *reached* the Secretariat in Geneva. . . . The vast majority," at 43.3 percent, "concerned Syria or Palestine."[25] Most of these, one way or the other, questioned the behavior of the mandate system writ large and the British Mandate for Palestine specifically, and most were dismissed. But even though petitions were ultimately unable to effect change in European colonial rule in the interwar period, they accomplished important feats for transnational communities struggling for rights in an age of national self-determination and legal claims making. Petitions served as consistent reminders that a given mandate's practice of power and its sovereignty were under surveillance by transnational communities engaged in a new "international sphere" defined by the liberal promises of self-determination and national rights.[26]

And though the league left the administration of Palestine to London and Jerusalem, by petitioning, Palestinian migrants effectively reminded London and Jerusalem throughout the interwar period that they were subjects of the British mandate, which owed them protection, guidance, and eventual independence, according to international law. After all, they were, had always been, and always would be, Palestinians. Put differently, the "universalism" of the liberal discourses of twentieth-century colonialism gave the colonized "a handle—outside of the immediate power relations—to single out local tyrannies and claim global rights."[27] This practice substantiated significant collective political, social, and legal "stances, projects, claims, idioms, practices" that fueled the growth and consolidation of transnational political Palestinian consciousness in an expanding diaspora.[28]

THE VOICES OF MEXICO'S PALESTINIAN PETITIONERS

On 11 November 1926, the British vice-consul in Mexico City sent a letter to Mr. Antonio J. Dieck, then president of the Centro Social Palestino in Monterrey, explaining the reasons for rejecting several applications for Palestinian citizenship made by Palestinian residents of Monterrey earlier that year. The vice-consul explained that the applicants had all been "absent from Palestine for periods of from twelve to twenty-five years:"

> I beg to advise you that I have received a dispatch from H.B.M. Consule General in the City of Mexico, stating that the following applications for citizenship have been refused:
>
> Salamon Canavati . . . Azize Marcos de Dieck . . . Zacarias J. Dieck . . . Espiridion Canavati and Salha Mansour Elias Freige. . . .
>
> H.B.M. Consule-General sends me a dispatch from the Officer Administering the Government of Palestine, from which I quote the following in regard to the above applications:
>
> "2" The Applicants have in every case been absent from Palestine for periods of from twelve to twenty-five years, and more and it is apparent that they have severed all connections with this country. In these circumstances I do not propose to accept their applications.

He added that they could reapply for citizenship before 1 August of that year if they fulfilled the six-month residency requirement in Palestine and if they could prove Ottoman nationality and birth in Palestine:

> "3" It will, however, be open to them to apply for citizenship under Art. 4 of the order, provided application is made before the 1st. of August, next, and provided also that they qualify by residence in Palestine for a period of six months before the date of application and are able to produce satisfactory evidence of Ottoman nationality and birth in Palestine.[29]

In response to this letter, members of Monterrey's Centro Social Palestino, now under the leadership of Salamon Canavati, met throughout January 1927 and drafted a petition to send to the high commissioner. In their 5 February petition, they declared that the 1925 Palestinian Citizenship Order-in-Council contravened international law as it was prescribed by the League of Nations. Canavati, Secretary Kawas, and approximately 220 members of the

Centro who signed their names to the petition explained further that excluding the migrants from citizenship—a legal requisite for self-determination—would constitute a disavowal of the British mandate's purported responsibility, as dictated by the League of Nations, to the aspiring constituents of a Palestinian nation. If the migrants were to permanently be denied citizenship, the petitioners argued, their "personal statute would come to be fixed in such terms which in no way could agree either with the general principles of equity and justice or with the modern practices of International Law."[30]

Whether London or Jerusalem liked it or not, the disenfranchisement of an individual or community in a newly interconnected world would not go unnoticed if the individual or community petitioned the League of Nations. The process of petitioning the league for redress regarding a mandate's behavior, questioning the mandate, and appealing rejections created a global space within which ordinary individuals and groups communicated with states, legal bodies, and international regimes. In this way, the "mandate system created 'mandated peoples' as figures in international law, granting them standing—a place from which to write."[31] Concomitantly, the more petitions were dismissed on arbitrary grounds, the more convinced petitioners were that they had the right to appeal the league using more strongly worded petitions. The Monterrey petitioners therefore felt vindicated and certain in their petition to Plumer when they declared: "We firmly believe we have a right to [Palestinian] nationality and to be held as citizens of Palestine."[32] Ultimately, this relational process between petitioners and their distant overlords cemented the authority of the league and the British mandate, as well as the practice of rejecting appeals, but it also contributed to strengthening networks of solidarity and collective identification among Palestinians in the diaspora.

As Canavati began convening with other members of the Centro Social Palestino de Monterrey to draft a petition, he also reached out to Jesus Talamas, president of the Comité Hijos de Palestina in Saltillo, a group established in 1917 that had secured significant economic and political leverage, especially with the British vice-consulate in Saltillo. A month prior, on 2 January 1927, Talamas submitted the first petition on behalf of the Comité Hijos de Palestina to Plumer. On 3 February, two days before Canavati's petition, Talamas submitted another one to the minister of the colonies in London, of which he sent copies to Plumer and Musa Kazim al-Husseini, president of the Arabic Executive at the time and former mayor of Jerusalem between 1918 and 1920.[33] In both, he affirmed his and his community's Palestinianness, committing to protesting any attempts to deny it.[34] With their considerable influence among Palestinian communities in Monterrey and Saltillo, two of Mexico's larger urban centers in the north, Canavati and Talamas managed to collect signatures of support from palestinos in colonias palestinas throughout the northern corridor. The network of Palestinian jaaliyaat in northern Mexico stretched from the eastern towns of Linares, Monterrey, and Saltillo to San Pedro and Torreon in the center, and all the way to Chihuahua farther to the west. This chain of Palestinian collectives covered three of Mexico's largest states: Nuevo Leon, Coahuila, and Chihuahua, which bordered the United States. Palestinian communities in Mexico thus formed an integral part of Mexico's northern east-west corridor, and their flurry of activism in the early months of 1927 through petitions that reached British authorities in regional consulates in Monterrey and Saltillo, the Consulate General in Mexico City, the Foreign Office in London, the PMC in Geneva, and the Government of Palestine in Jerusalem reflects the economic and political clout of this diaspora collective.

Throughout late January and February, Palestinians in Linares, Saltillo, San Pedro, and Chihuahua submitted telegrams in Spanish and Arabic to the Centro Social Palestino, pledging their support to the campaign to petition the high commissioner in Jerusalem. Each telegram included the signatures of those involved, which totaled approximately 135, excluding the original 220 signatures of members of the Centro Social Palestino.[35] The telegrams written in Spanish were succinct and reflected the formal language used in the Centro's petition. As an example, the jaaliya in Linares submitted the following telegram on 26 February 1927:

> The undersigned, members of the Palestinian colony based in Linares, N.L., energetically protest against the decision of His Excellency Field Marshal Lord Plumer in charge of the English Government in Palestine to ignore our rights to citizenship for being absent from our country more than 12 years, and we support in all its parts the protest presented by the members of our colony in Monterrey, N.L. Mex.[36]

On the other hand, on 10 February, Talamas and thirty-five members of the Comité Hijos de Palestina had sent a concise letter of support to Monterrey in Arabic and in a less formal register: "We, the sons of Palestine generally and those resident in this city, support the protests of our brothers in Monterrey" (figure 5).[37] Collectively, these telegrams signified the

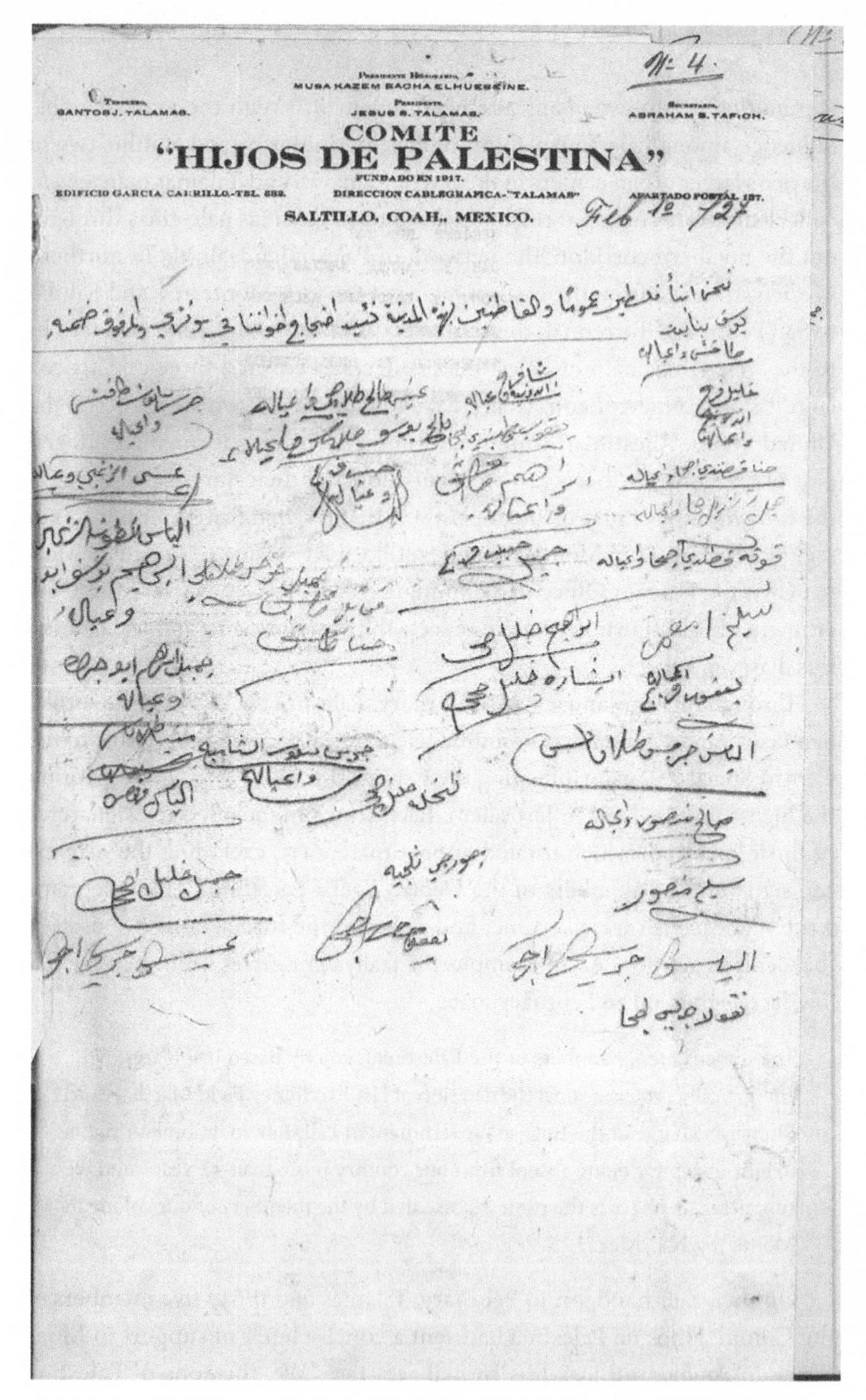

No. 4.

Presidente Honorario, MUSA KAZEM BACHA ELHUESSEINE.

Tesorero, SANTOS J. TALAMAS. — Presidente, JESUS S. TALAMAS. — Secretario, ABRAHAM S. TAFICH.

COMITE
"HIJOS DE PALESTINA"
FUNDADO EN 1917.

EDIFICIO GARCIA CARRILLO.-TEL. 833. — DIRECCION CABLEGRAFICA.-"TALAMAS" — APARTADO POSTAL 127.

SALTILLO, COAH., MEXICO. Feb 10 /27

FIGURE 5. The 10 February 1927 declaration of support for the Monterrey petitioners from members of the Comité Hijos de Palestina in Saltillo. Source: Israel State Archives, Jerusalem, M-233/38.

interconnectedness of northern Mexico's Palestinian communities and their commitment to supporting one another in the defense of their rights to Palestinian citizenship.

For its part in representing these collectives in their joint protest, the Centro Social Palestino amended its 5 February petition and submitted a revised one on 23 February. Canavati and Kawas began the original petition by indicating that they were speaking on behalf of "all natives of Palestine . . . having been born there."[38] But on 23 February, the vice-president of the Centro, Abraham Masso, and Kawas began their petition with the following statement:

> We, the undersigned native-born Palestinians, resident of the Cities of Monterrey, Saltillo, Chihuahua and San Pedro, Coahuila, Republic of Mexico, do hereby most respectfully beg to lay before you the following information and to solicit your aid in the solution of a problem, which for us is most serious.

Similarly, the original petition ended with the signatures of Canavati and Kawas, but the revised one included the following statement: "Signed on behalf of the members of THE PALESTINIAN COLONIES."[39] Unmistakably, the new petition represented a larger collective, and below these words, Masso and Kawas added: "Attached are the signatures of more than three hundred of our compatriots,"[40] the first of which was Salamon Canavati's (figure 6). Throughout January and February 1927, the Centro's leadership thus managed to add more than one hundred signatures to the original petition from Palestinians residing between Chihuahua and Linares, two towns at the opposite ends of a corridor that stretches more than 900 kilometers across much of northern Mexico.

As indicated by the opening lines of the revised petition, this newly disenfranchised collective used the opportunity to communicate with Mexico City, London, Geneva, and Jerusalem via petitions to demand national rights within a new liberal age of legislated international colonialism. The language in the petition was thus not subversive and ultimately reflected a community that was asking to be included in Britain's transnational empire. But this community also used the petition as a platform to circulate, transnationally, language that they strategically borrowed from the new liberal discourses of international law and then creatively manipulated in a way that substantiated their standing as Palestinians respectfully making demands of their mandate.

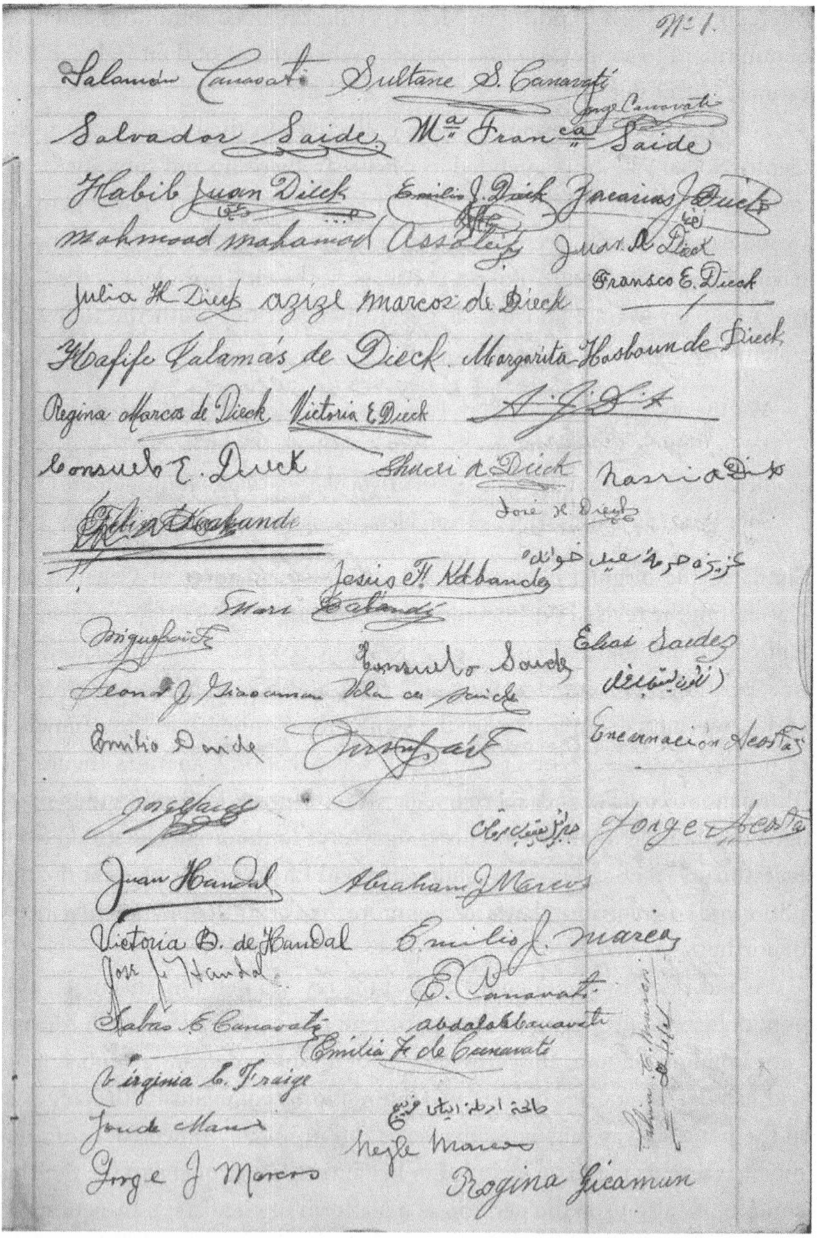
Nº 1.

Salamon Canavati Sultane S. Canavati
Jorge Canavati
Salvador Saide Mª Franca Saide
Habib Juan Dieck Emilio J. Dieck Zacarias J. Dieck
Mahmoud Mahamad Assaleff Juan A. Dieck
Fransco E. Dieck
Julia H. Dieck Azize Marcos de Dieck
Nafife Salamás de Dieck Margarita Hasboun de Dieck
Regina Marcos de Dieck Victoria E. Dieck
Consuelo E. Dieck Shucri A. Dieck
Jose H. Dieck
Jesus H. Kabande
Elias Saide
Consuelo Saide
Encarnacion Acosta
Jorge Acosta
Juan Handal Abraham J. Marcos
Victoria B. de Handal Emilio J. Marcos
Jose J. Handal
E. Canavati
Abdalah Canavati
Emilia F. de Canavati
Virginia C. Fraige
Jorge J. Marcos
Regina Zacamun

FIGURE 6. Two of several pages of signatures representing some three hundred Palestinians showing support for the 23 February 1927 petition of the members of the Centro Social Palestino in Monterrey. Former president of the Centro, Salamon Canavati, was the first to sign the petition. Source: Israel State Archives, Jerusalem, M-233/38.

Salvador Zarurro   Rosa Zarur

Arturo Zarur

Jorge S Zarur   جميلة ... عيسى ابو ...

Maria S. Zarur

Carlos Zarur

Julio Zarur

Jobi Batarse   Emilio Nasa Canovatti

Emilio J Batarse

Virginia J. Batarse

مريم مرقص حرمة يوسف خليل البطارس

Jorge J. Batarse   Emilia Batarse

Victoria J. Batarse

Yssa M. Marcos

Benito Marcos

Luis A. Marcos   Emmanuel A. Marcos

Rafael Marcos

Maria A marcos   Margarita A Marcos.

Rosa A. Marcos   Clara A. Marcos

Regina A. Marcos

Inés A Marcos

José A Marcos

Afife H. de Marcos   Taufic Marcos

Nasario marcos

Nehme Salman

Jorge Abu charur   Richara A. Marcos

Issa B. Marcos

In other words, Consul General Browne in Mexico City would not have forwarded the petition to London had he not believed that it fulfilled the League of Nation's instructions for submission and that the petitioners were Palestinians with rightful grievances. In fact, on 3 March 1927, when Browne forwarded the petition to the office of the Foreign Secretary in London, he indicated that the enclosed memorandum "by the Palestinian Community in Monterrey," as well as "a further petition signed by the Palestinians in Linares," were addressed to the high commissioner for Palestine.[41] This colonized community claimed global rights as Palestinians.

On 23 February, Musso and Kawas explained their full awareness of Britain's legal right to remain provisionally in Palestine. But, as Palestinians now under British mandate rule, they introduced international law as the guiding principle to any mandate government, reminding the high commissioner of his duty to respect the will of the League of Nations, which, to the petitioners, would secure for the Palestinians a national home:

> Even though it be true that Palestine obtained only a semi sovereignty, it is no less true, that the international juridical theory of a protectorate or mandate, concedes to same only a provisional character, under the supposition that such small nations, not for the time being able to conduct their own affairs unaided, shall receive the advice and protection of a mandatory power, until such time as they are able to adopt a political constitution and assume full control of their own public administration.[42]

The petitioners were aware of the purported purpose and duration of mandate governments, as per the League of Nations. They paraphrased the section in article 22 of the Covenant of the League of Nations that pertained to former subjects of Ottoman domains:

> Certain communities formerly belonging to the Turkish Empire have reached a stage of development where their existence as independent nations can be provisionally recognized subject to the rendering of administrative advice and assistance by a Mandatory until such time as they are able to stand alone. The wishes of these communities must be a principal consideration in the selection of the Mandatory.[43]

They thus reminded Plumer that their wishes were protected by the covenant itself and that they were aware of Jerusalem's transgressions in denying them citizenship.

They made their claim against the decision to deny their citizenship applications by declaring that England's requirements were impossibilities unbefitting of international law:

> This being the case and the Mandate of England comprehended within its proper international legal limitations, it does not appear either just nor reasonable for a nation, like England, with extremely liberal rules of conduct, which permit the full exercise of all kinds of rights, should impose requirements, so difficult of fulfillment that they become impossibilities, on the natives of the semi-sovereign state over which she exercises a mandate and for whose proper administration and control she is accountable to the League of Nations.[44]

The petitioners were referring to Plumer's November 1925 decision to shorten the time during which the Government of Palestine would accept applications for citizenship from former Ottoman subjects who had been born in Palestine and were now residing abroad from what had originally been two years to nine months. As mentioned in chapter 3, Jerusalem had not publicized this amendment, and applicants were largely unaware of it before they received their rejection notices. For the petitioners, therefore, Jerusalem was imposing unreasonable requirements on its own subjects, which represented an abuse of power.

Situating themselves within this framework of international law, the petitioners viewed themselves as rightful owners of a history and future that they had been promised through the ostensible role of the mandate and its international authority, the League of Nations. Laws and decisions that prohibited them from acquiring their rights were therefore condemnable, and if their mandate government were the perpetrator, they would hold it accountable before its governing body, the League of Nations.

> We believe, Sir, and we beg so to state, with all due respect, that the decision of the Palestine Government, in the exercise of the Mandate conferred thereon, as expressed by you, does not in any way agree with the spirit of the treaties nor the clearly manifested intention of the League of Nations to foster, encourage and revive small nations, which before the War were subject to others.[45]

They thus proclaimed: "It would not be discreet, practical or reasonable to scorn and refuse our good intentions, because the combined efforts of many, even though insignificant individually, go to make up a powerful force for the restoration of the Palestine Nation." Their continued legal and economic connection to Palestine as wealthy migrants who frequently returned with hefty remittances, they ensured the high commissioner, would benefit Palestine and, thus, its British government.

Reminding the Government of Palestine of its duty to safeguard international law and the protection of its subjects was a privilege afforded only to those who were considered subjects of that government. To that end, the Monterrey petitioners considered themselves subjects of the British Crown, and they continued to dispute the equitability of the citizenship requirements. In reference to the twelve years to which the vice-consul in Mexico City referred when he informed the migrants that their applications had been denied in November 1926, the petitioners asserted: "Nor is the simple fact that we have been absent from our country for more than twelve years sufficient reason to deny us that which we seek. Such a period, as time, is purely arbitrary; the same could be said of five years or twenty-five years." The decision to deny them citizenship based on a twelve-year absence from Palestine was, for the petitioners, an absurdity. Furthermore, it was inconsequential in terms of the connections they felt with Palestine. They reaffirmed their love for Palestine:

> Our absence from our native land has not meant that we have severed our connection with same. To the contrary we can cite thousands of facts to prove that the Palestinian colonies in all parts of the world and very particularly those of Mexico, have always maintained and continue to maintain, their love of country, their intimate relations with same and their adhesion to all of those things, which form the basis of a native land and country.

They knew of the many committees and organizations that self-identified as Palestinian and spoke on behalf of Palestinian "colonies" throughout the Americas, many of which had been in existence since the end of World War I in 1918. These Palestinian groups persisted and formed a network of interconnected collectives throughout the North and South American mahjar, which now had more reason than ever to challenge British mandate rule. On 1 April 1927, Talamas of the Comité Hijos de Palestina sent out a "general call to our brothers, the sons of Palestine, in all countries of America" in which he asked all who could to follow suit and "protest with all you have in strength" Jerusalem's denial of their Palestinian citizenship (figure 7).[46]

In the petitioners' minds, their rights to Palestinian citizenship and to belonging legally to Palestine were unquestionable, certainly in light of postwar treaties, the most important of which, the Treaty of Lausanne, concerned

"COMITE HIJOS DE PALESTINA".

PRESIDENTE. JESUS S. TALAMAS. | TESORERO. EMILIO COSTANDI YGA. | SECRETARIO BISHARA F. ANDONIE

APARTADO POSTAL# 187. | SALTILLO. COAH. MEXICO.

جمعية ابناء فلسطين
سلتيو المكسيك

١ نيسان ١٩٢٧

نداء الى اخواننا ابناء فلسطين في كافة انحاء امريكا

سلام واحترام. فرحنا بان نرسل اليكم نسخة تحتوي عن الكتاب الذي وجهنا الى الهيئة
التنفيذية والى الراي العام الفلسطيني باسره والى الجرائد الوطنية [illegible] [illegible]
وذلك من بعد ان وجهنا جملة احتجاجات تلغرافية الى البرلمان الى وزير المستعمرات في
انكلترا والى المندوب السامي في القدس عن حرماننا الجنسية الفلسطينية ولا
يخفى عليكم ايها الاخوان عاقبة هذا الموقف وعظم هذه القضية التي تشغل اكبر دماغ عربي
مخلص لوطنه يدب في عروقه دم الشهامة والغيرة والتي تقضي على مصالحنا السياسية
والادبية وتحرمنا ذوينا وكل عزيز لدينا لذلك نطلب من حضراتكم ان تحتجوا بكل ما
لديكم من القوة الى المحلات الايجابية وتعضدوا الجرائد الوطنية الحرة بالمطالبة
بحق جنسيتنا والضرب على ايدي الاستعمار وتظهروا للملا ان ابناء فلسطين شعب حي
يشعر بهذه الاضطهادات ولا ينام على الضيم ولا [illegible] لدفع كل ما هو مجحف بكرامته
ولنا ثقة كبرى بان امانينا ستتحقق بهمة الله وهمتكم

وتفضلوا بقبول احتراماتنا

عن جمعية ابناء فلسطين
رئيسها
عيسى [illegible] طلامس

كاتم الاسرار
بشارة [illegible]

FIGURE 7. The 1 April 1927 letter of Jesus Talamas, president of the Comité Hijos de Palestina in Saltillo, "to our brothers, the sons of Palestine, in all countries of America." Source: Israel State Archives, Jerusalem, M-233/38.

the petitioners. The treaty was considered to be a domestic and international legal decree for all residents of Palestine. With the treaty, "the status of Palestine and the nationality of its inhabitants were finally settled . . . from the international perspective."[47] Pursuant to article 30 of the treaty, "Turkish subjects habitually resident in territory which in accordance with the provisions of the present Treaty is detached from Turkey will become ipso facto, in the conditions laid down by the local law, nationals of the State to which such territory is transferred." In order to qualify for citizenship, the treaty required two conditions: individuals first had to be Turkish citizens and second, they "had to be habitually resident . . . in Palestine as of 6 August 1924," the day on which the treaty came into force. Though Palestine was not mentioned explicitly in the treaty, it "provided generic provisions applicable to all territories detached from Turkey, including Palestine."[48] Consequently, the Treaty of Lausanne confirmed that non-Turkish citizens residing in Palestine were ineligible for citizenship unless they applied for it.

The Treaty of Lausanne also made provisions for Palestinians residing abroad. As explained in chapter 3, article 34 of the treaty gave those persons the right to "opt for the nationality of the territory of which they are natives . . . if they belong by race to the majority of the population of that territory." Notwithstanding, all applications for citizenship needed to be approved by the Government of Palestine. If the Government of Palestine could deny qualified applicants citizenship according to stipulations that were not written into the Treaty of Lausanne, such as the length of applicants' absence from Palestine, the right to opt for citizenship based on race or birth did not, in fact, guarantee receipt of citizenship. The petitioners pointed this out, adding that the choice of nationality "should depend, first and foremost, on the plain and expressed will of those interested":

> We have been unable to learn, Mr. High Commissioner, whether the conditions laid down by you are those expressly provided in the treaties, which defined the political situation of the Palestine region. . . . We may reasonably assume that in these treaties it has not been possible to legally determine our status, that is, to settle the nationality of the Palestinians or their relations to the Palestine Nation. We may also reasonably believe that this personal status should depend, first and foremost, on the plain and expressed will of those interested, who, in this case are the native-born Palestinians, attached to their mother country by all of the ties of nationality and antecedents, even though they were Ottoman

> or Turkish subjects before the changes, that were brought about by the treaties, which marked the end of the World War.[49]

The petitioners effectively questioned the mandate's application of its own postwar treaties. They were versed in the liberal language of the interwar years, and in the next paragraph, they called for a plebiscite based on the "modern rules of international law" that "take into account in a very special way the wishes of peoples affected by one condition or another." Accordingly, they believed that their individual opinions mattered in this new world, and surely, as individuals, each of them had the right to "cast his vote for the nationality he desires."

The petitioners thus affirmed their right to choose Palestinian citizenship using international law and treaties to which Britain was a signatory. Subsequently, they tacitly threatened Jerusalem with recourse to the League of Nations:

> The Palestine nation, as an outcome of the War of 1914–1918, recovered its identity as a State, and its sovereignty, although limited, is at present comprised within well defined geographical limits, as provided by the agreement between England, France and Turkey. It has, as a creation of the Treaty of Versailles, a special government under the Mandate of England. . . . We were born in that territory; have always wished to be Palestinians; and we are sure, if as a last resort, it shall become necessary to carry our petition before the League of Nations, that august body will grant us the right to consider ourselves nationals of Palestine, even though we may have been forced to seek our economic betterment in other parts of the world.

For the petitioners, Palestine had been awaiting liberation and self-determination since before the war. Its identity and sovereignty as a state *recovered* at war's end and its nationals who, like countless migrant communities around the world, had left it to seek economic betterment in the Americas had been awaiting this recovery. There could be no doubt for these petitioners that they were fully Palestinians. They were so sure, they pointed out, that they even helped British authorities in Mexico liberate Palestine from the Ottomans during the war: "We can also assert, that many of us . . . enlisted and fought in the allied armies. Many others helped with our share in a financial way. . . . We only ask to be treated with justice and as corresponds to Palestinians."

On Behalf of Palestinians and for Palestine

While petitions rarely won their authors redress or clemency, they did grant them a legal and transnational platform through which to speak as a political collective. The ways in which the 23 February petitioners spoke on behalf of members of the Centro Social Palestino and other Palestinians in Mexico were deliberate and contributed to the formation in Mexico of a distinct Palestinian community whose rightful claims to Palestine constituted a transnational call to Palestinian political consciousness. The petition began with a collective pronoun, *we*, and was subsequently replete with language that asserted the collective's rights to Palestinian citizenship. This collective was made up of "native-born Palestinians" who "continue to cultivate those ties of blood, language, tradition and all other ethnic and social associations, which go to make up a native land," conditions for citizenship that they believed outweighed the arbitrary time limit of twelve years. They were natives of Palestine who were born there and who belonged to its majority population by race, the two stipulations for citizenship laid out in article 34 of the Treaty of Lausanne. Mexico's Palestinian petitioners had done their research.

Speaking on behalf of "at least ninety percent" of "many thousands of native born Palestinians" in Mexico who stood to have their citizenship applications refused, the petitioners explained the untenable circumstance in which the high commissioner had put them following his amendment to the application deadline:

> It would be a physical impossibility for them to establish a residence in Palestine six months prior to August 1st next. First and foremost because they cannot secure passports from British Consular Officers. Such Officers refuse applications for passports of natives of Palestine, who have not yet been accepted by the Palestine Government and state that such applications must be referred to Jerusalem. But even if it were possible to secure passports, the forced departure of all Palestinians from foreign countries would not only work a great hardship on them individually but would result in the nullification of their many years of effort in foreign fields, the abandonment of everything they had acquired and the return to their native land in a financial condition that would mean a detriment to same rather than a benefit.[50]

This new collective, which left its homeland in pursuit of economic betterment and which could claim native connections to Palestine, also shared a new experience in the Americas: denial of its members' rights to Palestinian citizenship. The extent of this struggle for citizenship was unique in the interwar period among transnational mandated subjects, and it earned them recognition as a legal and political collective that they identified as Palestinian. They would not accept being denied their native nationality and citizenship, especially in a new world order defined by passports. They asserted:

> The absolute impossibility of our complying with the conditions indicated by you is manifest. If this fact should prevent our acquiring Palestinian citizenship, it would create for us a truly abnormal and unjust situation. . . . We would be outlaws, men without a country, persons without the fundamental ties of a native land.[51]

This impossibility was akin to them applying for Ottoman citizenship, which, they stressed, was "extremely repulsive." This stateless status simply "cannot be, any more than . . . we should be declared unfit to be with our own people, our race, our relatives, our friends, and lastly to go to our native land, where we were born."

The petitioners' right to speak about their collective as Palestinians and to question Jerusalem's practices was, to them, as incontrovertible as Jerusalem's right to reject their applications for Palestinian citizenship. This new collective also reached out as Palestinians to the Arab Executive in Jerusalem. On 4 February 1927, a day before the original petition sent to Plumer, Salamon Canavati sent a letter in Arabic to Musa Kazim of the Arab Executive in Jerusalem. Canavati addressed the letter to Musa Kazim and the Arab Executive and described his concern over the recent citizenship rejections: "In regard to Palestinian nationality," he said, "you now see a second copy of the [attached] complaint addressed to the high commissioner, signed by no less than every son of the watan." He then explained that the complaint was also submitted to the League of Nations and circulated among "all Palestinians throughout the mahjar."

> We implore you, your Excellency, to support our objections and to consult the high commissioner and the Government of Palestine in regard to the nationality issue, because this law effectively kills all migrants and destroys our rights that we consider as sacred.[52]

Canavati's tone was serious, signaling the exigency of the threat of losing citizenship. Canavati conveyed that the decision to deny them citizenship would effectively kill them; banning them from travel back and forth to Palestine would put an end to their profitable trades.

Turning next to an appeal for Musa Kazim's help, Canavati spoke on behalf of Palestinian migrants, using the collective pronoun:

> We here, your Excellency, need your political support. We need you to ease our travel back and forth from abroad. Unfortunately, the [1925] Citizenship Order-in-Council destroys our political and civic rights. We therefore ask you, Oh Father and Member of the Nation, to extend the hand of help, that hand which you have grown accustomed to extending, you who have devoted your noble life to the service and protection of the homeland. We ask you to consult the powers that be so that the homeland receives the rights it deserves from the mandatory government.

Canavati's request of the Arab Executive was phrased in nationalist terms. Musa Kazim was Palestine's foremost nationalist leader, and Canavati turned to him for help. But rather than request it for himself and his community in Mexico, Canavati considered Palestinian migrants' struggle for citizenship to be the homeland's, too. Any support Musa Kazim extended Canavati and Palestinians in Mexico would thus constitute a political act in defense of the homeland. As will be discussed in chapter 6, Palestinians across the Americas and nationalists in Palestine regularly drew this connection between Palestinian nationalism and the struggle for citizenship. Canavati and the Palestinians on whose behalf he spoke were determined to become nationals of Palestine, and the letter ended with the following statement: "We present to you a copy of our objection so that you see that every Palestinian residing abroad sacrifices everything for the homeland." Canavati's petitions and letters linked the voices of diaspora Palestinians with those of Palestinians within Palestine fighting for the creation of a nation.

These documents signal the global preponderance of the option for self-identification vis-à-vis a nation and a national collective during the 1920s and 1930s and the extent to which Palestinians worldwide were part of this trend. Following Canavati's example, on 27 March 1927, Jesus Talamas of the Comité Hijos de Palestina sent a similar missive addressed to the Arab Executive and to "Palestinian public opinion," in which he explained Palestinian migrants' struggle with securing Palestinian citizenship and the importance of this struggle to the Palestinian nation.[53] Palestinian migrants in Havana, Cuba, also sent similar letters to the Arab Executive. On 12 July 1930, for example, Yousef ibn Azar wrote a letter in Arabic on behalf of the Sociedad Palestino Arabe de Cuba addressed to The Father of Beloved Palestine, His Excellency Musa Kazem Pasha al-Husseini.[54] In the top right corner of the document was the slogan "Defending the homeland is the foundation of its building." The nationalist character of the heading ran throughout the letter in which ibn Azar, like Canavati, offered his duty and service to "our blessed homeland in the face of the enemies." He continued: "Our homeland has made you its representatives of those of us abroad, representatives of steadfastness, struggle, and faith based in love for the homeland and its sons." Articulating the shared vision of Palestinians transnationally, ibn Azar then made clear the purpose of the letter: "We therefore join our voices with those of our brothers in the homeland and abroad. We ask the Sire [*al-mawla*][55] that he take our homeland and help you receive our destroyed rights, that he spread peace and prosperity to our country from which evil foreign greed has distanced us." Ibn Azar enlisted Cuba's Palestinian community in Palestine's struggle for freedom from evil foreign greed, as he hoped Musa Kazim would help them restore their destroyed rights.

Ibn Azar, Talamas, and Canavati represented a rising mode of collective identification among these diaspora Palestinian communities in which the nation and homeland were unambiguously located in Palestine. The language used to identify with the emergent national homeland was deliberate, yet it was less guided by jingoistic rhetoric than by a genuine concern for the implications of being permanently distanced from a homeland to whose development into a nation they wished to contribute. In the 23 February 1927 petition from Monterrey, Masso and Kawas explained:

> We as Palestinians wish to form part and parcel of our country; not to be foreign to its reawakening but associated with its restoration to international life. We wish to take part in its development and general improvement and lastly to lend our aid to that of our fellow countrymen to bring about its complete independence.[56]

In addition to having relatives and landed properties throughout Palestine, these Palestinians had always wished to take part in growing Palestine into an independent nation, and they considered their efforts at economic betterment to constitute acts of nationalism. For this vocal community in Mexico's northern states, national self-determination had extended into the mechanisms of self-understanding and identification. They wished to be Palestinians wholly committed to building a free Palestine. Their distance from it was, for them, not an indication to the contrary.

In the conclusion to the petition, the petitioners reiterated their firm belief in their rights to submit the petition and to request citizenship based on international law. In doing so, they reaffirmed their submission to the mandate's authority and to that of the mandate's superiors in Geneva and London. They expressed this using the collective pronoun:

> If we have been somewhat lengthy in this exposition, it is because we wish to commend to your favorable consideration the reasons, which we believe will justify a reconsideration of our status and a declaration that our citizenship may be perfected by some means or acts within our power to comply. If this is a matter that requires the decision of some other Authority, we respectfully beg that you forward this application to such Authority with some recommendation as our reasons herein set forth may justify.[57]

They recognized and respected the authority of Britain and its mandate government in Jerusalem, strategically positioning themselves as loyal subjects beseeching their government for clemency and redress. Nevertheless, they affirmed their commitment to securing Palestinian citizenship. The petitioners were effectively performing the respect, dedication, and patriotism characteristic of a community that believed it deserved to "stand alone," fully independent, as described in the Covenant of the League of Nations, following Britain's assistance.

Operating within the logic of mandate rule, the petition functioned as a mechanism for colonial control, but it also functioned as a means of transnational political claims-making and group identification for a rising collective. While petitions reified the authority and sovereignty of the League of Nations and Government of Palestine over Palestine and its nationals, they also contributed to the creation of transnational networks of disenfranchised subjects laying claim to the same national rights *as* Palestinians. By petitioning, petitioners thus "looked to exploit the Mandate system's structure and logic, playing texts and jurisdictions off one another, and creatively reimagining their purpose and scope."[58] The effect has been an enduring mode of identification with a Palestinian homeland among members of a diaspora community who spoke about themselves using language that deliberately referred to Palestine and their collective historic, linguistic, familial, material, ethnic, and legal connections to it. The formation of this diaspora was critically linked to the community's creative engagement in transnational political and legal communication and contestation with European authorities in Mexico, England, Switzerland, and Palestine.

PALESTINIAN PETITIONERS AND PALESTINIAN HISTORY

The process of petitioning evinces the ultimately imperial character of the British mandate in practice, as well as the irreconcilable tension between what mandates purported to do and what they actually did.[59] Petitions were telltale signs of the deceptively benevolent presence of mandates in that, while the process of petitioning became a common practice among mandated subjects throughout the world, rejecting petitions was equally common. Petitioning "did not normally win the petitioner redress," and in fact, "in the large majority of cases . . . , the PMC recommended that no action be taken."[60] Petitioning, in other words, "worked to contain and delegitimize pressures and protests coming from below."[61]

As for Mexico's Palestinian petitioners, on 3 March 1927, Consul General Browne in Mexico City forwarded the translated petitions from Monterrey and Linares, which he had received from Vice-Consul Jeffrey in Monterrey, to the office of the Foreign Secretary in London. Jerusalem received a dispatch from the Foreign Office regarding these and other petitions from Mexico and Honduras on 4 May 1927 and submitted a reply weeks later on 31 May.[62] Plumer began by confirming receipt of a petition by certain "Turkish citizens who state they were born in Palestine but who are resident in Monterrey and Linares, in Mexico." He refused to acknowledge their claims to being Palestinians. As for their applications for Palestinian citizenship, he continued, "as these persons do not appear to fulfil the conditions laid down, I am not prepared to reconsider the decisions already given." Finally, he noted from the dispatch that in his response to the applicants, Consul General Browne had directly cited Jerusalem's reasons for denying their applications. "This in my opinion," he proceeded, "was unnecessary and should, I consider, be avoided in the future." The "consent of the Government of Palestine to these applications may be granted or withheld at its absolute discretion and it is considered preferable that no reasons for a refusal should be given."[63]

Petitions point to the unique way in which Palestine was administered as a mandate. As a territory promised to the Arab population of Palestine and to Zionist leaders in Europe, the League of Nations and PMC dealt with it quite differently from other mandated territories. Palestine "was the case in which the policy-making process became most thoroughly internationalized";[64] negotiations and deliberations in Geneva surrounding self-determination for Palestinian nationalists never took place outside the league's relationship with Zionist leaders in Europe.[65] By 1924, the PMC no longer questioned the logic of the Balfour Declaration, and by 1930, it was "staunchly Zionist," owing to years of collaboration between league officials and Zionist leaders inside and outside Palestine. The two figures most importantly associated with this collaboration were Chaim Weizmann, president of the World Zionist Organization, and William Rappard, director of the Mandate Department of the League of Nations. Through his work, Weizmann swayed many league officials to adopt a Zionist platform in the governance of Palestine. In the spring of 1925, Rappard accepted Weizmann's invitation to Palestine and toured Jerusalem and Tel Aviv with Arthur Balfour, the famed author of the 1917 Balfour Declaration. Prior to this trip, Rappard had remained publicly impartial toward both the Zionists and the Palestinians, but after the visit, which "entirely changed his point of view," he returned a Zionist.[66]

The Zionist influence on the League of Nations was so strong that the PMC declared in 1924 it would not consider petitions that questioned "the very principle of the Palestine Mandate," which included the establishment there of a Jewish "national home."[67] Petitions from Palestinians worldwide were destined to be ignored if they challenged in any way the policy of the British mandate government in Palestine when it came to Jewish immigration, naturalization, or a range of other complaints directed at British bias toward the Zionists. To that end, petitioners were careful in the language they used, refraining from questioning the mandate's principles and, instead, appealing for redress as loyal subjects of the British Crown.

Examining the mandates system in Palestine through petitions submitted by Palestinian migrants in Mexico thus serves several historiographic purposes. It allows us to understand the impact of the interwar world order on

Palestinian individuals and communities and, specifically, on their abilities to travel and belong legally to Palestine. And it allows us to appreciate petitioning as a form of social practice that substantiated a mode of political identification among thousands in the mahjar who saw themselves unequivocally as Palestinians. The British mandate and its citizenship legislation thus inadvertently secured an increasingly self-aware and substantive Palestinian presence across the world that could not be silenced. And in this way, petitions offered their authors "exposure, contacts, credibility, publicity, [and] voice."[68] Put differently, petitions gave petitioners access to an "international arena" in which their voices allegedly mattered:

> Petitioning mattered not because it offered petitioners redress but because it allowed them to enter and speak in a multi-vocal, international arena. It was one of the key mechanisms . . . through which a previously binary relationship—colonizer, colonized—was triangulated. Suddenly, there was another location for confrontation, and new participants in the room.[69]

The case of Palestinian migrants petitioning British mandate authorities in the interwar period further suggests that the development of networks of transnational political identification was not outside their relationship with systems of colonial dominance. The process of exclusion and inclusion through citizenship and immigration policies developed in tandem with the claims to collective racial and national identification via international law among those whose legal status was undetermined or contested. Conceiving of this context in terms of an interaction between new colonial authorities and their subject-citizens invites queries into the new kind of relationality that ensued from the interwar world order within what Timothy Mitchell calls a "terrain of power."[70] The petitions authored by Mexico's Palestinian jaaliya are windows into the processes of communication and contestation that constituted the terrain of relationships in and between interwar Mexico, England, Switzerland, and Palestine.

Petitions ultimately point to the productive interface between citizenship legislation and transnational communal activism when it comes to the social history of mahjar Palestinians in the interwar period. Indeed, that a group of individuals who identified fervently as Palestinians engaged in the practice of petitioning the League of Nations and mandate authorities from the towns of Monterrey, San Pedro, Saltillo, Chihuahua, and Linares, Mexico, in

1927 reflects the vitality of Palestinian communities in the Americas and the transnational character of Palestinian national consciousness throughout the interwar period. While in many ways a history of Palestinian migrants' dispossession, this history is significantly also one of community empowerment and transnational nation-building. Exactly how this community grew and acquired transnational significance for Palestinian political consciousness is the subject of the subsequent chapters.

CHAPTER 5

THE CHILEAN ARABIC PRESS AND THE STORY OF PALESTINOS-CHILENOS

"**PAY ATTENTION AND** wake up, Palestinians!" Philip Badran, a Lebanese journalist in Lima, Peru, wrote in an article published on 26 December 1925 in *al-Watan*, an Arabic newspaper based in Santiago de Chile.[1] The plea came as a warning to Palestinians to reject being referred to as "Ottoman resident[s] of Palestine" by British consular authorities, which Badran considered to be the "gravest plague and most evil illness threatening the existence and future of the Palestinian migrant." He explained that the phrase implied their ineligibility for Palestinian citizenship under the Palestinian Citizenship Order-in-Council. Badran insisted this was part of a plot to give Palestine to the Zionists, and he described its deleterious consequences for Palestinians:

> This phrase makes the true Palestinian a foreign Ottoman in Palestine, thereby costing him his British Palestinian citizenship rights, which afford him British protection like every British citizen. The law provides for this. Therefore, the Palestinian carrying that document containing that corrupt "phrase" becomes an Ottoman Turk. The British consul therefore does not acknowledge his right to protection, nor to his Palestinianness. The Palestinian is therefore deprived of British protection, of his nationalism, and of his nation as well. . . . [Palestinians] are forbidden from returning to their birthplaces and to the life of the country of their fathers and grandfathers.

But why did Badran, a Lebanese journalist in Peru, appeal to Palestinian migrants, and why did he send his plea to be printed in a Chilean newspaper?

By 1925, Chile was home to a thriving Mashriqi jaaliya with considerable economic influence; its Palestinian community, to be sure, was fast becoming the Americas' largest and most successful. Badran was deliberately appealing to this community. Through his plea, Badran and *al-Watan*'s editors affirmed that the issue of Palestinian citizenship was critical and that it needed to be dealt with urgently in order to safeguard the dignity and cohesiveness of the entire Arabic-speaking jaaliya, which was being threatened with fragmentation. Badran then instructed Palestinians on what to do:

> To prevent this danger, every Palestinian migrant must refuse under any circumstance to have that expression placed on his document. . . . Instead, he must insist that he is a Palestinian, son of Palestine, with Palestinian forefathers, and that he is not an Ottoman because the Ottoman state withdrew from Palestine and Syria years ago. . . . [Palestinians] have the right to return to their nation as nationals and not as foreign Ottomans. Pay attention and wake up, Palestinians!

Like petitions, periodicals throughout the Arabic-speaking mahjar were important mediums for political activism, and the crisis of Palestinian citizenship in the interwar period took center stage in many of Chile's Arabic newspapers.

More than ten Arabic newspapers were in circulation in Chile during the first two decades of the twentieth century. Two of these from 1920s Santiago, *al-Watan* and *al-Sharq*, were prolific in printing content that strengthened the jaaliya's standing within Chile and with respect to the watan, including calls for ethical behavior in the mahjar, patriotic love for the watan, and the defense of Palestinian rights to citizenship. In doing so, *al-Watan* and *al-Sharq*, among several other Arabic newspapers, contributed to reinforcing intercommunal bonds, connecting the jaaliya with other jaaliyaat throughout the Americas, and promoting transnational identification with the watan. Badran knew to send his appeal to *al-Watan*, a periodical with a particularly nationalist bent and an unwavering commitment to defending Palestinian rights.

SANTIAGO'S ARABIC PRESS

The first Arabic newspaper in Chile was *al-Murshed* (The guide) in 1912. Printed entirely in Arabic, *al-Murshed* was funded by a Palestinian migrant from Bethlehem, Jorge Hirmas. Its mission was to create an "Arabic publication in the country to advertise the business community and to discuss events and news on the homeland from [the migrants'] perspective, while also working as a link for the Christian Arab Orthodox community."[2] The founder of *al-Murshed* was an Arab Orthodox priest named Paul Jury, and the majority of migrants in Chile from the Mashriq were Greek Orthodox. Although *al-Murshed* was short-lived, other publications soon proliferated. The magazine *al-ʿAwaatif* (Sentiments) was founded in 1916, followed by *al-Munir* (The illuminated), founded in the same year in the town of Concepcion, today Chile's third largest city. *Al-Shabeebah* (The youth) followed two years later in 1918, and while the former two were printed entirely in Arabic, *al-Shabeebah* began including Spanish content.

In 1920, Issa Khalil Daccarett, a Palestinian migrant, founded *al-Watan* (The homeland), Chile's longest-running Arabic newspaper in the interwar years. *Al-Watan* was in circulation for nine years, during which time it began printing in Spanish, attracting a larger readership that spanned the continent. Other newspapers included *al-Islaah* (Reform) in 1930—which was most prolific in reporting on Palestine and the political upheaval of the 1930s—*Oriente/al-Sharq* (The east) in 1927, and *Mundo Arabe* (Arab world) in 1935. These mixed Arabic and Spanish newspapers—whose content ranged from daily updates about jaaliyaat throughout the Americas to the Zionist infiltration of Palestine and from the latest economic, political, and social issues in Chile to the 1925 Syrian Revolt and the Palestinian earthquake of 1927—are today preserved in microfilm in Santiago's Biblioteca Nacional.[3]

Chile's Arabic periodicals enhanced what were envisioned as meaningful and durable connections between the watan, the mahjar, and *al-mahalli* (the local). These three spheres appeared regularly and often sequentially in the periodicals. For example, *al-Sharq* contained the following sections: *akhbaar al-Watan* (homeland news), *rasaaʾil min al-mahjar* (letters from the diaspora), and *akhbaar mahalliyya* (local news). This juxtaposition provided readers with relatively comprehensive news on a regular basis, and it contributed to the creation of interconnected networks between local, regional, and transnational Arabic-speaking jaaliyaat. Consequently, these networks strengthened the scattered jaaliyaat's "groupness" around shared calls for moral behavior in the host country and patriotic sentiment for the homeland as critical components of successful settlement in the diaspora.[4]

Much like their counterparts in New York, São Paulo, and Buenos Aires, the Americas' largest hubs for Mashriqi migrants in the early twentieth century, Santiago's Arabic newspaper editors also responded to the dramatic changes that developed in Greater Syria after World War I, and regarding

Palestine, they actively defended Palestinians' rights to self-determination and citizenship.[5] *Al-Watan* and *al-Sharq*'s editors regularly updated their readers about developments in Britain's citizenship policies; they reprinted petitions submitted to British authorities from Palestinian collectives throughout the mahjar and the Middle East; they called on local Palestinians to refuse any other nationality and to demand their rights to Palestinian citizenship from the British consulate in Santiago; and they sent out requests for donations from the larger jaaliya to assist in the defense of the rights of Palestinian migrants. This information was critical to defining the Palestinian experience in Chile and to developing a Palestinian mode of identification within a community that was growing increasingly connected to other Palestinian jaaliyaat throughout the Americas, as well as to the Palestinian watan. Chile's Arabic periodicals contributed to forming a distinct Palestinian diaspora experience in Chile in response to inequitable British legislation in the interwar period, a diaspora that continues to maintain a strong attachment to a Palestinian mode of identification to this day.

Politicizing the Jaaliya, Protecting Its Reputation

Periodicals, more than any other medium for activism and notably in the mahjar literary hubs of New York, São Paulo, Buenos Aires, and Santiago, served as platforms for nationalist mobilizers to broadcast their agendas locally, regionally, and transnationally.[6] In the interwar period, Middle Eastern migrants used Arabic presses throughout the mahjar to broadcast their nationalist agendas for the homeland, as well as their anti-colonial protests against British, French, and League of Nations authorities. These periodicals were so prolific and political that their content was often circulated in periodicals across the newly divided watan. As Reem Bailony points out, "Syrian émigrés across the world formed an important set of trans-border circuits" throughout the interwar years which were forged as a result of Arabic periodicals.[7] Multilingual and cosmopolitan Arabic-speaking migrants took advantage of free presses in the Americas to circulate, in Arabic, the liberal rhetoric of self-determination and national independence that was emanating from Western Europe and North America and that their compatriots back home could employ in their anti-colonial nationalist struggles. Mahjar periodicals, that is, shared "a deeply historical (even irredentist) character, and faith in the culture of patriotism and the power of petitioning as politically progressive forces."[8]

Middle Eastern migrants often called out French and British authorities in periodicals for their contradictory practices, those that they pointed out belied the universal principles of the League of Nations' charter—namely, to award national independence to liberated peoples after the war. These criticisms of European rule were circulated from throughout the mahjar to different political centers in Greater Syria, providing Lebanese, Syrian, and Palestinian nationalists back home with critical language they could employ. As Bailony puts it, "straddled between the floating discourse of self-determination and the ever-present forces of imperialism" from afar, these migrants most strongly championed liberal politics in their writings, in turn bolstering Lebanese, Syrian, and Palestinian claims to national self-determination and independence transnationally.[9] In their periodicals, Chile's editors thus urged their readers to embrace collective solidarity around their shared history and their threatened present in order to succeed in the diaspora and secure independence for the homeland.[10]

Arabic periodicals reveal a great deal about the ways in which Arabic-speaking jaaliyaat envisioned their collective within their host countries, within the American mahjar, and in relation to the watan. This is particularly conspicuous with an examination of the ways in which newspapers addressed their readers at different times throughout the rapidly changing war and interwar years. Although periodicals largely addressed their readers as Syrians and Arabs in the years before the war, increasingly throughout the 1920s and 1930s, they specified which of the three new nationalities they were addressing—Lebanese, Syrian, or Palestinian—especially when they called on their readers to remit money to the watan in support of different causes. Throughout the interwar years, therefore, Palestinians in Chile could pick up newspapers to learn ways to donate to committees that supported Palestinians in Beit Jala or Bethlehem in securing rights to work and travel. Similarly, Syrians could consult newspapers to learn about opportunities for joining local committees that sent funds to Aleppo, Damascus, or Homs to recover from the aftermath of the 1925 Syrian Revolt. During that revolt against French rule, periodicals throughout the mahjar had urged readers "to engage homeland politics through fundraising, letter-writing campaigns, and the organizing of political parties and nationalist conventions."[11]

To be sure, highlighting distinct nationalities among a newly divided collective had a synergetic effect that enhanced the larger Arabic-speaking jaaliya's political value to the watan. And while nationalities could now be parsed following the instatement of the mandates, editors of mahjar newspapers continued to circulate language that united their readers as Arabic speakers from the Mashriq who shared their love and loyalty for the homeland and their transnational struggle for self-determination. To do so, editors also went to great lengths to obscure divergent political aspirations of diverse jaaliyaat across the Americas. The result of collective migrant political activism for Middle Eastern migrants in the Americas was thus a hodgepodge of diaspora nationalisms that underwent a process of homogenization in various publications and periodicals in order to reflect greater nationalist aspirations in the face of European colonialism. In other words, the variegated visions of political possibilities for the watan among diverse jaaliyaat across the mahjar were made "isomorphic" in newspapers in order to project greater unity.[12]

The most evident and unifying characteristic of these diverse communities was the Arabic language. One of the most salient themes in Arabic periodicals during the early half of the twentieth century was a call for unity in the mahjar through a shared love for and pride in the Arabic language. For example, in each issue, *al-Watan* newspaper printed the slogan "The newspaper of Arabic speakers on the Pacific Coast," embracing Arabic speakers in Peru, Ecuador, and Colombia in South America, as well as other countries in Central and North America. While Arabic newspapers in Argentina and Brazil covered the Atlantic coast, Chile's completed the puzzle, as it were, of uniting mahjar Arabic speakers in solidarity around their language and shared heritage. As another example, on 9 September 1928, *al-Sharq* newspaper advertised Arabic lessons on behalf of El Club Sirio-Palestino, the Syrian Palestinian Club: "The leadership of the Syrian Palestinian Club has decided to hold in its forum Arabic lessons for all interested compatriots. As for conditions and hours of instruction, the student can find them in the national press."[13] This collaborative effort between the Syrian Palestinian Club and *al-Sharq* to safeguard "the language of our forefathers" served to reinforce unity and promote patriotism throughout the Arabic-speaking mahjar, irrespective of nationality or confessional creed.

Similarly, newspapers deliberately named all three nationalities when it came to defending the reputation and success of the whole Arabic-speaking jaaliya in the mahjar. Concern over the jaaliya's ongoing stability and economic success hinged on the continuous flow of migrants from the Mashriq. To ensure this, newspaper editors informed their readers of honest and dependable travel agents about whom they could tell their families. For example, on 28 February 1925, *al-Watan* printed an account from a traveler, Sulaiman Ibrahim al-Hajal, who had left Santiago and journeyed to the watan through Buenos Aires. Titled "A Letter of Importance to the Community," the account praised a travel agent in Buenos Aires, Yaqoub Ghattas, for his integrity and fair prices:

> We arrived in the Argentinian capital to travel to our homeland. So, we went to the ship company to stamp our passports and we were shocked by the many difficulties and struggles we faced. Then we came upon your advertisement in your newspaper *al-Watan* about the integrity of the compatriot, Mr. Yaqoub Ghattas, who deals with matters of travel with ship companies, especially for travelers to the homeland. So, we relied on him and he eased each of our difficulties and appeared very polite and generous. He was economical with our travel expenses, which brings us to thank him, hoping that you will publish our letter in your forthcoming print so that our compatriots will know of the integrity and experience of Mr. Yaqoub Ghattas in the matters and needs of travelers and their transportation in the best ships and for the best prices.[14]

Two years later, on 22 January 1927, *al-Sharq* also praised Ghattas: "Many of our compatriots who are returning from the homeland spoke highly of the good treatment offered by Mr. Yaqoub Ghattas. . . . They complimented his care for every Arab son, rich or poor. . . . We recommend to whoever needs to travel, to do so through Mr. Ghattas."[15] Assistance with travel thus became an important means of expressing solidarity and commitment to the success of the jaaliya. Chile's Arabic periodicals were platforms for enhancing cooperation and communication between migrants transnationally, in turn strengthening the connectedness of Arab-speaking communities across Latin America.

The historic and linguistic connectedness of the collective jaaliya was also evident when the community's morality and heritage were seen to be under threat. That is, the collective was also connected through its shared experience in the mahjar, a place of opportunity, yes, but also a space of unfamiliar and possibly threatening social and cultural practices. For many contributors to the newspapers, the preservation of the jaaliya's heritage and moral character was possible by avoiding cultural syncretism with perceived "modern" immoralities. On 21 February 1925, *al-Watan* printed a long reproof to Middle Eastern youth in the mahjar who were thought to be losing their morals and heritage by taking part in shameful foreign practices. The editors titled it prescriptively: "Be Civilized but Do Not Imitate" and addressed it to "Arab dancers":

> It does not comfort us to read in the national papers about dance parties and competitions in which young guys and girls scramble to perfect the new dance styles for which prizes are awarded. This new art has come to this country with others like it from the [European] settlers, like cocaine, morphine and other drugs and poisons like them.[16]

The jaaliya's youth were evidently socializing with diverse communities in a Santiago that was growing into a cosmopolitan city center with an urban subculture. *Al-Watan* saw itself as the community's morality police, so to speak, and subsequently warned the community against the dangers of "Western urbanism," including modern dance styles:

> We have lived in free countries and among peoples whose morals differ from ours, and we have spent considerable time in the diaspora mingling with different classes of people. This allowed us to know the truth of modern Western values and we were and still are advocates for tolerance and reform, and desirous of borrowing all benefits. . . .
>
> Western urbanism has many virtuous benefits and ugly vices. It would behoove us to take the first and reject the other. Among what we must reject is foreign dancing into which Western nations have plunged after their tastes have been corrupted, after they lost their manliness.[17]

The editors understood progress and modernism to mean safeguarding the community's cultural heritage against the corruption of Western urban practices. For *al-Watan*'s editors, the mahjar was a space where they could instruct their readers in the ways of becoming modern by preserving cherished, "civilized" habits and rejecting disgraceful Western practices.

The article proceeded to censure young women's behavior as indulgent and immoral. It linked this behavior to "intellectual sterility" and a "lack of manliness" among young men since young women were resorting to seduction to get their attention:

> The surest sign of moral, intellectual and sexual degeneration is what we see of rampant immorality and debauchery . . . and the obligation of women to appear refined and dolled up. . . . The problem points to intellectual sterility, and the

> fact that women get dolled up and flirt with men is a sign of a lack of manliness. . . . Women [have had] to reveal a lot of their virtues to men and to suffice with little in the way of clothing in order to stimulate the man. This effort exhausted them and corrupted them morally of late.[18]

Al-Watan was concerned with edifying the jaaliya's youth with the conceptions of virile manliness and modest femininity, which were linked to civilizational progress. Although certain urbanized Westerners chose to behave immorally by dancing and wearing provocative clothing, it was the jaaliya's collective responsibility to resist these temptations:

> If Europeans need these pernicious habits, what need do we Arabs have for them? . . . [They are] not necessary for peoples that are bracing themselves for reawakening and renaissance. . . . Therefore, we do not see shame in not being fluent in dancing and getting dolled up so long as we have no need for it. . . . True civility is not achieved through modern dancing, scandalous dress, or getting dolled up. Rather, true civility is knowledge, self-morality, and the health of mind and body.[19]

The "we" in this instance referred to the collective jaaliya, and the "others" against which the community needed to defend itself were immoral European migrants polluting Santiago with drugs and dance. *Al-Watan* was thus not rejecting Chile, for Chile was its new home; rather, it was seeking to instruct its readers in how to become ethical members of Chilean society. *Al-Watan*'s editors were convinced that the jaaliya's youth could be rescued from moral corruption, and it was their duty to tell their readers how. Concern for the jaaliya's reputation and survival in Chile was therefore critically connected to social conduct, and readers knew they could turn to their periodicals for collective reflection and edification.

Al-Watan also printed acerbic critiques of the jaaliya's unethical activities by way of its members' voices. On 28 March 1925, the newspaper printed a letter from Abdo al-Baraka, resident of a small town in north Chile, in which he criticized the jaaliya for its "backwardness and degradation." This behavior included uncouth eating habits, deceptive work practices, and physical violence. Evidently, members of this jaaliya in northern Chile were regularly breaking into aggressive brawls in public. To remedy the situation, al-Baraka urged his compatriots to cleanse their community of reprehensible behavior, which he had observed for fifteen years since his arrival in Chile from Argentina:

> Yesterday morning, a quarrel happened between Ghaleb Sharfan and Butrus Elias Sim'an, and the matter was brought to the police station this morning. . . .
>
> Shame and disgrace on these lowly habits that cause [Chileans] to feel contempt toward us and to write about us in their newspapers. They criticize us bitterly considering what some of us do. I remember once the newspaper *Trabajo* called one of us trash! And another said "we are a coterie of lousy *turcos*."

Al-Baraka reproached the entire jaaliya. He called on them to fear God, and to question their values:

> Oh people! When will we be satisfied with this miserable situation? Over eighteen years have passed since many of us have migrated and it seems as though we just arrived and were not impacted by intermingling, assimilating, and coexisting with foreigners.
>
> Fear God, oh people, and have pity on your wealth. Relieve us of this shame that follows us. Work to suffocate envy and do not let people gather around you because you scream so loudly to obtain five copper coins. Be ashamed of yourselves, change this ugly habit, and look how [Chileans] live with tranquility. No envy exists between them for sales or for customers. You have made us morsels in people's mouths for mockery and ridicule. . . . We are in this country as foreigners, and as the proverb says: "The foreigner must be a person of value." Are these values? Where are values, and where are we? . . . I hope that this letter, published in the pages of the famed *al-Watan*, will suffice to deter you from falling again.[20]

Al-Baraka used *al-Watan* as a platform to critique the jaaliya directly. He and *al-Watan*'s editors shared the conviction that it was the jaaliya's collective responsibility to see to the progress of its members in Chile, whether in the cities or the countryside and irrespective of national or confessional origins.

Following his account, al-Baraka added information he had learned since writing the account about the shameful brawl: "Sim'an threw dirt in the street that was covered in feathers. The feathers flew and landed on Ghaleb's son's clothes. There had already been troubles between these two merchants on account of sales and customers, so the war erupted." The personalized tone of this postscript, in which the perpetrators were named again and in which details of their petty quarrel were explained, suggests that anonymity was implausible within the small and interconnected jaaliya. No member of the jaaliya, whether in a small town in northern Chile or in Santiago itself, was immune to censure, and thus, corruption and immorality were theoretically kept in check.

Chile's Arabic newspapers taught their readers that if individual members of the jaaliya were not committed to succeeding in Chile, they were not committed to the success of the collective, and consequently, not of the watan either. This conflation was most evident in 1927 when the Chilean government imposed strict migration legislation that impacted the jaaliya directly. Much like the governments of other Latin American countries and the United States, the government of Chile was interested in populating Chilean cities and the countryside with white, western European migrants, and immigration authorities put this policy into practice. This became particularly pronounced following the end of World War I, with the surge in immigration from southern Europe, the Middle East, and Asia to the Americas. And although the Chilean government began limiting immigration altogether, it imposed stricter restrictions on non-white migrants. By 1927, therefore, and with the growth of Arab, African, and Asian populations in Chile through higher birth rates and illegal entry, non-white migrant communities began to feel the Chilean government's increasing resistance to their assimilation and expansion into Chilean society.

On 29 October 1927, *al-Watan* printed a letter written by a Syrian scholar in Santiago, Mary Atallah, to the Syrian Palestinian Club following the news of the crackdown on incoming migrants from the Mashriq. After a lengthy explanation of the reasonableness of the Chilean government's decision—since it needed to protect the nation from backwardness and decay—Atallah delivered a message calling for action among "those of healthy conscience" within the jaaliya:

> The decision [of the Chilean government] comes at the price of the moral and economic right of the sons of my country firstly because it prohibits them from their livelihood. . . . Secondly, because the government would not have made this decision if it did not find in it value in reducing the problems caused by those lacking in conscience. . . .
>
> To those of healthy consciences among my compatriots, . . . to those who obtain their strength with integrity, and not with theft and looting, . . . to those pure at heart, . . . I direct these words hoping that they will join forces and form a committee with the aim of defending their rights and protecting their reputation.[21]

The distinction between the moral and the corrupt was a common theme in Chile's Arabic newspapers. Atallah instructed those of healthy conscience to spearhead the community's rise from degradation in order to forestall its banishment:

> Tell the government that you are free of association with those who have chosen lowness to achieve victory.
>
> Tell her that you are like her in hating those who desire richness by depriving others of grace....
>
> Tell her that you will help her get rid of these lowlifes who destroy your reputation. She will help you thus in respecting the sentiment of the noble migrant.
>
> And ask her to open her doors to every person seeking refuge, and to not close the door in the face of those who desire prosperity for the sake of their children.[22]

Atallah's message indicated that for her and *al-Watan*'s editors, moral behavior and self-reflection were tantamount to economic success. The threat of failing as a migrant community, whether through economic losses or banishment by the Chilean government, was critical to those within the jaaliya who were concerned about the fate of the community following the new restrictions on immigration. The jaaliya needed to ensure that migrants from the homeland could continue to enter and settle in Chile, and to do this, it needed to convince its members to impress the government with moral behavior; they needed to prove that they were proud migrants of conscience who reject corruption. Atallah ended her message with an arguably racialized undertone by commanding the jaaliya to embody whiteness and shun darkness: "Be the white page on which the government reads the lines of your innocence and obscures the darkness of others."

One month later, on 29 November 1927, *al-Watan* published an appeal from the Syrian Palestinian Club to all "Arabic speakers in the Republic of Chile." The appeal included instructions on how to achieve a better reputation as merchants in Chile. Addressing the appeal to its "Dearest *muwaatineen*" (compatriots), the Syrian Palestinian Club began by explaining the serious situation they were all confronting with the Chilean government's decision to limit incoming migrants from the Middle East. The club then clarified that Syrians, Palestinians, and Lebanese alike were all considered undesirable migrants under the new legislation and that there was a critical need for collective action:

> The [Chilean] government wants to encourage the immigration of useful elements into the country so it can benefit from their trade, and so that they can contribute to building strong future generations. Likewise, it prohibited the entry of harmful elements into its lands.
>
> As for us Syrians, Palestinians, and Lebanese, it is unfortunate that we are of those of little use and desire. . . . His Excellency the Minister of Foreign Affairs asked consuls of the state in foreign countries to not issue travel permits from now on to [Syrians desiring to enter Chile]. This has already been applied; in Buenos Aires now, some Syrians to whom the Chilean consul did not wish to grant travel permits have written to their relatives in Santiago asking for help with their entry.[23]

The Syrian Palestinian Club addressed the entire jaaliya of *muwaatineen* because they were all impacted by the new restrictions, regardless of national origin. Middle Eastern migrants were viewed collectively and pejoratively by Chilean authorities and non–Middle Eastern locals as *turcos*. Separating *turcos* by new nationalities would have been counterproductive. The club then further explained that it sent its representatives to meet with the head of the consular department, who confirmed the validity of the restrictions. The consul evidently explained that the Chilean government "wants immigrants who are useful for the nation, . . . like Saxons (i.e., Germans and English, among others). As for Asian elements who come to the country to simply sell, the government does not desire them."[24] The Syrian Palestinian Club thus urged the jaaliya to behave less like Asian and more like European migrants. As elsewhere in the world, race and class were invariably connected and critical to migrant narratives.[25]

The Syrian Palestinian Club prescribed a list of eleven dos and don'ts in order to achieve these goals. They included exhortations against "fraudulence," "arson," "tax evasion," and mistreatment of female customers in Middle Easterners' stores. It also urged the jaaliya to "respect the feelings of the people of this country with whom we live by closing our shops on church and national holidays" and to keep their stores and clothes clean. Finally, the club called on the jaaliya to "care for our moral and social institutes so they can appeal to the foreigners and be a source of admiration." It then announced that it would petition the Chilean government to explain "the usefulness of our communities which are dispersed throughout this country." This usefulness was found in the jaaliya's factories, stores, and farms; it was also found in the value of the properties its members owned; and it was found in the "number of boys and girls from this jaaliya who were born under the Chilean flag."[26] By 1927, Chile's Syrian, Lebanese, and Palestinian jaaliya was represented and instructed in ethical behavior by a patriotic organization that was committed to improving its national reputation in order to ensure its survival through continued migration from the homeland. *Al-Watan* was the platform for publicizing this important reality.

One article in particular stands out for promoting the theme of the triumph of the moral over the corrupt in a just and equitable mahjar. On 23 August 1924, *al-Watan*'s editors printed a love story titled "The Tragedy of a Syrian Girl in North Chile" (figure 8). *Al-Watan* evidently received information about the story from *El Mercurio*, a newspaper in Copiapo, Chile, where much of the story unfolded. Replete with poetic language and dramatic imagery, the tragedy began in the idealized, borderless homeland and was resolved in Chile:

> There, in the south of Lebanon, where Palestine and the hills of the Hawran and Hula begin, in Marjʿoyoun, where innocent passion meshed with the souls of two youths in love, two souls were made one.
>
> But the disease that has been seeping into the veins of Syria's sons since half a century afflicted the youth, George Niqola. So, he was compelled to emigrate to collect money with which to indulge his lover. At the hour of farewell, they stood there, shedding tears and sighing, reciting [old poetry].[27]

The surge in emigration, described as a disease that had been afflicting the homeland for half a century, was undoubtedly a familiar reality to *al-Watan*'s readers. The story continued with the lovers, Saʿida and George, swearing loyalty to one another and hoping to be united again soon. "But how many of those migrants who have aged in the diaspora assumed that?" *Al-Watan*'s editors asked. "Most of them leave . . . and only few return." The realities of migration were familiar to the newspaper's readers, who knew too well that separation from the homeland was always lengthy and sometimes even permanent.

Back in Marjʿoyoun, Saʿida waited for George to return, and year after year, she was disappointed. She learned that George settled in Copiapo, a

FIGURE 8. The main illustration for "The Tragedy of a Syrian Girl in North Chile," *al-Watan*, 23 August 1924. Source: Biblioteca Nacional, Santiago, microfilms.

town in the Atacama, in northern Chile, and she decided to venture there herself to find him. She took to the seas and arrived in Buenos Aires, where "the tragedy started." Upon her arrival in Buenos Aires, Saʿida received a series of telegrams from different family members in Copiapo warning her against meeting George before meeting with them because his "morals had been corrupted in America; he had taken many mistresses and traded in them." The family also hinted at another man, Kamel Eliya, whom they believed was better suited for her. But Saʿida's difficulties were just beginning. On her first night in Copiapo, her relatives, Jibrail and Deeb Murqus, introduced her to Kamel, who explained that he knew her from Marjʿoyoun and professed his love for her. Her relatives supported Kamel's plan to marry Saʿida, but Saʿida did not agree. They "pressed and pressured her further, and she grew more frustrated. They then imprisoned her and forbade her fiancé from visiting her."

An unmarried Arab woman was in high demand in this endogamous jaaliya, and Saʿida's hosts were determined to marry her to Kamel. To do so, they orchestrated a ruse: "They told her that in this country, there is a habit of throwing a welcome party for arriving travelers. One of the rituals of this party is inviting a government official of high rank who brings with him a register in which he writes the name of the traveler." The traveler is asked several simple questions about the journey and is then asked to sign the register. They also explained that "a friend of the traveler" must also be present to introduce the traveler to the government official, as well as others who attest to the validity of the answers and signature. So, Jibrail and Deeb Murqus planned this "welcome party" and had Kamel stand beside Saʿida as her supposed friend before the alleged government official. Kamel requested from the official to ask Saʿida his questions in Spanish, which she did not understand, and Kamel instructed her to answer in the affirmative and to then sign the register. Saʿida was tricked into signing a marriage certificate to a man she did not know or love.

The Murqus' ruse was deplorable, but Saʿida, filled with love for George, quickly realized what had happened and retaliated. Consequently, her relatives trapped her in "a dark basement under the house floor," where she spent three days and nights. On the fourth day, she tricked her captors into easing her confinement by pretending to be weakened by hunger and torture, and she successfully ran away. She roamed the streets of Copiapo searching for George until a Middle Eastern family took pity on her and took her in, "as Arabs are generously wont to do." George learned of Saʿida's presence in Copiapo and found her. "Their reunion," *al-Watan* described, "was in exultation, and their former vows were renewed that they would never be apart." Finally, Saʿida appealed the local court, explaining what had happened, and the judges ruled in her favor, annulling her marriage certificate to Kamel Eliya and punishing her captors. Saʿida and George were reunited and could finally wed, beginning their lives together in the Chilean mahjar, a place that rewarded virtue and love and punished crime.

"The Tragedy of a Syrian Girl in North Chile" was didactic. It offered hope for the triumph of true love over evil, and it informed *al-Watan*'s readers that they could seek recourse in a just Chilean legal system so long as their behavior was noble and righteous. Perhaps Saʿida's story inspired *al-Watan*'s readers to be and to do good. After all, she suffered greatly, but above all, she remained true to her noble mission, which she began in the pure homeland, and in the end, she was reunited with her love. Chile's Arabic newspapers were thus involved in teaching their readers the value of moral behavior within a mahjar that rewarded it judicially and with continued immigration from the watan.

Loving the Watan, Demanding Nationality, and Defending Palestine

Chile's Arabic periodicals appealed to the jaaliya whenever their watan needed them. These appeals were reinforced with various committees and organizations that emerged before and during the interwar period to reflect solidarity with the homeland. The first Syrian youth society in Chile, La Sociedad Juventud Homsiene, was formed in 1913. Its founders were from Homs, in present-day Syria. And as word of Britain's injurious policies spread, Palestinian collectives sprouted in Chile as a hub for Palestinian settlement. The struggle to defend Palestine from British and Zionist forces—and, by extension, to defend Palestinian migrants' rights to nationality and citizenship—became a focal point in the collective jaaliya's struggle against the postwar world order. For example, El Club Deportivo Palestino, formed in 1920 by Palestinian migrants, and La Sociedad Juventud Palestina, in 1924, had the following objectives: "The mutual protection of Palestinian residents in the Chilean territory as well as the moral and intellectual advancement of its members, while maintaining the local objective of meeting periodically."[28] Groups like La Sociedad Juventud Palestina and El Club Sirio-Palestino used periodicals to circulate their agendas and to boost membership.[29]

Similarly, periodicals sought to enhance the sense of collectiveness among their readers by appealing to their patriotic sentiments. On 5 August 1928, for example, *al-Sharq* printed a brief reflection on its mission and purview as a newspaper:

> ***Al-Sharq* Newspaper—Weekly, patriotic, independence-driven, unifying**
>
> We saw to naming the newspaper *al-Sharq* out of respect for and pride in our beloved east: the source of the soul, and of poetic, philosophical, and human inspiration, and the place of values and the land of civility.
>
> And to make our newspaper more popular, useful, and realistic for our readership, we have split it into two sections. The first in the honorable, exalted Arabic language, and the second in Spanish.

By 1928, Chile's jaaliya was bilingual, indicating a degree of acculturation that, while promising for a migrant community seeking success in the host country, also suggested that it was letting go of its Arabic origins. *al-Sharq*'s editors thus printed in both languages, emphasizing the importance of retaining their shared knowledge of Arabic. The editors then urged their readers to honor patriotism and to partake in the collective drive for national independence back home. Regarding the newspaper's political agenda, they went on:

> It is patriotic and independence-driven—with indulgence and support. It is serious in criticizing the deplorable of our patriotic deeds, for there is no reform without criticism. And are we sons of gods? We are not gods, infallible. Our political and nationalistic errors are countless, for we are still young in this track—the track of nationalisms—especially with respect to the friction between our sects and denominations.[30]

For *al-Sharq*'s editors, the surest way of accomplishing solidarity with the watan was through patriotic edification in the mahjar that championed respect and adoration for the homeland and its language, as well as ongoing collective self-reflection and improvement. The editors stressed that outgrowing sectarian differences would be a critical step in this collective journey to patriotic progress.

Palestinian migrants' battle for citizenship after 1925, then, was considered at once a Palestinian issue and a collective one for the Middle Eastern jaaliya. Supporting Palestinians, regardless of national or confessional creed, was an act of patriotism since the reclamation of Palestine's self-determination from British and Zionist forces was considered part of a greater regional, transnational, and Arab cause throughout the mahjar. The different instances in which members of the jaaliya formed political collectives and in which periodical editors urged their readers to support different causes in the beloved watan suggest the quality of the connections they envisioned between themselves and their ancestral homelands. And in the case of Palestine, they constitute a critical part of the formation of Palestinian national consciousness transnationally. Mahjar periodicals' coverage of developments that were specific to Palestine and Palestinians contributed to the emergence of distinctly Palestinian modes of identification and activism among their readers.

But to ensure that their readers connected with the Palestinian watan and sought to protect it and their rights to it, periodical editors needed to first inculcate in them a love for a distant geographic homeland that grew increasingly far from their daily realities. One way in which they did this was by bringing the beloved homeland to life in their pages, including through regular messages from compatriots in Palestine. These messages complemented the newspapers'. On 20 June 1925, for example, *al-Watan* printed an article written by Jamil Khalil Daccarett in Bethlehem in which he called on all Arabs to fulfill their duty of loving the homeland:

> Love of the homeland is sacred and imposed upon us. It is the duty of every one of us to love our homeland and to respect and revere it because it is the place of our residence, and the place where we grew up to become men. Therefore, it is our right to love our homeland as it is imposed on every human to love his homeland and protect it. . . . We must establish patriotic schools to graduate great leaders to defend the homeland, scholars to establish patriotic and charitable organizations to illuminate the minds of our youth, male and female. Perhaps with that, we will rise up and produce works that are praiseworthy, and obtain what souls aspire to (independence). Independence does not come except through these works. And peace be to he who follows the right path, listens, and becomes aware.[31]

That *al-Watan* published an article by a resident of Bethlehem calling on Palestinians to love their homeland by establishing patriotic schools signifies that its editors considered their readership in the diaspora to be part of a collective that shared all concerns related to Palestine. For the newspaper's editors, love for the homeland and the pursuit of progress linked the jaaliya with the watan. The ultimate sign of transnational patriotism was true love for the homeland, a kind of love that protected and defended the watan through the establishment of schools that would graduate generations of enlightened leaders committed to achieving national independence. By reading *al-Watan*, members of the jaaliya in Chile could become part of this transnational responsibility, fulfilling their sacred duty to the watan.

The most urgent and critical responsibility the jaaliya needed to assume was the protection of Palestinian migrants' rights to Palestinian citizenship. As British mandate authorities enacted legislation and put into practice policies that actualized their promises to the Zionists at the expense of Palestinians, Chile's newspapers responded immediately. The 1925 Palestinian Citizenship Order-in-Council featured prominently in many newspaper articles following the rejection of thousands of applications for Palestinian citizenship. In addition to warning all Palestinians among their readers of the dangers of losing their rights to Palestinian citizenship, newspapers linked citizenship and nationality with patriotism, which, in turn, was connected to economic and ethical success in the diaspora. To care about one's rights to Palestinian citizenship was thus also to care about the well-being of the jaaliya, whose existence depended on the integrity of the watan.

Al-Watan notified its readers of the issue of Palestinian legal and political representation before the promulgation of the ordinance in July 1925. On 11 February 1925, it printed a letter from Philip Badran in Lima, Peru. In the letter, Badran addressed *jaaliyatuna*, "our community," which, he elaborated, included Lebanese, Syrians, and Palestinians.[32] Subsequently, he described a problem that he said concerned *jaaliyatuna*: Palestinians' political and legal representation following Britain's new policies. Evidently, Palestinian members of the Peruvian jaaliya had gone to the British consulate in Lima to ask for help in resolving a conflict between Palestinian merchants and the Peruvian police that involved the murder of a Palestinian merchant. Badran explained that they were told by the British consul that nothing could be done for them:

> As for our notables in this town, they have taken this matter very seriously, but . . . the English consul replied to them that there is nothing he can do since issues relating to Palestinians are the direct concern of the Colonial Office, and not of England's ambassadors and consuls, who do not have the official power or legitimate agency to protect Palestinian migrants. Furthermore, the state of Peru does not grant the right of protection to Palestinians, nor does it recognize England as their representative since they do not carry official or legal documents to that effect.
>
> Briefly, English agencies do not consider Palestinians English citizens, and therefore, it cannot defend them, protect them, or interfere in their matters. This is what the representative of the British consulate said.[33]

Badran was alarmed that the Palestinian community in Peru could not seek justice for the killing of one of its members for reasons beyond its control. His plea, subsequently, was for action on the part of the sizeable and successful Chilean Palestinian jaaliya:

> Our jaaliya here awaits Palestinians in Chile to expose this tragedy and the position of the British consul [in Lima] to the British embassy there so they can inform them of their opinions on this matter. . . . They will know that as it stands,

they have no international representative, consulate, or agency to turn to during hard times or for their commercial needs, especially when it comes to traveling outside these countries and obtaining the legal documents required of every mobile migrant and traveler. . . . I have been asked to take charge of the duty of the editor in chief of this newspaper and reach out to the chivalrous Palestinians and Arabs to remedy this . . . defect.[34]

Though Badran was Lebanese, he considered the issue of Palestinian migrants' rights to legal recourse and representation to be a concern for all Middle Eastern migrants in Latin America, and he was compelled to reach out to Palestinians in Chile. Badran, in doing so, and *al-Watan*'s editors, in printing his letter, enhanced the sense of connectedness among Palestinians and their allies throughout Latin America.

By July 1925, when the Palestinian Citizenship Order-in-Council was promulgated, therefore, Chile's Arabic newspapers were speaking of immigration and nationality in the context of Palestinians alone. As for the Lebanese and Syrian members of *jaaliyatuna*, *al-Watan* also had news for them. Unlike Palestinians, Lebanese and Syrian migrants had recourse to French consulates in the diaspora since France officially represented them, so long as they were not anti-colonial nationalists. Generally speaking, French consulates in the diaspora encouraged Syrians and Lebanese to elect for the citizenship of their homelands, and *al-Watan* delivered the news to them, albeit with a warning: it urged Lebanese and Syrian migrants not to opt for citizenship since "citizenship papers are our enemy's weapons against us." *Al-Watan* warned that citizenship would function as tacit acceptance of French suzerainty over Lebanon and Syria, and subsequently, any claims against French rule there in the fight for independence would be discredited. On 11 November 1925, *al-Watan* printed the following warning to Lebanese and Syrian migrants applying for citizenship:

Citizenship Papers for Syrians and Lebanese, and the Intentions of the French Consulate

The French consulate in this capital [Santiago] placed an announcement in the local papers calling on the sons of the jaaliya to choose the nationality that they want. This is based on the Treaty of Lausanne. . . .

Citizenship papers are our enemy's weapons against us. They can say to the League of Nations: "How can the Syrians disapprove of French guardianship while their migrants, who are free in their foreign countries, present themselves willingly and obediently to request this guardianship?"

This is from one side. From the other, he who signs up for citizenship places himself under the mercy of the French consul who can one day impose the residency law on the Syrian who recognizes French protection, and thus ask him to leave the country.

We warn our compatriots not to fall into this French trap, and we advise them to not sign up for citizenship.

Al-Watan's editors alerted their readers to the double-edged sword of French guardianship through Syrian and Lebanese citizenship, and they added that French authorities had considerably reduced the fee for applying for citizenship: "We are certain that this cheap price will not lure the sons of Syria and Lebanon, and France will not find among them those who will join it 'for free.'"[35]

Matters became more urgent for Palestinians with Britain's continued refusal to reconsider the ordinance and with the August 1926 deadline for submitting requests for citizenship fast approaching. On 5 March 1926, *al-Watan* printed a letter from Mikhail al-Nabt, a member of the newspaper's administrative board who was writing from the city of Conception, south of Santiago. In the letter, al-Nabt expressed concern over the implications of missing the unworkable deadline, and over acceding to British demands that Palestinian migrants submit documents proving that they were Palestinians. Dated 11 February 1926, the letter read:

We saw . . . that the English consul has signed a declaration that every Palestinian is required to present proofs that he is a Palestinian. And if the window for doing so passes, i.e., by August, and he does not present the necessary evidence, he will lose his citizenship. Furthermore, the consul will not acknowledge him, especially if he requests a passport. We here have looked into this colorful British policy, and we no longer know how to limit its power. We are concerned about the damages we would inflict . . . if we signed that we are from Palestine. Furthermore, if we are late in doing so, not one of us can dispense of his nation. We implore you to enlighten everyone at *al-Watan* and to remember what our destiny will be at the end of this policy.[36]

Briefly, meeting the deadline was infeasible, as was leaving Chile. In response to al-Nabt's alert and in the same issue, *al-Watan* offered suggestions regarding what members of the jaaliya should do to protect their rights to nationality.

Echoing Badran's plea and further stressing the uniqueness of Palestine, *al-Watan*'s editors amended what they had recommended on 11 November 1925. Rather than warn against the ulterior motives of European citizenship legislation as they had done three months prior, they urged their readers, especially Palestinians among them, to elect for the nationalities of their mandated *awtaan* (homelands). They explained that while France required applicants for Lebanese and Syrian citizenship to declare their recognition of French sovereignty, Britain did not, and this was reason enough to rush to apply for Palestinian citizenship:

> It is . . . incumbent on the sons of Syria, Lebanon, Palestine, and Iraq to take the nationality of their homelands by asking for it from the local governments in the homeland, and from the agents of the guardian state abroad, and to not become considered Turks after this coming August. . . .
>
> As for the sons of Palestine, the matter with them is different from Syrians. Firstly, England, as far as we know, does not force Palestinians to accept the Balfour Declaration, nor British protection, as is the case with the French. Secondly, they write on tickets and certificates that the bearer is a subject of, and under the protection of, England.
>
> The nationality document is therefore required for the Palestinian, and this is unavoidable for whoever wishes to keep his nationality. And since the British do not ask of the Palestinian, as the French do of the Syrian, to sign a document confirming their acceptance of their protection, we do not see any harm in taking British nationality as a benefit to the Palestinian nation.[37]

Al-Watan was effectively the Chilean Palestinian jaaliya's most reliable, if not its only source for learning about British policies that impacted it directly. Most importantly, applying for citizenship from the British consulate, the newspapers' editors ensured their readers, would not entail acceptance of the Balfour Declaration to give Palestine to the Zionists.

The debates surrounding citizenship and nationality intensified in 1927 following a slew of rejections of applications for citizenship by Palestinian migrants. Chile's Arabic newspapers thus began printing more strongly worded reactions. On 29 January 1927, *al-Sharq* printed two articles regarding the issue of nationality. The first, titled "El concepto de nacionalidad" (The concept of nationality) and written in Spanish, was submitted by a contributor to the newspaper, Salvador Sackel. Sackel described his philosophy on nationality and the importance of what he called "el sentimiento patrio" (The patriotic sentiment). This sentiment, Sackel began, is inborn in every person, and it develops as an affection toward the defense of freedom. He explained: "This laudable sentiment, based on deep affection and caused by that which is closest to the individual, becomes something familiar to the inner self when contemplated daily over time." And as the patriotic sentiment becomes second nature, Sackel proceeded, people must guard it as they would their own home, fighting for it when it is endangered. "It is a primary duty of sustaining deep down our undying ideal of freedom," Sackel declared, "which is the sublime communion of the soul. And when we meet this most sacred duty of all duties, only then can we be proud of having rights." For Sackel, inborn nationality was congruous with achieving freedom, and "only a citizen who has duties and civic rights is worthy to be called man! Others are vile slaves!"[38] The issue of Palestinian citizenship was so acute, it elicited philosophical sermons in the pages of *al-Sharq*. Indeed, Sackel linked inborn patriotism with nationality, freedom, and civic duty. True rights, he believed, were achieved only with nationality.

The second article on nationality in *al-Sharq* on 29 January 1927 was also in Spanish. In "La negacion de nuestra nacionalidad" (The denial of our nationality), *al-Sharq* urged the jaaliya to action regarding the denial of Palestinian nationality to Palestinian migrants because

> the British consulates abroad have received strict instructions from His Majesty's government to not grant visas or passports to any Palestinian citizen who wishes to travel.
>
> The alarm caused among the children of Palestine by this arbitrary measure will gradually break out abroad. [The policy] is . . . illegal and contrary to every rule of international law.[39]

As would also be expressed in the 23 February 1927 petition from the Centro Social Palestino de Monterrey, Mexico, to the high commissioner in Jerusalem, Palestinians in Chile were adamant that they would not sit by while they were denied their nationality; they were united and steadfast in their fight for Palestinian rights. *Al-Sharq* then printed the notice migrants received from consular offices regarding the denial of their citizenship applications, which was similar to those given to Mexico's Palestinians:

Sir,

With reference to your request opting for Palestinian Citizenship under Article 2 of the Palestinian law on nationality transmitted through the British Vice Consulate in Santiago, I lament to inform you that the Government of Palestine is unable to accommodate your request.

The reason given by the Government of Palestine is your long absence from the country.

[But you may apply for residency] under Article 4 of the Act in question, provided you comply with the requirement of residence for a period of six months in Palestine before presenting your new application, and providing evidence of birth in Ottoman Palestine. This application must be submitted before August 1, 1927. . . .

The British consular representatives [in Santiago] are not able to lend greater support in the matter.

Sincerely,
Constantino Graham
Consul General of British Consulate
December 27, 1926[40]

While British consular offices throughout the Americas were receiving orders to deny Palestinian migrants' applications for citizenship for the same arbitrary reasons, Palestinians and their allies throughout the mahjar were also protesting using the same logic. The crisis of Palestinian citizenship was thoroughly transnational, and the response to it, unified.

Following the notice, *al-Sharq*'s editors continued to criticize Jerusalem's decision. They also emphasized the Zionist element in the British policy and the infeasibility of meeting the new 1 August 1927 deadline for submitting applications for citizenship:

Under the pretext that the Palestinians scattered abroad recognize their nationality and are opting for Palestinian citizenship, the British rulers . . . have dealt a huge blow to the majority of native Arabs of Palestine from diverse backgrounds.

So, the vast majority of true Palestinians have informed mandatory authorities that the Palestine they are attempting to deliver to Jewish hands belongs legitimately, by Law and Justice, to its native sons who have lived there for centuries.

> We have understood this wicked arbitrariness as an attempt to formalize the desires of the Zionists, against the overwhelming majority of the natives who defend every inch of the land of their birth, the sacred heritage of their ancestors.[41]

Invoking "Law and Justice" was significant. Like their counterparts in northern Mexico, these migrants were employing the liberal rhetoric emanating from Europe in the interwar period. That law and justice were on the side of Palestinian migrants whose nationality was under threat unambiguously placed the onus of redress on Britain:

> [The British] have resorted to eliminating the Palestinian element, denying them citizenship . . . passports, thus preventing their return to their legitimate homeland, despite their families and relatives, properties and interests. . . .
>
> [And] for a true Palestinian to reach his native country, he has until next August 1, i.e. just six months. In addition, [this trip is very costly] and there are few who are disposed to spare the cost. And still, we must reside [in Palestine] for six months before applying for citizenship.
>
> And with that passport do we go![42]

The explanation yielded exclamations of disbelief, offering readers the opportunity to share in the frustration, especially considering Britain's ostensible role in Palestine as temporary mentor in the path to self-determination.

To express this frustration further, *al-Sharq*'s editors declared their disappointment with Britain, the supposed trustee of Palestinians worldwide:

> We are deeply disappointed with the purposes given to forbid our leaving, and with the discovery that the British Government is doing this, [despite] the freedom and emancipation that it promised the people of Palestine. Now that these procedures are unveiled, our indignation cannot be more profound, since this mandatory regime, under the pretext of offering complete freedom, only has come to trample on the sovereignty of a nationality that aspired to own a free country without foreign meddling in its domestic business.
>
> Britain, which has always boasted behaving with Law and Justice in international affairs, in the case of Palestine, has only managed to create a heavy atmosphere of animosity among [us] toward its rulers, the consequences of which in the Middle East are not predictable in their full amplitude.[43]

By accusing Britain of failing to abide by its own standards of "Law and Justice," tenets by which all governments are to behave, the newspapers' editors explicitly blamed Britain for the injustice being committed against Palestinians. Anger and disbelief permeated the mahjar, with Palestinians across the Americas lambasting Britain for contravening international law in leaving its rightful subjects stateless. *Al-Sharq* thus gave a platform for all members of Chile's jaaliya to join Arabs transnationally in voicing collective outrage against the denial of "nuestra nacionalidad." The loss of Palestinian citizenship was a loss for all; distance from the homeland was not a barrier to transnational solidarity.

But Chile's Arabic newspapers also gave Palestinians their own venues for expressing frustration and for deliberating solutions to the loss of their nationality. To do so, periodicals addressed Palestinian members of the jaaliya directly. On 19 November 1927, for example, *al-Watan* published a call to Palestinian migrants urging them to take action against losing their rights to Palestinian nationality by registering for a committee that was established that year to defend their national rights:

> Are you Palestinian?
>
> If you are a real Palestinian, concerned for the well-being of your nation upon which your dignity rests—and he without dignity does not have a life—if you are this Palestinian, then hurry to register for the Committee for the Defense of Palestinian National Rights which defends your nation and your nationality against the colonizing ghoul.[44]

Newspaper editors solicited their readers' support for multinational groups and organizations that emerged in the mahjar throughout the interwar period. Earlier that year, on 22 January, for example, *al-Sharq* had reported that La Sociedad Juventud Palestina had held a public hearing and invited "all members of the Palestinian community" in Santiago to discuss the crisis of Palestinian nationality.[45] The purpose of the hearing was to collect "financial and moral support from every national who has enthusiasm and patriotism and who desires that the English government recognize their Palestinian nationality and forbid the Zionist greed that prevails in our homeland." The committee accepted donations from Palestinians in "all parts of this Republic," and it required a monthly membership fee. But the committee also mentioned prescriptively that it "does not protect those who are late in supporting this endeavor to obtain their nationality," urging the public to act quickly. Chile's Arabic newspapers were vehicles for responsible public action and awareness.

In the same issue of *al-Sharq*, dated 22 January 1927, the editors included an excerpt from the Egyptian newspaper *al-Shuri* to explain the issue of Palestinian nationality as a consequence of the 1925 ordinance. Palestinians in Egypt had also been facing challenges returning to Palestine, and *al-Shuri* had already reached conclusions regarding the validity of the citizenship legislation and Palestinian migrants' claims to Palestinian nationality. The article explained how *al-Shuri*'s editors had managed to discredit the Government of Palestine's reasons for denying migrants' applications for citizenship using the Treaty of Lausanne:

> Article 30 of the Treaty of Lausanne states that Turkish subjects residing in countries that, according to this treaty, are separated from Turkey, shall rightfully become, according to this treaty, subjects of the state to which the country has been transferred.
>
> Article 31 states that persons over the age of 18 who do not have Turkish citizenship and who rightfully gain the new nationality according to article 30 shall have the right for two years starting on the day this treaty is enacted to opt for Turkish nationality.
>
> Therefore, article 30 of the Treaty of Lausanne clearly showed that the two-year window within which to opt for citizenship does not begin until the issuance of the local legislation. . . .
>
> The two-year window ends at the end of September 1927, as is deduced from these materials. We believe this policy has become illegal, and it was an unwarranted rejection [of our citizenship].[46]

Al-Shuri's editors had done their research, and in printing their conclusions about Britain's policies, *al-Sharq* reassured its readers that they were not alone in their outrage or suspicions regarding Britain's real motives behind denying Palestinians' applications. The article ended by accusing Britain of deliberately distancing Palestine's finest to make room for the Zionists, a conclusion also reached by *al-Shuri*:

> What we believe is that the consulates are trying through this to concoct a specific plan that cuts off the connection of immigrants—whose numbers are not

> small—with their homeland. They are doing this so that the Zionist nation can be rid of the smartest, richest, and strongest of the sons of Palestine.[47]

Newspapers from Egypt to Chile collectively contested the validity of Britain's reasons for denying Palestinian migrants' their citizenship. Concomitantly, Palestinian jaaliyaat from Egypt to Chile could develop stronger bonds around shared experiences.

Chile's Arabic newspapers also regularly printed articles about the crisis of citizenship that were authored by Palestinians in Palestine. On 20 August 1927, *al-Watan* printed a letter from Secretary Khalil Murqus of the Committee for the Defense of the Rights of Palestinians in Foreign Countries, which had formed earlier that year in Beit Jala. In the letter, Murqus reiterated the seriousness of the citizenship crisis:

> The Palestine citizenship law has been issued, with all its injustices and inequities that fall on our sons and brothers in the diaspora, as well as the financial and moral damages that ensue. . . . We have received your letters filled with complaints about this law that has hit the core of our hearts, and your voices have been heard on the pages of the newspapers yelling at the Mandate Government, appealing to the sons of the nation to join them in protesting this injustice . . .—which makes them in their diaspora as sheep without a shepherd and a savory bite for every greedy lawmaker. . . . It will also deprive them of international laws, which protect them from injustice and uphold their matters before other nations.[48]

Murqus proceeded to add his voice and the voices of Palestinians throughout Palestine to protesting the legislation, whether in Jerusalem, London, or Geneva:

> We are with you in voicing your demands, standing as one with our brothers in Jerusalem, Jaffa, Haifa, Bethlehem, Ramallah, Nazareth, Hebron, and elsewhere in Palestine, unified in protest against the Mandatory Government about this unjust law, demanding that it amend it or add to it an article that defends our brothers. . . . And we will raise our voices and our protests will continue until the highest level of protest, doing anything and everything we can for the sake of obtaining our desired rights, whether with the local government in Palestine, the supreme authorities in London, or the League of Nations.[49]

Finally, he asked for the financial support of Palestinians abroad to contribute to the defense of their nationality, the purpose for which his committee had been formed:

> Considering what this lively project will require in hardships and expenses, we write to you this letter begging for your devotion and enlivening your motivation to gather the necessary money and send it to us as soon as possible so we may go forward. Money is the basis of winning these projects and their success. Therefore, we will have carried out our duties to our sons and nation.[50]

Migrants' remittances were central to sustaining Palestine's economy and also to the operation of its nationalist movement. The Committee for the Defense of the Rights of Palestinians in Foreign Countries, which linked the mahjar and the watan, also needed the support of Palestinian migrants to carry out its duties. Chile's Arabic periodicals contributed to the consolidation of transnational networks of solidarity around the cause of protecting the rights of Palestinians both in the mahjar and the watan.

These networks were also strengthened when Chile's Arabic newspapers reprinted articles regarding the crisis of Palestinian citizenship that had first appeared in newspapers in Palestine—namely, in *Filastin*. Arabic newspaper editors in Santiago reprinted the calls for political action and support from Palestinians throughout the mahjar that they received from *Filastin* newspaper in Jaffa. These articles kept the Palestinian community across the world connected to the greater Palestinian nationalist cause promoted by *Filastin*, and they had the added effect of constructing shared experiences among Palestinians throughout the mahjar. Therefore, mahjar Palestinians could also grow into an interconnected community by turning to the watan's newspapers. On 8 April 1928, for example, *al-Watan* reprinted an article that had appeared in *Filastin* by a Palestinian residing in El Salvador. Nakhla al-Daʿdaʿ addressed his *kitaab maftouh* (open book) to "God Almighty," suggesting that the tone of the community's frustration with Britain's arbitrary citizenship requirements had reached new levels since Britain had become unrelenting with its rejections.

He began by asserting, unequivocally, that he and those on whose behalf he was writing this letter, were Palestinians and from Palestine: "Oh, Lord / You have willed it and thus created us as Palestinians in the land of Palestine, in the birthplace of the Revelation and religions, of prophets and protectors."

He proceeded to describe the long history of oppressive colonization they had endured as Palestinians, which culminated with the Ottomans:

> But some of your creations have envied us for this "blessing" and have thus trespassed upon your godly instructions, infringed upon your heavenly will. They do not want to see us safe and assured in our nation and home, so they have attacked us and colonized our country, unsettled our comfort, disturbed our souls, and soured our lives. The Turks were the last to have ruled us, and so we submitted to their rule, living under oppression. We longed for them to leave our lands, believing them the most oppressive in existence, but they were not.[51]

In this chronological narrative, al-Daʿdaʿ likened British and Zionist forces to their Ottoman predecessors in Palestine:

> You heard our cries, oh great God, and sent us "Great" Britain. We thought she was benevolent and just, and so we opened to her our souls and gave her our hearts, but shortly after, she turned her back on us and punished us, stepping on our necks, cursing our money, taking pleasure in our pains, choking us more tightly, selling our country to a foreign . . . people. . . .
>
> [The Zionists] incited Britain to discard us and deprive us of our Palestinian nationality. Britain did as they asked . . . and the immigrants screamed and cried, and raised their case to you, Lord, and to the great and small states, to the British Colonial Office, as well as to the Government of Palestine, the Italian state, papal heads, the League of Nations, to the civilized and barbaric worlds, and to every living soul, in open and official petitions. We cried for our beloved nation and for justice . . . but all of it was like screaming in a valley.[52]

Al-Daʿdaʿ was exasperated. Palestinians had done all they could to defend their rights and protest their disenfranchisement. There was nothing more they could do but implore the lord for help.

This dramatic opening set the tone for al-Daʿdaʿs discussion about the difficulties Palestinians in El Salvador were facing as a result of Britain's unjust policies:

> [The] government of El Salvador has issued a new law . . . and imposed it on every migrant that he must present citizenship papers, notarized by the government of his nation, or else he would be prohibited from work in El Salvador. This came as a direct blow to Palestinians as it ended the remainder of their hopes and rendered them homeless without a nation or citizenship.[53]

Al-Daʿdaʿ reassured the Lord that he and Palestinians in El Salvador had also sought to remedy this situation through diplomacy. The Palestinians of El Salvador even formed a delegation to meet with the British representative, to no avail:

> The delegation petitioned him and sent him a telegraph requesting a time to meet, but the representative refused to meet the delegation and provided the following strange reply through his scribe: "The consul says to you that Britain has only colonized the land of Palestine, but it has nothing to do with its people"!!!
>
> The delegation did not succeed in meeting the consul face to face since the consul refused, so it then requested from the consul to broadcast his reply to the community, but his reply on the following day was the text of the unjust Palestinian Citizenship Order-in-Council, and nothing less![54]

He then pleaded with the Lord for answers:

> The Republic of El Salvador does not want to consider us its subjects. . . .
>
> So, tell us, oh God, what we should do and to whom we should go. We have become sheep without a shepherd, a pasture for wolves, and the coveted of the oppressors! Shall we commit suicide and die, and bid farewell to our country, its nationality and its people???[55]

Al-Daʿdaʿ was desperate, a feeling that resonated with Palestinian communities across Latin America whose connections to Palestine were being increasingly threatened. And that *al-Watan* received al-Daʿdaʿs open book to the Lord from *Filastin* indicates that for these newspapers' editors, the crisis of Palestinian citizenship was a transnational issue that also impacted Palestine, as will be made clear in the following chapter. Throughout the interwar period, Palestinians worldwide thus grew increasingly interconnected through their shared struggle. Diaspora periodicals propagated and reinforced these bonds.

CHILE'S PALESTINIAN DIASPORA STORY

Chile's Arabic newspapers fostered unity, ethical behavior, and patriotism among their readers. The collective was Syrian from Greater Syria, to be sure, but it was also increasingly divided nationally throughout the interwar years. Newspaper editors acknowledged and at times even celebrated these new nationalities, but they also continued to address their readers as one jaaliya facing similar successes and challenges in Chile and at home in the watan. *Al-Watan* and *al-Sharq*'s editors were aware that their readers constituted Lebanese, Syrian, and Palestinian members who espoused a range of desires, fears, and loyalties outside the homogenizing effects of newspapers, especially when it came to their new *awtaan*. Yet they continued to address their readers as collectives that were first and foremost Arabic-speaking, preoccupied with the well-being of their jaaliya in the mahjar, and ultimately, concerned for the future of their newly divided *awtaan*. In doing so, they made all issues pertaining to the historic watan relevant to all readers.

These Arabic-speaking collectives were local, national, regional, and transnational, linking Santiago's jaaliya with others across Chile, the South American Pacific coast, the remainder of the continent, North America, and the watan. In effect, Chile's Arabic newspaper readers could pick up a newspaper, practice their Arabic, discover opportunities for teaching their children Arabic, read about other jaaliyaat in Chile and throughout the Americas, stay up to date on developments in the distant watan, and learn of ways to engage in local and transnational political activism. They could even read harrowing love stories between impassioned youths who met in the pristine homeland and were reunited in a just and promising mahjar. Perhaps most importantly, mahjar Arabic presses gave the jaaliya in Chile the opportunity to join others throughout the Americas in developing into interconnected groups that could now stake claims and express themselves in collective idioms.

In significant ways, this is the history of this community's formation into a diaspora. The process by which groups come to see themselves and speak about themselves in terms of groups is the subject matter of diaspora. When it comes to Chile's Arabic-newspaper subscribers in the 1920s, their diaspora connections developed whenever they paged through newspapers and read stories of *muwaatineen* in different towns and cities in Latin America who were experiencing similar challenges and successes. By reading a newspaper, an ambitious Palestinian shop owner in Concepcion, Chile, for example, could feel connected to and even aspire to become like a wealthy Palestinian business owner in Monterrey, Mexico, because he also spoke Arabic, because he had also left the homeland for economic betterment, and because he also subscribed to one of Chile's Arabic newspapers.

The proliferation of national identifiers in the Mashriq into Lebanese, Syrian, and Palestinian categories was accompanied by the simultaneous circulation of rhetoric among jaaliyaat in Latin America about a shared struggle for transnational recognition and representation as a collective newly made up of multiple nationalities. The emerging diaspora of Palestinians experienced the most difficulty when it came to transnational recognition and representation as a collective. And much like their Mexican counterparts who gathered in committees to draft petitions to British officials, Chile's Arabic newspaper editors were prolific in expressing concern over the loss of Palestinian nationality among their Palestinian readers following the Government of Palestine's rejection of their citizenship applications. In a concerted campaign that combined Chile's Palestinian community with Palestinians throughout the Americas and the beloved watan, they continually urged readers to action in the form of demanding redress, rights, and citizenship as Palestinians. They also called on all members of the jaaliya to support Palestinians in their struggle.

The exclusionary measures put in place by London and Jerusalem in the aftermath of the 1925 Palestinian Citizenship Order-in-Council thus spurred

FIGURE 9. As a tribute to Palestine, the Plaza Palestina was constructed in the shape of historic Palestine at the intersection of Los Militares and Alonso de Córdova streets. It is located in the upscale neighborhood of Las Condes in Santiago de Chile, amid many of the city's embassies. Source: Personal collection of Constantino Marzuqa Giacaman.

a transnational campaign to raise awareness among those who identified as Palestinians throughout the mahjar about the importance of fighting for nationality and citizenship. Newspapers, like petitions, were platforms for voicing local, regional, and transnational solidarity around causes that were considered to be shared and critical. This community's struggle with denial of Palestinian citizenship in the 1920s was a formative part of its diaspora story; in significant ways, it contributed to the emergence of palestinos-chilenos, a community bounded and empowered by an ongoing and shared experience of distance from a homeland that holds symbolic and material significance for the collective (figure 9). How and why Palestinians in the distant watan brought their mahjar compatriots' voices home to Palestine is the subject of the next and final chapter.

CHAPTER 6

BRINGING THE RIGHT OF RETURN HOME TO PALESTINE

THE EXTENT TO WHICH the crisis of nationality and citizenship was transnational for Palestinians in the interwar period can only be grasped by returning the historical lens to Palestine. That Palestinian migrants were denied Palestinian citizenship also affected Palestinians in Palestine. Beyond financial remittances, on which many families in Palestine depended, the denial of citizenship to relatives, neighbors, friends, and business partners meant dramatic consequences for property ownership, inheritance, and social cohesion. It meant dissolving family and community structures, including permanently keeping families apart. How did Palestinians in Palestine respond to the denial of citizenship to thousands of their compatriots in the diaspora? Who among them took the lead in mobilizing in defense of transnational Palestinian jaaliyaat? How did they strategize confronting British authorities in Palestine? How did their activism contribute to the broader Palestinian national movement within Palestine?

Two efforts in particular, those of the members of the Committee for the Defense of the Rights of Palestinians in Foreign Countries, founded in Beit Jala in 1927, and those of the editors of *Filastin* newspaper, were responsible for bringing the crisis of Palestinian citizenship to Palestinians in Palestine and to the offices of the Government of Palestine in Jerusalem. In petitions delivered to British authorities in Jerusalem and in hundreds of articles printed in local newspapers, they contributed significantly to building transnational networks of communication, financial remittance, and solidarity among Palestinians and their allies; they bolstered local and mahjar claims to national self-determination as Palestinians; and they managed to bring the equitability of mandate rule into question in Jerusalem, London, and Geneva. While their Palestinian counterparts in the diaspora formed pro-Palestina collectives, members of which would visit British consulates throughout Latin America and submit petitions to be delivered to London, Jerusalem, and Geneva, applying pressure on the Government of Palestine, on the League of Nations, and on Palestinian leadership from within Palestine was doubtlessly critical to ensuring that action would be taken to solve the worsening crisis of mahjar Palestinians' citizenship.

In the long run, although Palestinians in Palestine were unable to effect significant change in British policy toward Palestinian migrants throughout the interwar period and although the exile of their fellow Palestinians persisted for the duration of British rule in Palestine—and beyond, for that matter—members of the Committee for the Defense of the Rights of Palestinians in Foreign Countries and the editors of *Filastin* brought mahjar Palestinians' voices home. By merging the Palestinian mahjar with the Palestinian watan in a struggle to protect migrants' rights to citizenship—all within the context of national self-determination—they effectively made the crisis of mahjar Palestinians' citizenship a crisis for Palestine.

THE COMMITTEE FOR THE DEFENSE OF THE RIGHTS OF PALESTINIANS IN FOREIGN COUNTRIES

In 1926, Issa Bandak, a prominent nationalist from Bethlehem, spearheaded a campaign to protest the 1925 Palestinian Citizenship Order-in-Council through publications in his newspaper, *Sawt al-Sha'b*.[1] By early 1926, Bandak was printing politicized pieces explaining why British authorities were refusing Palestinian citizenship to Palestinian migrants. In piece after piece, he made the argument that the ordinance "constituted a ploy to increase Jewish immigration at the expense of the citizenship of Arabs born in Palestine."[2] Bandak called on migrants to register themselves as Palestinian natives at local consulates across the diaspora, in defiance of the ordinance. Other leaders in Bethlehem, Jerusalem, and Ramallah joined Bandak in publicizing the citizenship crisis through manifestos and open letters. These activists were mostly middle-class nationalists, including "newspaper editors, municipal council leaders, lawyers and members of prominent families," and they received the full support of the Arab Executive in Jerusalem.[3] Musa Kazim al-Husseini, president of the Arab Executive, became active in lobbying colonial officials in Jerusalem throughout 1926, and late in that year, Bandak, Musa Kazim, and other Palestinian leaders met with mandate officials in Jerusalem to request changes to the citizenship ordinance. They even met with Colonial Secretary Leopold Amery, who "refused to discuss changes to the order or increase assistance for the emigrants." In response, Musa Kazim wrote an open letter to the Government of Palestine asking for an extension to the deadline for applying for citizenship, explaining further that the law itself "was difficult to understand for even competent legal authorities."[4]

The efforts of Bandak and many other Palestinian leaders within Palestine reflected a growing network of politically engaged activists who identified as Palestinians and who had reason to make demands of European colonial authorities as a disenfranchised political and national group. Indeed, by early 1927, Palestinians transnationally had become so prolific in demanding justice for migrants that Palestinians in Palestine began to speak of migrants' "right to return" to their homeland in periodicals like *al-Jamʿiyya al-ʿArabiyya* and *Filastin*.[5] Musa Kazim also called on Palestinians in Palestine to "stand up in order to defend [the emigrants'] rights, which are our rights," effectively merging the Palestinian nationalist movement with migrants' right to nationality and to return to Palestine.[6]

In 1927, in the pages of *Sawt al-Shaʿb*, Bandak, along with Khalil Murqus of Bethlehem and Atallah al-Najjar of Beit Jala, announced the formation of the Committee for the Defense of the Rights of Palestinians in Foreign Countries.[7] The committee was formed as a result of British citizenship policy, but the larger context included more urgent concerns. In his memoirs, Bandak described the unsafe conditions many Palestinian migrants were reporting from the diaspora. Throughout the 1920s, Latin American republics faced frequent coups and uprisings that put migrant communities at risk. For example, as Bandak wrote, Honduran "revolutionaries looted the shops and homes of many Palestinian expatriates."[8] And without British consular support, Palestinians were unable to receive protection during these unsafe times. Adnan Musallam explains that "Palestinian migrants deprived of their citizenship faced extremely difficult circumstances," including loss of protection during times of war, inability to travel, and in some case, extortion under threat of deportation.[9] With this news and with the knowledge that the Government of Palestine had refused to amend the ordinance, Bandak, Murqus, and al-Najjar decided to take action.

The committee "billed itself as the voice of the emigrants," largely because Bandak, Murqus, and al-Najjar came from Bethlehem and Beit Jala, the two towns from which most Palestinian migrants in Latin America originated.[10] The committee leaders thus appealed to residents of these towns for support because many of them would have had relatives in the diaspora who were impacted by the citizenship ordinance. As the committee's membership grew in the period after its formation, its leaders prepared to appeal the Government of Palestine. But first, the committee went to the Arab Executive in Jerusalem. The Arab Executive formed in 1920 in Haifa, and although British authorities did not formally recognize it as a representative body of the Arab population of Palestine and dissolved it in 1934, during its tenure, it served to promulgate Palestinian political activism and contributed to legitimizing the struggle of Palestinian nationalists for national self-determination. Furthermore, it offered a mouthpiece for migrants across the diaspora who sought representation back home in their struggle against British policies. Under the leadership of Musa Kazim, the Arab Executive extended its support to the committee. And on 2 June 1927, Musa Kazim joined the committee's leaders and visited the office of the high commissioner in Jerusalem to submit a petition requesting that the Government of Palestine reconsider the rejections doled out to Palestinian migrants applying for citizenship.

George Symes, chief secretary of the Government of Palestine, received the delegation and forwarded the petition to London. The three-page document covered nine areas that firmly but respectfully explained the extent of the crisis for Palestinians in Palestine and in the mahjar, as well as the benefits for Britain and its mandate of securing mahjar Palestinians' riches. It began with the committee members informing High Commissioner Plumer of Britain's responsibilities in Palestine, according to international law:

> It is required of every law or regulation—as Your Excellency is aware—that it should safeguard the well-being and happiness of the people. Any law that prompts a whole people to demur from oppression is harmful and contrary to the rights of the people, and thus is to be condemned. If such is the case, we do not wish to believe that this British Government intended or intends by the

promulgation of the law on Palestinian citizenship to deprive the greater majority of the inhabitants of the land from a natural acquired right. Your Excellency will not also ignore the reflection on the reputation of Great Britain, if she persists to turn a deaf ear to the pleadings of a people, based on a rightful and logical claim.[11]

They began the petition by confidently expressing an expectation among a people of their government. Well-being and happiness, for these petitioners, were to be safeguarded by the powers that be, and immediately after proclaiming this, they used *oppression* and *harmful* to describe the government's policy. Finally, they asked Plumer to reflect on the reputation of Great Britain were it to continue to disregard the grievances of its people, indicating that the committee members considered all Palestinians and Palestinian migrants to be subjects of the British government, entitled to the freedoms afforded to all other subjects of the Crown. These petitioners were speaking to their new government, a privilege awarded to liberated peoples in the aftermath of World War I.

The petitioners went on to describe the ways in which the Palestinian migrants' rightful and logical claims to their rights had been denied:

The British Consuls in Europe and America have asked, through the papers, copies of notices we possess, which we will exhibit to Your Excellency if desired, of all Palestinian emigrants to make applications for the maintenance of their Palestinian nationality. Applications were duly submitted, and the Palestinian residents abroad in the belief of having complied with the law, awaited the issue of the proper nationality certificates. They were greatly surprised to learn from their Consuls that the Palestine Government had refused its approval, on the plea that the applicants did not reside in Palestine for the required period.

If we consider the Consuls' reply to be in conformity with the stipulations of the nationality law, on the other hand, we find that the law contains harm and oppression to a degree not applicable on the most uncivilized people.[12]

Bandak, Murqus, al-Najjar, and Musa Kazim left no doubt as to the injustice they believed had been committed against Palestinians. They pointed out that the reason given to deny their applications—residence in Palestine for a required length of time—was unjust and that the British government's behavior was uncivilized.

They were ready to present their case based on the stipulations of article 34 of the Treaty of Lausanne. Namely, they emphasized their diaspora counterparts' claims to racial ties to Palestine. After quoting article 34, they stressed the infeasibility of meeting the application deadline:

> The logical conclusion to be deduced from the stipulations of the article is that the emigrants of this land who belong to the majority, enjoy the right to Palestinian nationality. We do not for a moment consider that the British Government would want to deprive them of this right simply because the time given for compliance was not sufficient, as the Treaty became effective on the 6th of August, 1924, and the nationality law was only published on the 16th of September, 1925. Therefore, it could not be claimed that article 34 was enforced, and furthermore, the time limit was not sufficient to be of use to the emigrants.[13]

In referring to the Treaty of Lausanne, the petitioners brought their case directly to the heart of European policy. It was Britain, after all, and not the Palestinians, who had agreed to the treaty. The petitioners further used the Treaty of Lausanne to point out the inadequacy of the time frame given to Palestinian migrants to apply for citizenship and return to Palestine, and they indicated that the Colonial Office agreed: "In support of this statement we call attention to the fact that the British Colonial Office in its reply to a petition in this connection, acknowledged that the time and circumstances under which the nationality law were published were inadequate." They were, in effect, building a case against the practices of the Government of Palestine, not against the law itself. The petitioners were convinced that the reasons given for rejecting citizenship applications needed to be revisited.

Following these grievances, the petitioners turned to describing the relationship between Palestinian migrants and the Government of Palestine. For the petitioners, Britain owed its tax-paying migrant subjects acknowledgement and protection. They went on to describe Palestinian migration as a benefit not only to Palestinian society but to British rule in Palestine and globally. In doing so, they included Palestinians transnationally within British suzerainty and British Palestine within the ranks of the world's greatest nations. For the petitioners, it behooved Britain to encourage Palestinian migration and to protect Palestinian migrants because "all Arab emigrants possess real estate and immovable property in Palestine, upon which they pay taxes and rates."[14] The petitioners explained that migrants did their part in supporting the Government of Palestine in its "administration of the land," but they added that the government "seems to refuse to do its part, by depriving them, through the iniquitous nationality law, of the protection they require in their abodes abroad." They proceeded to alert the high commissioner to the riches of the majority of Palestinian migrants in the mahjar, who "have attained a large success in business and industry, many of whom own progressive factories reaping large profits." These riches, they went on, "will eventually be added to the wealth of the land upon their repatriation," and in the meantime, "it is impossible for busy people to abandon their affairs for several months to come to Palestine to reside in compliance with the law." The committee members ended this section of the petition with a forceful reproach against British policy: "The nationals of the greatest nations in the world are scattered all over the world, and instead of being hampered for reasons of nationality, are afforded the greatest help in the pursuit of their business." If Britain were a great nation, surely it would invest in the business of its subjects, wherever they may be.

The petitioners went further and invoked Britain's reputation as an imperial power that had defeated the Turks, the enemy that stood to gain from 25,000 Palestinian migrants' profits if they were denied Palestinian citizenship and awarded Turkish citizenship instead. With such a high number of wealthy migrants, they went on, "the benefit to be derived of their activity is not negligible," and evidently, "Turkey, realising such benefits, has informed her Consuls abroad to recognise as Turkish subjects all emigrants, formerly Turkish subjects, but who did not acquire or were not admitted to the nationality of the new political division their country has acquired." They then shrewdly asked:

> Would the British Government tolerate that the active section of the Palestinian population be accredited to Turkey? Would that be suitable to British policy? Would British public opinion permit the denial of these emigrants who would rather die than relinquish their land associations, family ties and Palestinian nationality?[15]

The petitioners deliberately and strategically pointed out the new Turkish republic's interest in Palestinian migrants. On the one hand, they were correct to assume that Britain would not wish to accede any victories to Turkey and that Turkey benefiting from the riches of 25,000 successful Palestinian migrants could reflect poorly on Britain. On the other, they continued to declare that they considered themselves to be rightful beneficiaries of British rule. Palestine, after all, was theirs and their compatriots' in the diaspora, and since Britain had taken power a few years prior, theirs was to be a reciprocal relationship. For the petitioners, Britain needed them as much as they needed Britain.

Before making their demands of the Government of Palestine, the petitioners described specific difficulties migrants were experiencing without citizenship. They pointed out that Palestinian migrants were unable to travel "between Europe and the different parts of America on business, as they cannot obtain a Passport from the British Consul;" their lives and businesses were at risk without British consular protection, especially in Latin American countries experiencing political unrest; and they faced imminent deportation from "some of the American republics, notably Chile and Mexico" that "have promulgated laws to expatriate all foreigners not provided with a certificate of some nationality, which laws will shortly be enforced." Regarding the last difficulty, the petitioners explained that Palestinians would "be forcibly ejected, as tramps and outlaws." They concluded this section with the following statement: "Your Excellency will not ignore the dangers and losses to which they will be subjected, and the dishonour and disrepute that will befall them."

They also called the high commissioner's attention to the losses that Palestinians within Palestine would incur without migrants' remittances, emphasizing that this would mean a loss for Britain. They began: "The losses that will be the lot of the relatives of those emigrants are many, notably the stoppage of all money remittances that have heretofore been the backbone of the wealth of the country." This loss, they continued, "will be felt through the renunciation of the rich emigrants to repatriate themselves, bringing their wealth and establishing in the homeland commerce, industry and agriculture. The losses to the Government in taxes and revenues are great."

Finally, the petitioners listed their demands, including that Britain amend the ordinance and notify British consular offices abroad of the amendment:

> In view of the above, we solicit of Your Excellency:
>
> a. In conformity with the power granted to the High Commissioner by Article 24 of the citizenship law published in the order in Council of July 24th,

1925, to amend the said law to enable all Palestinian emigrants abroad to maintain their nationality while residing abroad.

b. To circularise general orders to the British representatives all over the world to afford the protection to the Arab emigrants until the amendment of the law in a suitable manner. . . .

c. That the Palestine Government give this request the heavy consideration the seriousness of the case deserves.

d. That Your Excellency kindly consider this solicitation as the expression of Arab public opinion in this land and abroad.

The final solicitation is significant. While the issue of Palestinian citizenship was unique to Palestine, the petitioners considered its implications relevant as an Arab cause. This, to be sure, was connected to the broader cause of Arab nationalism following World War I and also to the way in which Arabic-speaking migrants identified in the diaspora. The Committee for the Defense of the Rights of Palestinians in Foreign Countries played a role in propagating this unity within Palestine and among Palestinians transnationally.

The third solicitation, urging Britain to give the petitioners' request the "heavy consideration the seriousness of the case deserves," merits mention. Although it is unknowable precisely why British authorities in Jerusalem and London took this matter as seriously as they did in the weeks and months following the 2 June petition, it is likely that the deluge of petitions they received from Palestinians across the Americas during the first half of 1927, as well as the 2 June petition itself submitted in person by the committee members alongside the president of the Arab Executive, played a considerable part. On 21 June 1927, Symes sent a confidential dispatch to Colonial Secretary Amery in London, in which he explained the extent of Palestinians' complaints and his inclination to agree with them. He began: "Arab sentiment in Palestine has been stirred to protest against what is represented to be an arbitrary deprival of the rights of persons born in Palestine and resident abroad to become nationals of the country of their birth."[16] He explained that "the local Arabic press has published many articles and letters on this subject" and that "a committee has been formed 'for the defence of the rights of Palestinians in Foreign Countries.'" He added that "a deputation of this committee, accompanied by Musa Kazim Pasha, president of the Arab Executive, visited me last week and handed me the petition of which I enclose a copy." Symes recognized the importance of addressing the issue, and the role Palestinians in Palestine played in stirring the Government of Palestine to action cannot be overlooked.

Symes described to Amery the nature of the petition and its authors, suggesting further the weight with which the committee members' visit with Musa Kazim was received in Jerusalem. He explained that the committee members described to him the status of many of these migrants and their attachment to Palestine, including that most had not severed ties with it. He also elaborated that the petitioners were concerned with the unworkability of the application deadline:

> The members of this deputation came from Bethlehem, Ramallah, and other places which have supplied a large proportion of the emigrants to Central and Southern America. They represented that the present situation of these emigrants is a very difficult one. They did not deny that many emigrant families had been absent from Palestine for more than a generation, but they maintained that they had never completely severed their connection with this country, had paid visits to it whenever they could afford them, sent considerable sums of money to their relatives, and in some cases, retained ownership of immovable property in Palestine.[17]

Symes then relayed the committee members' arguments against the ordinance—namely:

> (a) that Article 2 of the Palestinian Citizenship Order 1925 as amended, to conform with the Treaty of Lausanne, by the Proclamation of the 12th of November, 1925, gave insufficient notice to Palestinians abroad of the option which they might register before the 6th of August, 1926; and
> (b) that the residential qualification in Part III of the Palestinian Citizenship Order, 1925, rendered it practically impossible for persons having business connections abroad to become Palestinian nationals.[18]

Symes relayed the full extent of the petitioners' grievances, demonstrating his disquiet about the matter. He exhibited concern not only for the migrants and the difficulties they were facing but also for Palestinian society, which depended heavily on migrants' remittances.

Following his explanation of the petitioners' complaints, Symes intimated that he agreed with the petitioners and was open to reconsidering the migrants' applications:

> I feel that there is a certain force in these contentions and am satisfied that fairly regular connection is maintained between individuals and 'colonies' of these persons in America and their country of origin. On political and other grounds I should not be disinclined to reconsider sympathetically applications for Palestinian citizenship made by persons who by birth, race, and sentiment are genuinely attached to Palestine, although they are resident abroad and are likely to remain abroad for an indefinite time.[19]

Symes circulated the first draft of this letter to Amery on 14 June. On 16 June, the chief immigration officer of the Government of Palestine recommended the following revision be made to this section of the letter: "applications for Palestinian citizenship submitted at the proper time wherein the applicants definitely declared their intention of returning to Palestine although they have been resident abroad for a considerable period and in the majority of cases are not likely to return to this country." Symes did not apply this change to his 21 June missive. Arguably, he would have considered it less sympathetic to Palestinian migrants than his original wording. The work of the committee members paid off. Symes was convinced that Palestinian migrants deserved British sympathy and assistance in securing Palestinian citizenship, even if they chose to remain abroad. It is noteworthy that Symes relayed their concerns accurately and thoroughly before offering his personal opinion, suggesting his confidence in their logic and in the rightfulness of their claims to Palestinian nationality.

In the next section of the dispatch, Symes expressed some concerns about the migrants' intentions. He explained that his hesitation came from a dispatch Amery had issued a year and a half prior, in January 1926. While he agreed with Amery that "it is not intended to accept options from persons who desire to obtain Palestinian citizenship merely as a means of obtaining British protection," he continued to exhibit trust in the committee members' words:

> My deputation did not conceal the fact that, apart from individuals who found it inconvenient to return immediately to Palestine, the desire of a majority of persons affected was to obtain a national status which would regularise their position in the American States where they were resident and also secure for them the good offices and protection of British Consuls.[20]

Symes's use of the personal pronoun is significant; he considered the committee members to be allies, of sorts, in pursuit of a common goal. This became more pronounced in the following section where Symes made his case for reviewing the matter more closely. He began: "It is not in the interests of the British Government to estrange numbers of Arab natives of Palestine who are resident abroad and arouse the resentment of their relatives in this country on account of what, they contended, was a repudiation of the Mandatory's proper responsibility." While he specified that it was the committee members' contention that the mandate was not fulfilling its responsibility, he did not express disagreement. Instead, he made a request since "this aspect of the matter evidently concerns the Foreign Office." He requested that Amery inquire about "the size of these 'Palestinian' colonies, notably in Chile and Mexico, and whether protection of their interests would involve trouble and expense so considerable as to make it inexpedient to afford them special facilities to obtain Palestinian nationality."

Interestingly, days earlier, on 16 June, the chief immigration officer of the Government of Palestine sent Symes figures pertaining to these Palestinian colonies to include in the letter to Amery. According to the chief immigration officer, Jerusalem received 3,603 applications that fell under article 2 of the 1925 citizenship ordinance. "Of these," he explained, "1,965 have already been rejected, and it is estimated that if the rules hitherto adopted for guidance continue to be observed, about another 250 of these applications will be rejected." He estimated in conclusion that if these migrants' applications were to be reconsidered, "it is possible that about 1,700 of these rejected applications on reconsideration will be accepted."[21] The chief immigration officer then suggested that Symes specify that the secretary of state would "doubtless consider whether the protection of the interests of an additional 1,700 families" would be a worthwhile expense. Symes did not include these recommendations in his revised dispatch. It is arguable that he was concerned that "1,700 families" was not sufficient information to convey to Amery about the actual number of individuals who would be considered for Palestinian citizenship, especially since the petitioners had indicated 25,000 individuals. His request was thus that Amery make the inquiry.

Finally, Symes offered his recommendation. While he was convinced of the difficulties Palestinian migrants were facing due to the citizenship legislation and while he sympathized with the committee members and their grievances, his duty was to safeguard the interests of London and the Government of Palestine, including upholding the requirement that applicants abroad had left Palestine after 1920. To Amery, he made this suggestion:

> Pending further instructions from you on this point I propose to maintain the present practice of refusing all applications for certificates of Palestinian citizenship from persons who left this country prior to 1920 and have not resided here for more than a period of six months since that date, or from persons who, having left the country more recently, are not able to satisfy me of their intention to return and permanently to reside here in the near future.[22]

Despite his sympathy for Palestinian migrants and for his deputation, Symes would maintain the status quo until told otherwise by London. He would fulfill his duties in doing as told. Nevertheless, Symes was evidently affected, even sentimentally, by the visit of the Committee for the Defense of the Rights of Palestinians in Foreign Countries and by what he seemed to agree were rightful requests for redress. Through their efforts, Palestinians in Palestine were able to stir British mandate authorities in Jerusalem to action in an attempt to safeguard migrants' national rights.

Five weeks later, on 29 July 1927, Mitchell Banks at the Home Office in London sent a letter to William Ormsby-Gore at the Colonial Office expressing sympathy for the case of Palestinian migrants whose citizenship requests had been denied. Calling it a "very important" issue, he concluded that granting them nationality would, first, "be an act of justice and fairness to them, because otherwise they may lose any nationality," and second, "it will also be of considerable advantage to British interests to have these people satisfied and therefore friendly to us in the different countries in which they live."[23] Replying on 2 September, Ormsby-Gore first referred to article 34 of the Treaty of Lausanne, stressing that the option for nationality given to former subjects of the Ottoman Empire now residing abroad was "subject to the consent of the Government exercising authority in the detached territory" (i.e., the Government of Palestine). Since many of the migrants, he went on, had "no connection with Palestine and had no intention of returning there except perhaps for occasional short visits," it was deemed "undesirable to create a class of persons permanently resident abroad who are entitled to British protection."[24]

Furthermore, he explained that the "adoption of 1920 as the year since which applicants for citizenship must have resided in Palestine" was "quite fair and equitable" since it ensured that only those migrants truly intending to remain in Palestine were naturalized. Ormsby-Gore explained that the existing law was sufficient in addressing "all the possible cases" of Palestinian migrants, and he also declared that migrants who left Palestine before 1920, when Palestine was "part of the Turkish Empire," had no intention of returning and settling there irrespective of their "material interests in Palestine." Therefore, he continued, "they are scarcely entitled to British protection while abroad." More importantly for the purposes of the Treaty of Lausanne, Ormsby-Gore contended that these persons who had had their citizenship certificates rejected "remain Ottoman subjects" since they "are not and never have been Palestinians."[25] As far as Ormsby-Gore and the Colonial Office were concerned, Palestinian nationality began with the establishment in Palestine of a British mandate that afforded its inhabitants rights to citizenship and not, as many migrants protested was indicated in the Treaty of Lausanne, with birth in Palestine or belonging to Palestine by majority race.

But not everyone in Europe agreed with Ormsby-Gore. On 2 September 1927, the Committee for the Defense of the Rights of Palestinians in Foreign Countries sent a petition to the League of Nations requesting amendments to the citizenship ordinance. Murqus also sent a telegram to follow up with the league in which he adjured its members to consider revising the law, since "it is unreasonable that [an emigrant] should be prevented from his nationality because he has emigrated from his country to work in commerce."[26] On 6 September, Mary Adelaide Broadhurst, an activist who founded the National Political Reform League in England in 1911 and who advised members of the Arab Executive in Palestine, sent a letter to the colonial secretary in which she enclosed Murqus's telegram and explained that there is "great anxiety amongst the Arab leaders on the matter, which they rightly consider to embody a real grievance." Speaking on behalf of the league, she expressed confidence that "now that the attention has been drawn to the grievance," London and Jerusalem would resolve the issue since "there could be no desire to impose unnecessary and vexatious disabilities on emigrant Arabs." Days later, Amery replied that London and Jerusalem had already considered the issue and decided that the law was sufficiently thorough and that it did not need to be amended. As for cases of migrants whose status could not be determined because they had left Palestine before 1920 and because they were unable to fulfill the two-year residency requirement in Palestine to qualify for citizenship, "His Majesty's Government in Great Britain do not doubt that the High Commissioner for Palestine would exercise a proper discretion" in addressing these situations. London gave Jerusalem the freedom to determine the fates of thousands of Palestinian migrants.

Several weeks later, on 7 October 1927, Ormsby-Gore sent a confidential dispatch to Plumer. Following a thorough explanation of the previous months' correspondence and developments on the issue of Palestinian migrants requesting Palestinian citizenship, Ormsby-Gore reiterated that, despite Symes's, Banks's, and Broadhurst's recommendations for clemency, he was "reluctant to agree to any relaxation of the rule" surrounding residence in Palestine in or after 1920. As for why, he declared that "there can have been little emigration from Palestine between 1914 and 1919" due to the war, so

> the adoption of 1920 as the year since which applicants for citizenship must have resided in Palestine means in effect that most natives of Palestine who have been in that country for a period of six months or more during the past thirteen years can obtain Palestinian citizenship provided that they intend to return there within a reasonable period and to settle there permanently.[27]

Additionally, he emphasized the concern that creating a class of British protected persons abroad was undesirable for Britain. As for those who had been out of the country for longer than "thirteen years," they "cannot be held to have had direct connection with that country except under the Ottoman regime or to have any legitimate claim to be considered Palestinians or to British protection." He added that the foreign secretary concurred with this policy and that the Colonial Office would be forwarding this letter to the secretary-general of the League of Nations.

The issue persisted until the end of October 1927, during which time Plumer sent a letter on 21 October to John Shuckburgh at the Middle East Department explaining that he "entirely agree[d]" with the decision to not amend the law. As for Jerusalem's official response to the issue, Plumer submitted a communiqué to Amery summarizing the cumbersome second article of the 1925 Palestinian Citizenship Order-in-Council and why it caused such trouble:

> Article 2 of the Order provides that persons of over eighteen years of age who were
>
> (a) born in Palestine; and
> (b) acquired on birth or subsequently and still possess Turkish nationality; and

(c) on the 1st of August, 1925, were habitually resident abroad,

might opt for Palestinian citizenship which in certain conditions would be granted. It was announced on the 12th of November, 1925, that the right of option had to be exercised before the 6th of August, 1926, that is, within two years from the coming into force of the Treaty of Lausanne.[28]

He explained that many applicants for Palestinian citizenship in Latin America had their applications denied either because they missed the deadline, because they had not maintained connection with Palestine, or because they could not prove an intention to return to reside permanently in Palestine. He added that "the period for option cannot be extended, but the Palestine Government are anxious to accord every facility for the acquisition of Palestinian citizenship by persons who by birth, race and sentiment are genuinely attached to Palestine."[29] However, this would turn out not to be the case. Palestinian migrants repeatedly proved their "genuine attachment to Palestine" in their petitions, but it was never enough.

In the remainder of his communiqué to Amery, Plumer explained the requirement of returning and residing in Palestine before being able to apply for citizenship, and he reiterated the importance of abiding by the 1920 rule. He added that, following fulfillment of the return requirements, applicants could hope to be naturalized "on conditions which, if their principal interest be in Palestine, they should find it easy to fulfil." These included "good character" and knowledge of English, Arabic, or Hebrew; intention to reside permanently in Palestine; and two continuous years of residence in Palestine before applying for citizenship. All other claims to Palestinian nationality and citizenship that were presented to authorities in London and Jerusalem were ignored, including the migrants' historic, familial, and economic connections to Palestine; the benefits of migrant remittances to Palestine and to the Government of Palestine; and the legality of extending citizenship to migrants, as well as the concerns over having no nationality at all pending further rejections.

The work of the Committee for the Defense of the Rights of Palestinians in Foreign Countries extended beyond the petitions of 1927. Throughout 1928, the committee members continued to appeal to British authorities in Jerusalem and London and to the League of Nations. They also appealed to the people of Britain in a forty-page open letter addressed to "the Noble

British People." The appeal was published in multiple Palestinian periodicals and reiterated many of the arguments made in the petitions submitted to the Government of Palestine in prior years. It also indicated that the committee members considered that they shared a government with the British people, a significant and arguably unintended byproduct of mandate rule. That is, "the committee envisioned an international right to nationality that mandated that individuals had diplomatic protection from their nation's government."[30] It was inconceivable, therefore, that Britain would deny its subjects their rightful nationality. Surely, the committee members believed, the British people would agree, though this was never the case.

Notwithstanding the inability of the Committee for the Defense of the Rights of Palestinians in Foreign Countries to effect meaningful change in British citizenship policy in Palestine, its members' efforts to organize in the face of oppressive policies were significant. That the president of the Arab Executive joined them in confronting the Government of Palestine in their Jerusalem offices and that the chief secretary of the Government of Palestine was so convinced by their petition that he relayed his sympathies for their cause to London merit recognition within the history of Palestinian political activism. The Government of Palestine may have persisted in its exclusionary practices, but thanks to the committee members and their compatriots in the diaspora, the failure to secure the support of European officials in Geneva, London, and British consular offices in the Americas regarding British citizenship legislation toward Palestinian migrants, raised questions about the equitability of British mandate rule in Palestine. As explained in chapter 4, the administration of Palestine as a territory promised to the Zionists and to the Palestinians would rest with London and Jerusalem, falling outside the purview of the charter of the League of Nations and the Treaty of Lausanne. Interwar international law, in other words, did not apply to Palestine.

Perhaps Ayoub Musallam, an intellectual and political activist from Bethlehem who spent a considerable part of his career in Latin America throughout the mid-twentieth century, said it best. In his memoirs, Musallam described the epoch of the Committee for the Defense of the Rights of Palestinians in Foreign Countries as follows, highlighting Britain's duplicitous behavior:

> The committee . . . held meetings and carried out protests against the government regarding what it viewed as politics of separation, and it showed through

> these efforts a flaw in British mandate policy regarding migration legislation. However, it was unable to convince the government to abandon the law or annul what it had issued in confidential instructions to British ambassadors abroad regarding easing the acquisition by migrants of the nationality of their country. . . .
>
> Such was the rule of the British mandate over Palestine, operating on a concealed politics of evil toward Arabs. For while it encouraged the emigration of Arabs from the country, it was simultaneously easing the immigration of Jews to it in an alarming and dreadful way.[31]

The committee's work challenged, transnationally, the inequities imbedded in British mandate practice in Palestine, and its members were not alone in disclosing this. The editors of *Filastin,* a Jaffa-based Palestinian nationalist periodical, were committed to defending Palestinian migrants' rights and to exposing Britain's unjust policies. Yet the editors took it further: they used the crisis of mahjar Palestinians' citizenship as leverage against Palestinian leadership in Palestine, which was failing to achieve national self-determination for Palestinians. The strategic ways in which the editors linked the defense of Palestinian migrants' rights to citizenship to the need for reformed Palestinian leadership thus indicate the extent to which Palestinians in Palestine considered mahjar Palestinians' citizenship to be a transnational political issue that impacted Palestinian political freedom.

FILASTIN, CITIZENSHIP, AND THE REFORM OF PALESTINIAN LEADERSHIP

Throughout 1927, *Filastin* newspaper also responded to Palestinian migrants' exclusion from Palestinian citizenship. The periodical was founded in Jaffa in 1911 by Issa El-Issa, a prominent nationalist, who was later joined by his cousin Yousef El-Issa in managing the newspaper. The cousins first published it weekly, primarily critiquing Greek clerical power over the Orthodox Church in Jerusalem. As secular Christian nationalists who opposed any form of religious or foreign hegemony in Palestine, the El-Issa cousins were outspoken critics of Ottoman and British authorities and, later, of the Zionists. Indeed, they were so outspoken in their anti-Ottoman, anti-British, and anti-Zionist politics that both Issa and Yousef were exiled to Anatolia during World War I, only returning with the creation of the Arab Kingdom of Syria in 1920, after which Issa returned to Jaffa and to printing *Filastin*. With much to protest and critique regarding hegemonic colonial powers quashing Palestinian national aspirations during the first half of the twentieth century, *Filastin* became Palestine's most prominent periodical. By 1929, the year the newspaper became a daily, it is estimated that *Filastin* had circulated three thousand issues, surpassing its nearest competitor by double the publications.[32]

The issue of Palestinian migrants' citizenship received considerable attention in the pages of *Filastin*. The El-Issas considered it a thoroughly national issue. Yet unlike the Committee for the Defense of the Rights of Palestinians in Foreign Countries, *Filastin*'s editors regularly relayed to their readers the importance of protesting British policies *and* of calling for the reform of Palestinian national leadership to assist Palestinian migrants. In doing so, they linked the issue of Palestinian migrants and their struggle for Palestinian citizenship to the broader struggle to achieve Palestinian national self-determination. In effect, *Filastin*'s editors printed mahjar Palestinians' protests against British mandate policies, as well as their appeals to Palestine's leaders, to help them secure citizenship in order to bolster the newspaper's agenda of revamping Palestine's tottering nationalist movement in the face of an increasing Zionist threat. As a result, *Filastin* enhanced communication and solidarity between Palestinians worldwide who were struggling for the same outcomes and contributed to the development of Palestinian national consciousness transnationally.

The inability of thousands of Palestinians' family members residing abroad to secure a legal means to return permanently to Palestine without losing their economically viable businesses abroad was cause for alarm across Palestine. *Filastin*'s editors alerted their readers to this crisis. On 16 August 1927, *Filastin* printed a petition that had been sent earlier that year to George Symes from Salamon Canavati, president of the Centro Social Palestino in Monterrey, Mexico.[33] The text of the petition was written in Arabic, and it took up the entire front page of the issue as well as most of the last page. Titled "About Palestinian Nationality," the article about the petition was forceful and authoritative.[34] In the petition, Canavati had explained that the Government of Palestine had been behaving hypocritically when it came to citizenship legislation. He pointed out that Britain had promised to help Palestinian migrants as part of their "duty as guardians of the rights of Palestinians" but that their refusal to amend the 1925 Palestinian Citizenship Order-in-Council to allow the migrants more time to apply for citizenship pointed to the opposite. He asked: "What sort of assistance do you mean, Your Excellency, when you contradict yourselves?"

Canavati then dispelled any notion that the migrants had severed ties with Palestine as a result of their lengthy stays abroad. "This is an accusation with no godly authority," he declared, "for every migrant is in constant contact with his dear homeland through writing letters to his family and sending them money to pay taxes on his properties." In terms of the financial aspect of the connection, Canavati explained further that "the towering palaces and buildings being built in Palestine are from the riches of migrants, and this is the biggest proof of their attachment to Palestine, their dear homeland."[35] He proceeded with evidence that Palestinian migration had historically been part of a larger global tradition of movement in pursuit of economic betterment and that, like migrants from other cultures, Palestinians never wished to remain permanently abroad. Consequently, for Canavati, the obstacles placed in these migrants' paths by the British authorities were "illegitimate." Specifically, he said: "The Government [of Palestine] has no right to forbid [the migrant] from the holy inheritance [of nationality], holding on instead to an unjust law enacted for Zionist ends and founded on miserly ambitions!"[36]

Toward the end of the petition, Canavati emphasized his and his jaaliya's confidence in their claims to Palestinian nationality and their steadfastness in the face of oppressive British policies. He declared:

> We do not acknowledge nor accept any nationality but that of our fathers and ancestors, whether the government desires it or not. We were born Palestinians and will live and die as Palestinians; we will make every effort for our Palestine; and we prefer death, hunger, murder, and arson to embracing another nationality. Know, too, that we demand a right that is legitimately ours, and thus, we will remain steadfast in accomplishing our mission until we receive our rights.[37]

Canavati demanded that British authorities repeal the citizenship ordinance and remove all obstacles placed in the migrants' paths to citizenship. Accordingly, he concluded, "you will have carried out your duty to justice and you will be written into the history books and in gold onto the hearts of every Palestinian." By demanding national rights as Palestinians and holding Britain accountable for its duties to Palestine, Canavati circulated defiant language that at once broadcast the circumstances of Palestinians worldwide and bolstered the Palestinian nationalist movement. As for *Filastin*'s nationalist editors, they printed this petition because they, too, believed in it. For *Filastin*, migrants in the diaspora were Palestinians in every sense, and their struggle with British authorities was part of a larger Palestinian struggle for national self-determination.

The struggle was also regional. In addition to printing petitions against British rule from Palestinians in the mahjar, *Filastin*'s editors collaborated with regional newspapers in the Middle East in publicizing the injustice of British policies. On 5 August 1927, *Filastin* printed a statement from the British consulate in Alexandria, Egypt, regarding its policies on "Palestinians and passports." The statement appeared in Egypt's *al-Muqattam* newspaper, and *al-Muqattam*'s editors added their critique of the statement. They described the difficult conditions Palestinians in Egypt were facing with the consulate's refusal to cooperate. Palestinians in Egypt had evidently gone to *al-Muqattam* for help in securing visas to return to Palestine. "When we received the complaints," *al-Muqattam*'s editors wrote,

> we sent a representative of *al-Muqattam* to the consulate. . . . The specialist in issuing visas there explained to the representative that the Palestinians who left Palestine before the month of August 1925 are not considered Palestinians even if they were born there and carry Palestinian passports.[38]

Palestinians in Egypt were evidently experiencing difficulties similar to those of their counterparts in the Americas, and like Palestinians in the Americas, they were told to apply for other nationalities: "People such as those," *al-Muqattam*'s editors continued, "may not return home carrying Palestinian passports; instead, they must receive Egyptian passports. It is this reality that many Palestinians do not wish to accept, for they believe that the British consulate is placing obstacles in their way."

Filastin's editors printed *al-Muqattam*'s full critique of British policy. In the remainder of the article, the editors explained that *al-Muqattam* had discovered further "policies under which the British consulate in Alexandria operates." The British consulate had apparently been requesting information about certain applicants from the Government of Palestine, and it was requiring some applicants to prove their wealth before considering their applications for return visas:

> The consulate is requesting of returnees to Palestine to prove that they are wealthy before being awarded visas. And there are individuals about whom the consulate can request information from the Government of Palestine regarding

whether to grant them entry. If the government approved of them, the consulate could grant visas. But if it refused them, the visas would not be granted.[39]

These policies, *al-Muqattam* argued, were strange and unprecedented:

What is stranger is the consulate's request of Palestinians to prove that they are wealthy. . . . For has it been the case that any government in the world can treat its subjects this way? And if the Government of Palestine can forbid the sons of the nation from entry into their home on account of poverty or impoverishment, where should they go? . . .

As for the special arrangements put in place to allow consulates to solicit information from the government regarding suspicious individuals, we do not have an objection as it concerns the government's security and safety. Regardless, we want that this not be applied to the sons of Palestine to whom the doors must be opened for return home.[40]

As far as *Filastin* and *al-Muqattam* were concerned, Palestinians in the mahjar had rightful connections to Palestine, and Britain was falling short of honoring them. *Filastin* reported that *al-Muqattam* replied as much to the consulate in Alexandria:

If the consulate's statement is true, then this is very strange. For how can the British consulate forbid individuals who were born and raised in Palestine, all enjoying the birthright to Palestinian nationality, from return to their country, considering, too, that they haven't replaced their nationality with another . . . ? If they were not present in Palestine before August 1925 even though when they left it before this date, they did so as Palestinians carrying Palestinian passports, it is the British consulate's duty to protect and help them.[41]

The crisis of Palestinian citizenship thus brought Palestinian and Egyptian periodicals together in protesting mandate authorities' abuse of Palestinian rights transnationally, and in demanding redress. "In closing," the editors of *Filastin* concluded, "we would like to call on the British Government to attend to these severe measures . . . and to facilitate the travel of returning Palestinians of all social classes to their homeland."

For *Filastin*'s editors, the protection of the rights of Palestinians residing abroad was commensurate with demanding reform and empowerment at the local level. Accordingly, the experiences of migrants with exclusionary British policies were described in Filastin in a way that linked the two. In several articles printed throughout 1927, *Filastin* offered critical reflections on the status of the Palestinian nationalist movement in Palestine and its responsibilities toward its compatriots throughout the diaspora.[42] As an example, and in reference to the discord between two of Jerusalem's most prominent families, the Husseinis and the Nashashibis, which was hampering the Palestinian nationalist movement, *Filastin* printed a message to its readers in the mahjar on 12 August 1927 decrying the state of Palestinian leadership:

> We would like to inform our immigrant brothers that there are no political parties in Palestine today; . . . there is nothing but familial discord among our leaders. . . . This discord . . . is what invited and invites us today to form a new and inclusive political party . . . to restore to our national movement its former energy and to build our future on firm grounds, unmoved by the winds of personalities and families.
>
> We hope that our migrant brothers will join us in this blessed movement, which is undertaken by every reasonable thinker in the country.[43]

Earlier in the article, the editors reiterated to their readers abroad that *Filastin* belonged to them as well as to Palestinians within Palestine; the editors considered their readership to be transnational and spread a message of unity in the face of antiquated, old-regime politics. Their vision for a reformed nationalist movement would thus also benefit mahjar Palestinians.

To convey this unity among Palestinians transnationally for reforming Palestinian leadership, the newspaper also printed migrants' dismay at the state of Palestine's nationalist movement. On 9 August 1927, *Filastin* printed an article titled "The Immigrants Are Crying! Oh, Leaders, What Have You Done for and with the Nation!" in its periodic column "American Mail." The title relayed the migrants' struggle with loss of citizenship and it signified the editors' resolve to hold Palestinian leadership accountable. It also included a testimony from an unnamed migrant in San Salvador, El Salvador, that described the sadness migrants there felt at having lost their nationality to a nation that was unable to organize effectively politically:

> Sir, owner of *Filastin* newspaper, May God keep you:
>
> With all respect and honor, and with my firm belief that you are struggling for our honor and our oppressed nation, I write to you the following. . . .
>
> I went one day to the capital, San Salvador, as my national brothers invited me to the Association of Palestinian Brotherhood and I saw their miserable

citizens, all of them crying. I began to cry with them without knowing why. Someone asked me what I was crying about, and I said, "I am crying with you." He said, "Does your family cry with you as well?" I said, "No." He said, "So you are not of us because we and our families cry and ache together!"

I asked him why that was, and he said, "We cry because we have become without a nation and without a nationality, and without a common ground to resort to. Our nation was given to others at no cost; our honor was sacrificed for the sake of chairs and desk jobs; and our nationality has gone for the sake of division, discord, and troublemaking."[44]

That migrants felt the paralysis of Palestine's nationalist movement, and that this was ostensibly a larger cause for their tears than the loss of their citizenship enhanced the newspaper's call for reforming a failing nationalist movement.

The author of the testimony continued with a description of the abysmal conditions of migrants in El Salvador:

Our prestige has fallen in the eyes of people, for we have no consulates to protect us, no passports in our hands. We have become prisoners, insulted, humiliated, dying. And our children after us are dying as vagabonds, for they have no home or nationality, and no nationalist connection.[45]

The migrant then echoed *Filastin*'s editors in tacitly holding Palestinian leadership accountable:

But what makes us cry even more is what we read in the papers about slander in the nation, and hostility between leaders. The small slanders the big, and the big demeans the small, which makes us believe that our connection is dissolved, that our national movement is paralyzed, and that our honor in the homeland and the diaspora is lost. . . .

They have oppressed the sons of our country, and they have given their home to Jewish vagrants, forbidding them their natural nationality. And our leaders are unaware. There is no mercy or strength in anything but God.[46]

Filastin's editors deliberately printed these testimonies from Palestinians in the mahjar. Their readers in Palestine would know that their counterparts in the diaspora were equally frustrated with Palestine's leadership and that they were equally committed to the newspapers' agenda: out with the old, in with the new.

Filastin's editors also made the struggle of Palestinian migrants for Palestinian citizenship personal for their readers in Palestine. Following the San Salvador testimony, a short article under the title "Palestinian Nationality in Chile" appeared, listing the names of several Palestinians in Chile who had reached out to them asking for help in securing their rights to citizenship:

> We received a request from the Association for Palestinian and Transjordanian Unity in Tampico, Chile, signed by Misters Mina Andonio, President of the Association, Vice President Abd al-Jawad Jabr, Secretary Ayed Abu Dayyeh, and Treasurer Yaqoub al-Abd al-Fakhouri. In it, they described the difficulties migrants face on account of the Citizenship Order-in-Council. . . . We ask of the government to please make efforts within the Colonial Office to amend the present Citizenship Order-in-Council in a way that safeguards for Palestinians their rights in their homeland and distances ill thought from them.[47]

Filastin considered its mission to be transnational, bringing diaspora Palestinians into the fold. Indeed, how could *Filastin* help its readers abroad if Palestine's national leadership was unable to organize and lead effectively? Including the names of the members of Chile's Association for Palestinian and Transjordanian Unity would bring the issue home, so to speak. Distant Palestinian migrants fighting for their rights as Palestinians were connected to *Filastin* and its readers in Palestine in name and vision.

As another example of the conflation of the citizenship crisis with Palestinian nationalist reform, on 30 August 1927, *Filastin* published a migrant's testimony regarding the "Problem of Palestinian Citizenship and how it was created."[48] The migrant, Abdullah Abu Shaweriyya, residing in the small town of Curanilahue, Chile, was exasperated by the existing restrictions on naturalizing Palestinian migrants. He described the challenges Palestinians were facing when submitting applications for citizenship to local British consulates:

> British consuls here announced to all Palestinians that whoever wishes to have the right to his citizenship and to acquire Palestinian nationality must register at their consulates. We all did so. . . .
>
> Three months later, the British consul wrote explaining that the Government of Palestine refused to accept our nationality. They said that if we wished

> to be considered as Palestinians, we would need to travel there, reside there for six months, and then write to the Government requesting acknowledgment of our nationality. Otherwise, we cannot be considered Palestinians.
>
> This was how the consuls replied to us. Observe, brothers, the obstacles and difficulties that the occupying state places before us, for who can leave behind their work to travel to Palestine, live there for six months, and then get acknowledgment of nationality?[49]

The sequence of events was familiar to Palestinians throughout Latin America. But *Filastin* was also interested in what Abu Shaweriyya had to say about the Palestinian nationalist movement in Palestine. While he explained that the plight of Palestinian migrants was a result of unjust British policies, he emphasized that a sleeping, stagnant Palestinian leadership was also to blame for not protesting the policy:

> And is it not shameful that this happens to us while you are asleep? . . . You must not overlook the present condition of our country, which lacks a political party or committee to represent it before the government. This has made us like sheep without a shepherd while the Zionists grow in power through their unity. Until when shall we sleep, and until when this slumber and stagnation?[50]

The solution, he continued, lay in reforming the Palestinian nationalist movement: "So, let us move forward, gentlemen, and protest to your government, for there are among you those with the financial means to do so. And we Palestinians abroad will endeavor to subscribe to this project on which we hang our hopes for our nation." Abu Shaweriyyeh then called on his compatriots in Palestine to convene and form a unity opposition party in order to regain the dignity and pride Palestinians once enjoyed, effectively echoing *Filastin*'s mission.

The most salient connection between the mahjar and the watan was invariably monetary, and for *Filastin*, the most direct way of showing support for Palestinians in the diaspora came in the form of honoring their financial contributions to their watan, including to the very committee established in Palestine to defend them. In an article titled "To Defend the Rights of Migrants," *Filastin*'s editors published a message from the Committee for the Defense of the Rights of Palestinians in Foreign Countries announcing the amounts migrants in Honduras and the Dominican Republic had sent the committee:

> We have received the following letter from Mr. Atallah al-Najjar, secretary of the Beit Jala Committee, which was established in Beit Jala to protect the rights of Palestinian migrants:
>
> To whom it may concern . . .
>
> The Beit Jala Committee has received from San Pedro Sula, Honduras . . . on 4 July a wad of cash from the National City Bank in the amount of US$165 to aid our committee in its work. The money was sent with enthusiasm and encouragement. . . .
>
> The Committee has also received a letter from the Dominican Republic . . . on 5 July containing two wads, each with US$25 for the same purpose. The money was also sent with enthusiasm and encouragement.[51]

The names of all the donors were also listed. This practice of honoring Palestinian migrants who sent money to the committee was common in *Filastin*, indicating the quality of the union the newspaper editors wished for between their local and transnational readers. The reciprocal appreciation would at once overshadow the newspaper editors' inability to effect change in the Government of Palestine's legislation or in the Palestinian nationalist movement's shortcomings but simultaneously uphold the interconnectedness of the reforming—and now transnational—Palestinian nationalist cause.

Filastin's nationalist editors were committed to easing the struggles of their compatriots in the mahjar. To do so, they honored migrants for their generosity and printed their testimonies; they protested British policies individually and in collaboration with regional presses; and, most importantly, they called on Palestinians in Palestine to unite and reform their leadership. *Filastin*'s nationalist mission of political reform and party unity within Palestine thus found transnational fodder in the injustices meted out to the Palestinian diaspora community after the promulgation of the 1925 Palestinian Citizenship Order-in-Council. The causes were aligned, and the rhetoric describing them was made congruous. *Filastin*, as a platform for challenging British and Zionist colonial hegemony in Palestine during the interwar period and for critiquing Palestinian nationalist leadership, was ideal for publicizing the crisis of Palestinian citizenship—a thoroughly political issue—and for building transnational solidarity around it.

THE TRANSNATIONALIZATION OF PALESTINIAN SOLIDARITY

Through their activism and publications, Palestinians in Palestine brought the crisis of mahjar Palestinians' citizenship to the offices of the British mandate in Palestine and to the attention of Palestinians throughout Palestine. Members of the Committee for the Defense of the Rights of Palestinians in Foreign Countries and the editors of *Filastin* newspaper took the issue seriously and sought justice for their relatives and compatriots in the diaspora. As a result of their efforts, mahjar Palestinians' voices came home, and their right of return to Palestine acquired new significance as a legal and political matter that concerned the Government of Palestine as well as Palestinian leadership.

Bandak, al-Najjar, Murqus, and Musa Kazim caused a rift in British opinion regarding what needed to be done with the increasing number of mahjar Palestinians whose safety was in danger and who desperately sought a way to legally remain connected to Palestine. On the one hand, Symes, Banks, and Broadhurst sought clemency on behalf of Palestinian migrants and their defenders in Palestine, calling for an amendment to the way in which the 1925 Palestinian Citizenship Order-in-Council was implemented. On the other, Ormsby-Gore, Shuckburgh, and Plumer saw no reason to relax the law and even refused to acknowledge Palestinian migrants' claims to Palestinian nationality. This dissonance within British rule, to be sure, would ultimately do little to safeguard the rights of Palestinian migrants, and Geneva allowed the Government of Palestine to behave as it pleased, irrespective of international law. However, through their efforts, the committee members challenged a fundamental imbalance in British governance of Palestine. The discussions and disagreements which Palestinians engendered among British and European authorities through their opposition to British policy confirmed what Palestinians everywhere had been protesting since the 1917 Balfour Declaration: Britain's crooked administration of Palestine, giving clear priority and preference to the Zionists at the expense of Palestinians worldwide.

Beyond exposing inequities in British practice, Palestinians in Palestine decried their own leadership's shortcomings. Palestine's most prolific and anti-colonial nationalist newspaper, *Filastin*, highlighted the crisis of citizenship as a thoroughly nationalist issue, the resolution of which *Filastin* insisted was the responsibility of a reformed Palestine's nationalist movement that would effectively challenge British and Zionist rule, and as a result, defend Palestinians' national rights, wherever they may be. And in printing petitions and testimonies sent from Palestinian migrants who were protesting British policy and lamenting the state of Palestine's nationalist movement—while also acknowledging the financial commitments of diaspora Palestinians to Palestine—*Filastin*'s editors effectively merged the defense of Palestinian migrants' rights to citizenship with its main mission: unity and reform in the face of archaic and ineffective Palestinian nationalist leadership. *Filastin* informed its local and transnational readers that to support its nationalist cause was also to call for the defense of Palestinians residing in foreign countries, and vice versa.

Finally, the efforts of Palestinians in Palestine to protest exclusionary British policy and to reform the Palestinian nationalist movement through communication and collaboration with mahjar Palestinians demonstrates that Palestinian nationalist consciousness in the interwar period formed and developed transnationally. In writing a history of the rise of Palestinian national consciousness in the early twentieth century, therefore, we must recognize that what it meant to be Palestinian and, indeed, *where* it meant to be Palestinian were never limited to geographic Palestine. As Sebastian Conrad put it, "The search for particularity and for the elements of an unchangeable national identity . . . was . . . an actual effect of processes of cross-border circulation."[52] Palestinians across the Americas were also defining Palestine and collective Palestinian political consciousness.

Palestinians have always been part of the age of transnational migration in pursuit of economic stability and political security that impacted much of the world starting in the mid-nineteenth century. And wherever they settled, they adapted and responded to the extensive global shifts in political, economic, legal, and social dynamics that rapidly characterized the new interwar world order. As the world they knew was radically transforming, permanently altering the borders of their homeland and their manifold connections to it, their role in resisting interwar European imperialism and in demanding national rights and justice for Palestinian migrants was significant. It contributed to the development of a transnational mode of political identification among Palestinians, to the emergence and consolidation of a Palestinian diaspora, and to stretching Palestinian voices transnationally. Mobile, migratory bodies therefore forced nation-state makers to contend with claims to the nation from expansive geographies inhabited by persistently noisy voices fully versed in their national and transnational rights and wholly invested in their homelands.

CONCLUSION

THE TENS OF THOUSANDS of Palestinians who migrated to the Americas in the final decades of the nineteenth century and through the first two decades of the twentieth century left their homes as Ottomans, Arabs, and Syrians, and became Palestinians in the mahjar through their transnational activism against inequitable British mandate practices. In the interwar period, diaspora Palestinians were continuously engaged in defining themselves as Palestinians, fueled, in no small part, by the persistent denial of their Palestinianness. Indeed, Britain's exclusionary policies in London and Jerusalem in the years surrounding the enactment of the 1925 Palestinian Citizenship Order-in-Council contributed to the consolidation of transnational networks of identification with Palestine as a national homeland among Palestinian migrants who were responding to a new world order defined by nation-states and passports. Britain's denial of thousands of their applications for Palestinian citizenship—and thus, to residence, inheritance, ownership, and legal recourse in Palestine—repeatedly drove them to claim national rights *as* Palestinians and based on birth, race, language, ethnicity, property ownership, justice, and international law. And in articulating their claims to Palestinian nationality and citizenship along these lines, they effectively broadened, deepened, and gave new valence to what it meant to be Palestinian racially, linguistically, socially, culturally, legally, historically, and transnationally.

This process was significantly connected to the development of Palestinian national consciousness, and this book has investigated and contextualized the imbricated and complex instances of its formation into a social, political, and legal reality. The different instances where Palestinians in committees and social clubs throughout the Americas deliberately chose to speak of themselves in newspapers and petitions as Palestinians rather than Syrians, Ottomans, or Arabs constitute the historical elements of the consolidation of transnational political Palestinian consciousness vis-à-vis the Palestinian watan. Consequently, a transnational examination of the development of Palestinian modes of nationalist identification in the interwar period indicates that geographic Palestine was never the exclusive site of these developments. Palestinians across the world were profoundly connected to this process. The emergence of Palestinian national consciousness in the interwar period must be understood to have been fundamentally forged and to have fundamentally developed as a transnational process.

The emergence of Palestinian modes of national identification and claims making among Palestinians in and outside Palestine in the interwar period was connected to an age of globalization that had begun with mass mobility and migration in the nineteenth century. "The late nineteenth century," Conrad reminds us, "was an era of worldwide interaction and exchange" which must be taken into account in historiographies of the formation of nation-states.[1] Therefore, the enhancement of transnational interrelationships with the "globalization of the turn-of-the-century era" can "be seen as one of the most important factors contributing to the consolidation of national categories."[2] Palestinians had been on the move, settling the vast mahjar and continually returning home since the latter half of the nineteenth century. And like their Syrian and Lebanese neighbors to the north, they had a vested interest in the future of their watan. The story of Palestinian migrants in the interwar period must therefore be understood as a story of adaptation and self and group fashioning. Palestinians across the world were motivated by the call to Palestinian national self-determination, and their collective initiatives to fight for it through periodicals, social organizations, petitions, remittances, and so forth were part of the process of defining what it meant to be Palestinian as a political identifier, both in Palestine and across the world. Through these efforts, Palestinian migrants also partook in defining Palestine as a national homeland.

Beyond the historiographic debates about nationalism and the interwar world order, an investigation into the stories of Palestinian migrants in the late nineteenth and early twentieth centuries foregrounds the human component of this historical narrative and the potential for growth in the field of Palestine studies. While much of the existing historiography posits political self-determination as a critical theme in twentieth-century Palestinian history within geographic Palestine, this book has investigated this theme through the lenses of migration and diaspora formation to offer new perspectives that expand the scope of the historical analysis. That is to say, the migrants whose stories are recounted in these pages became Palestinians through transnational processes of negotiation, contestation, and struggle that indicate the need for further investigation into migration and diaspora formation as themes in Palestinian social and political history. Migration and diaspora formation in the context of Palestinian migrants struggling to remain connected to Palestine in the interwar period reveal a great deal about transnational networks of solidarity and activism among Arabic-speaking migrants in the early twentieth century and thus, about Palestinian stances and claims to collective social, political, and legal rights well before 1948.

This is to say that the results of this analysis bespeak a diaspora narrative that accentuates human dimensions to the historical study of the Palestinian people, dimensions that may otherwise be subsumed in discussions about larger historiographic trends like nationalism and settler colonialism. Palestine is a historically global phenomenon; the stories of its migrants and their jaaliyaat throughout the mahjar can help elucidate this reality. Over the course of the nineteenth and twentieth centuries, individual Palestinian migrants in the Americas came together and formed jaaliyaat that continue to maintain significant material and symbolic connections with Palestine and with other Palestinian communities throughout the world to this day. Indeed, today, and since the early twentieth century, Palestinians across the Americas and beyond speak, and have spoken of themselves, in ways that refer to a historic, cultural, racial, and material connection to Palestine, as well as an attachment to a specific diaspora mode of identification. In other words, Palestinian-Chileans, Palestinian-Mexicans, Palestinian-Americans, Palestinian-Jordanians, and so on have developed as categories for social and political claims making and as modes of identification that denote collective and individual sentiments with historical roots. This suggests the possibility for a proliferation in interdisciplinary and comparative analysis within the field of Palestine studies and certainly with Jewish diaspora studies.

Finally, this book has highlighted critical thematic continuities in the modern history of Palestinians. Exiled, transnational Palestinian communities have existed throughout the world since the last decades of the nineteenth century, and they have been protesting the denial of their right to return to Palestine and to *be* Palestinians since 1925. Exile and the fight to secure a right to remain connected to Palestine have characterized the Palestinian experience for a century. Importantly then, the narrative of a Palestinian struggle for a right of return to their homes in Palestine started in 1925, not 1948. This is significant in modern Palestinian historiography, in which the year 1948 has achieved axiomatic prominence as the start of Palestinian dispossession. Extending the narrative of Palestinian exile and dispossession twenty-three years earlier allows for a deeper appreciation of Palestinians' historical and future trajectories, about which new and compelling queries are posed. If forced exile has been part of Palestinians' transnational lived experiences since 1925, how have Palestinians incorporated these narratives into their collective consciousness and how have they conveyed them to new generations of Palestinians in Palestine and in exile? To what extent—and why—have Palestinians forgotten, or deliberately omitted, these narratives of exile? How has the denial of Palestinians' legal right of return for arbitrary and discriminatory reasons for a century impacted the ways in which Palestinians have been positioning themselves vis-à-vis international law, governing bodies, and the concept of justice? How can this unique history be weaved into transnational solidarity with Palestinians today, both in cultural production and political activism?

That the narratives of dispossession and permanent exile thought to have begun in 1948 were already part of Palestinian collective memory and socialization for nearly thirty years by the time of the *nakba* suggests that Palestinians experienced and made sense of their post-1948 and post-1967 diasporas in fundamentally unique ways. This might be literal, on the one hand, in that many Palestinians fled to Latin America in 1948 and 1967. But it also indicates that for the different waves of Palestinian exiles since 1948, return was already a fraught concept, including the notion of having a legal right to it, given the precedent set by British mandate authorities of denying them this right. In a way, then, twentieth-century Palestinian history is a scaffolding of intergenerational diaspora experiences that compel us to ponder how Palestinians worldwide have been experiencing, internalizing, and talking about permanent exile and dispossession for nearly a century.

Networks of communication and solidarity, of different forms of material and moral support, and of nostalgic love and longing for Palestine have signified the enduring connectedness and resilience of exiled Palestinians since the promulgation of the 1925 Palestinian Citizenship Order-in-Council nearly a century ago. Observing the development of these substantive modes of affinity between Palestinians worldwide since the 1920s and to this day suggests that for Palestinians everywhere, being Palestinian has had little to do with securing physical presence in or legal belonging to Palestine. Rather, for Palestinians everywhere, Palestine will always be a shared historical narrative preserved in generational memory and stories, a shared past and present experience in exile, and a shared longing for return to Palestine, whether literal or symbolic, that belongs only to Palestinians. As Juan Sikaffy of Trujillo, Honduras, declared in his 23 April 1927 petition to the League of Nations following the rejection of his application for Palestinian citizenship: "We are Palestinians, born, bred, and reared, and no power on earth can sever our claims and rights as Palestinians."[3]

Epilogue

In March 2015, I attended the funeral of a relative in Jerusalem. My uncle Boulos was a man of few words, but his laugh began deep in his gut, traveled audibly up his chest, and out his mouth with a distinct reverberation that filled any room with instant glee. He had worked for over forty years as a tour guide of Jerusalem and, before his debilitating illness, of historic Palestine. In addition to beautiful Arabic and English, he spoke French and Italian and read Latin. A devout Catholic, he had attended seminary as a young man and knew Palestine's Christian history by heart. With his European tour groups, he went by Paul—the anglicization of his name—and often made them laugh with a short explanation that our family name, Bawalsa, is the Arabic plural for Boulos; hence, he was Paul Pauls. Mr. Pauls was a loved man, and Jerusalem will remember him.

During my research trips to Jerusalem, I stayed with Ammo Boulos and my aunt, Amto Lorice. In their humble home, Ammo Boulos had several cabinets and bookcases filled with books, pamphlets, and other documents that were mostly religious in content and that he had been collecting for decades. In the mornings, Ammo Boulos often sat in the narrow kitchen balcony facing the lemon and fig trees that grew below just outside the balcony's limestone barriers. He enjoyed his time in this shady, quiet spot of the apartment, which, throughout the day, would get bombarded with his loud, hungry, and energetic children and grandchildren. In these few solitary moments, Ammo

Boulos would read through one of his countless documents or books, in any of the three languages, and remember the random facts with which he used to impress his tour groups. In between gasps of air from his mobile oxygen tank, he would often smile gently.

One morning, I asked Ammo Boulos to tell me what he had been reading out on the balcony once he came back into the kitchen where I was having my morning coffee. He was excited I asked and took small, heavy steps toward the table with a grin on his face. He slowly pulled out a chair and collapsed into it across from me. I asked if he needed any help, but he dismissed my offer quickly; this was his everyday. Catching his breath and adjusting the tubes in his nose, Ammo Boulos looked at me, took a deep breath, and explained that he had been reading a French Catholic priest's account of Jerusalem's Christian history. He said that he loved how the priest described Jerusalem and he wanted to keep the images of the Old City's churches fresh in his mind. I asked why he didn't visit the Old City himself to see these churches; it was a few kilometers down the road, after all. He quickly retorted, "Because I can't," pointing, frustrated, at the oxygen tank to his left. "I can barely make it to the church across the street." I apologized and said I should have known.

"You really love this city, don't you, Ammo Boulos?" I asked after a brief silence.

"It's the holiest city. I live just up the road from where Jesus was crucified, you know. How could I not love it?"

"Are you sad what's happened to it?" I asked, and knew that Ammo Boulos would recognize that I meant the Israeli government's ongoing division and transformation of the city.

"They can do whatever they want to it. It will always be Jerusalem."

"Is that why you never left?"

"Absolutely. I am with the Lord here. I will never leave it. It's bad enough I can't be in His churches because of this body of mine." I sighed in commiseration and allowed a soft silence to settle for a few moments before speaking again.

"Ammo Boulos, you know your family name might be Jordanian, but you are more Palestinian than anyone I know," I offered, hoping I did not insult him.

He gave out a quick laugh. "Tell me about it!"

On the day of Ammo Boulos's funeral, an older woman by the name of Diana Mubarak entered the hall underneath the church where we had earlier held a service bidding him farewell. She stood in the expanding line of people waiting to express their condolences to his family members, among whom I stood, shaking what felt like hundreds of hands. Only three of us Bawalsas in Jordan had been given visas by the Israeli authorities; we had American passports. All the other Bawalsas had their visas denied, including my father, and Ammo Boulos's brothers and sisters were unable to lay him to rest. But this is occupation.

By the time Diana Mubarak appeared before me, I had seen so many faces and shaken so many hands, I wasn't paying much attention. After all, I was the nephew who had come from New York and who grew up in Amman; I wouldn't recognize anyone here. But I did notice that Diana looked into my eyes a few seconds longer than anyone else as she wished for the rest of life to be ours (*el-ba'iyyeh fi hayaatkom*), an Arabic expression spoken at funerals. I didn't make much of it; I assumed she was wondering who this stranger was standing with the Bawalsas. A little while later, after the line ended and we sat somberly in our seats to drink coffee and converse quietly with those on either side of us, Diana came and sat beside me. I thought this was strange; women and men traditionally sat on opposite sides of the hall, their rowed chairs lining the contour of the big empty space between them that was meant for receiving mourners. Though I was family and was expected to sit in the front row of the men's side, I felt tired from jet lag and the day's events, so I had retreated to the third row for a little while.

As Diana sat beside me, I was worried the second question after asking who I was would be whether I was married. But instead, she wasted no time and asked if I was Yousef Bawalsa's son. I turned to her, smiling, and confirmed that she was correct. Her warm blue eyes sparkled as she smiled and let out a gentle laugh. "*Subhaan Allah*," she said, and I could tell that she was truly hoping I would be Yousef's son. "I knew from your face when I met you in line earlier," she said. "You look just like him, *subhaanak ya rabb*." Diana had been my father's neighbor and close friend in Beit Jala during his upbringing there. While he left in 1976, Diana remained and weathered decades of occupation, hardship, and loss. This was evident, I could see, in her tired eyes. But sitting beside me at this funeral, Diana shared sweet stories of her childhood with my father, and she relived nostalgic days with me in the somber setting.

I asked her where the rest of her family had gone to after she told me that she had no one left in Palestine, and she answered, "Everywhere. Even Chile."

I asked her more about her family in Chile, and instead of explaining the details of their migration, she retrieved her mobile phone and showed me photos of her brothers and their children in Santiago. I asked her if she had ever gone to visit them, to which she replied that she had not. She explained that it was too far, that leaving Beit Jala would be too much for her to handle at her age, and that Chile seemed like such a different place, where she would feel lonely and lost. I regarded her empathically and told her that it was indeed quite far from Palestine. But then I shared with her stories from my time in Chile, of the heartwarming connections I made with Palestinian-Chileans who retained Palestinian surnames, called themselves "palestinos-chilenos," and welcomed me into their homes. She smiled and asked which families I had met. I named a few and she proceeded to share stories of different friends and relatives who either came from those families or married into them. As she began to retell stories from her childhood and adolescence with Marzuqas, Qumsiyyehs, and Makhloofs, Diana became increasingly jovial. At one point, she laughed loud enough that mourners in the room heard her. They looked at us disapprovingly and we put our heads down knowingly. A moment later, she looked at me with youthful eyes and whispered, "Tell me more."

I told Diana about my visit to the town of Illapel, how incredibly similar to Palestine it is in landscape and climate, and how thousands of its residents are Palestinians who are proud of their heritage. I told her about the Dabed family who welcomed me into their home and shared with me their family history. She corrected me and said, "you mean Dawood," and I told her that she was correct but that they had Latinized the name sometime in the early twentieth century. She smiled and said that made sense. I told her about the other families that lived in Illapel, about the Khameeses and the Maʿloufs. I told her about Rodrigo Dabed, Emilio's brother whom I had not met before my visit to Illapel and who graciously invited me to his home to meet his family over a meal. I told her that Rodrigo's home was small like ours are in Palestine, but that his mother, his aunt, his wife, and their two daughters were all there to greet me, and that they were all coiffed elaborately and dressed nicely. She smiled and said, "Oh my, just like us!" recognizing that treasured Palestinian tradition of gathering for lunch in memorable hairdos and attire to welcome the guest from far away.

I told Diana that Rodrigo gave me a tour of the small town and its commercial streets and that he and I visited the shoe store that one of his aunts owned. I described to her that when we arrived at the store, his aunt was standing outside chatting with her neighbor across the street. His aunt's face closely resembled that of my aunt in Jerusalem, but his aunt did not speak a word of Arabic and did not look haggard from life under occupation. Diana sighed knowingly. I told her that this woman turned to me as Rodrigo introduced me, and that, as I heard him say "mi amigo de Palestina" while gesturing in my direction, the woman's face lit up and she embraced me strongly, kissing each of my cheeks once, just like us. Hearing this, Diana looked at me with wide eyes and a smile. "*Maʿool*? They've been there a hundred years and they still kiss like us?" she asked, laughing. I nodded and giggled with her. The mourners regarded us disapprovingly again, and as we quieted down, Diana shook her head gently, took a deep breath and exhaled with a smile, "God help us all, and may God rest your poor uncle's soul. *Ya haraam*."

I told Diana that Rodrigo had kept the bible his great-grandfather had brought to Chile from Beit Jala in 1896 and that he showed it to me, hoping that I could help him translate the parts where his great-grandfather had scribbled notes in the margins. I told her that Rodrigo explained to me that he had never had an Arabic speaker in his home and that my help deciphering the handwriting would mean a great deal to him. Diana looked at me confusedly and asked: "Why would he care so much about that bible? He should come here. I'll give him all the old bibles he wants!" I smiled and told her that, just as for her, traveling between Chile and Palestine was not easy for Rodrigo and his family, and that the bible was for him a deep connection to Beit Jala and Palestine, his ancestral homeland. She slowly looked away, sighed, crossed her arms, and said, "I suppose it's nice to know there are Palestinians somewhere in this world who know where they're from."

I shared with Diana a few more stories from my time in Chile, and as the looks we received from mourners in the room increased, we agreed that we needed to stop and join the others in outward expressions of sorrow. But following our brief chat, I felt that Diana and I had been transported to another world, a world that transcended the sadness of both the funeral and the ongoing loss that Palestinians endure and have endured for so long. Somewhere in our minds, we were riding the proverbial great waves of migration that for centuries have been depositing Palestinians and their Palestinianness across the world. And in our minds we were somehow comforted, somehow at peace. At least I hoped so.

Minutes later, Diana gently rested her hand on my knee. I turned my head to look at her and she asked, leaning her body closer to mine while still somberly facing forward, "when will you go back to Chile?" I told her I was not sure, but that I hoped soon. "It would be wonderful if you would come see me again before you leave," she continued. "I have so many things to give you to bring to your friends there. *Ya haraam,*" she said, "it's so sad that they can't visit Palestine."

Acknowledgments

This book has its origins in a project that began twelve years ago. To that end, I am grateful to Professor Zachary Lockman, whose guidance and wisdom continue to inspire my colleagues and me to produce meaningful and thoughtful work. I thank you, Professor Lockman, for offering me this opportunity and for trusting me to complete this project. I am also indebted to my mentor, Professor Salim Tamari, for his support of my various academic and scholarly endeavors over the years, and for his faith in me and in my intellectual abilities. Thank you, Professor Tamari, for the many opportunities for publication, research, and intellectual growth you have given me since I started my career in Middle Eastern studies fourteen years ago. I hope that you both read this book with a sense of accomplishment and pride in what you do and in what you continue to offer generations of aspiring historians, thinkers, and writers.

I am humbled and inspired by the work of Kate Wahl, publishing director at Stanford University Press. As an editor myself, I understand the painstaking work and long hours it takes to coordinate with authors, reviewers, and editorial committees to bring manuscripts to print. Kate's generous and thorough advice throughout the two-year journey of publishing this book was immeasurably helpful, and her professionalism, accessibility, and cordiality were unmatched. Thank you, Kate, and thank you, Stanford University Press, for your patience with me and for your confidence in the value of this project.

I am grateful for the instruction and direction I have received from my various mentors throughout my educational and professional career at the College of William and Mary, Georgetown University, and New York University. Thank you, Professors Anne Rasmussen, Tamara Sonn, Abdul-Karim Rafeq, Judith Tucker, Yvonne Haddad, Frederick Cooper, Rochelle Davis, Ahmad Dallal, Osama Abi-Mershed, Michael Gilsenan, Jane Burbank, Arang Keshavarzian, Lauren Benton, Leslie Peirce, Yanni Kotsonis, and Zvi Ben-Dor for your tireless guidance and instruction. Your multidisciplinary expertise has broadened my knowledge of our world and its past and deepened my appreciation for critical thought within the social sciences. I am also grateful for my students at New York University and Friends Seminary, who, over the course of eight years, gave me daily reason to trust in the importance of sharing the history of Palestine and Palestinians. I thank you for your engagement in all my classes, for your openness to learning and reflecting, and for your boundless capacity for curiosity. Please keep questioning, writing, and caring for the stories of others.

For the collegial support and opportunities for scholarly collaboration from which I have benefited greatly during my graduate work, I am thankful to Cecilia Baeza, Amal Eqeiq, Jacob Norris, Emilio and Rodrigo Dabed, Kamal Cumsille, the late Eugenio Chahuan, Camila Pastor, Kathy Kenny, and Lauren Banko. Our different panels and thematic conversations at the Middle East and Latin American Studies Association meetings, as well as our numerous exchanges by e-mail and chats over coffee from New York, Washington, DC, and Santiago to London, Jerusalem, and Ramallah, have enriched the scope of my research and the breadth of my historical inquiries. I am also sincerely thankful to the Social Science Research Council, the National Endowment for the Humanities, and the Palestinian American Research Center (PARC) for their trust in my project's worth, and especially for the guidance and friendship of Penny Mitchell at PARC, who has stood by me throughout all these years. The research on which this book is based was made possible with your generous support.

It is not often that a historian connects personally with their subject matter. As a Palestinian, this bittersweet journey has brought me a unique combination of heartache and joy that I had not anticipated, and for the encouragement and love of my family and friends, I am profoundly and eternally grateful. Thank you, Sami Bawalsa, Zoe Bawalsa Xavier, Mohammed Fouz, Melle Patrick, Alikai Fouz, Samira Hajjar, Haley Peele, Helga Tawil-Souri, Basim, Hala, Karim, and Omar Said, Maria Fernanda Xavier, Giovanna Almeida, Basma Hantouli, Jude Bawalsa, Hala Khoury, Belle and June Bawalsa, Tareq Baconi, Seth Anziska, Isabella Hammad, Amir Moosavi, Dena al-Adeeb, Joseph Sills, Hollian Wint, Hanin Khawaja, Ahmad Hammoudeh, Nasri Ashkar, Samer Atiani, Rawan Zeine, Mona Sabella, Diana Mubarak, Adrien Zakar, Johnny Zaia, Suad Amiry, Randa Wahbeh, Omar Imseeh Tesdell, Wasim Salfiti, Katy Whiting, Jumana Bishara, Aunti Rawia Bishara, Sophie Hajjar, Yasmin Santana, Rodrigo Fischer, Yasmine Hamayel, Yara Hawari, Megan Driscoll, Mohammed Hamarsha, Alaa Tartir, Denman Tuzo, Deanna Yurchuk, Kristen Fairey, Amy Smith, Shayna Strype, Constantino Marzuqa Giacaman, Ryan Schlief, Lindsey Buller, Arianne Urus, Sam Dolbee, Shay Hazkani, Alex Winder, and my late friend, Michael Milic, who is missed every day, for inspiring me to get this done. Thank you also for keeping me afloat with your support and laughter and with your readiness to eat, imbibe, take walks, vent, meditate, and ruminate with me. I am indebted to your trust that I could do this and for reminding me time and again how significant this topic is for our collective knowledge. Palestine and its people must be preserved in the historical record.

I am especially grateful to my family in Jerusalem, Ramallah, and Beit Jala for hosting me during my research trips and for keeping me entertained, fed, and safe during often challenging and overwhelming journeys throughout occupied Palestine. Thank you to my late uncle, Ammo Boulos, to my sweet aunt, Amto Lorice, and to my grandmother's loving cousins, Aunti Rima Tarazi and Ammo Amin Nasser, for giving me safe and loving homes in Beit Hanina and Ramallah at times when I could not fathom humanity's cruelty or the absurdity of military occupation and exile. Thank you to my cousins Amal, Diana, Laura, and Fadi and to your beautiful families—Nabil, Walid, Latifeh, Mark, Dani, Natalie, Issa, Sama, Christian, and Aram—for your love, laughter, and warm hospitality. You have all made what would have otherwise been a profoundly painful experience feel like home. I love you all.

I am also particularly thankful to my friend, Fredrik Meiton, for keeping me company on often lonely and emotionally difficult research trips in London and Jerusalem, for helping me locate primary sources, and for editing the first full draft of this book. And I am deeply thankful to my stepfather, Kelly

Harrison, for joining me during my research in Chile, where he acted as my translator and interpreter for several weeks as we visited archives, private collections, book talks, cultural events, marches, and people's homes in Santiago and beyond. Without a doubt, I would not have been able to complete the research as I did without your selfless help. Thank you, Kelly and Fred, for your generosity of spirit.

To my grandparents, Sylvia and Albert, Umm Ead and Salman, whose short lives were so dramatically shaped by the loss of Palestine, thank you for giving me life. Through this research, I have returned to each of your homes in Palestine and have connected to each of you in ways I had not expected. I saw where you grew up, where you played, and where you learned who you were. I walked through the streets you called home as children and the courtyards where you watched your own children grow years later. I learned the true meaning of dispossession when I stood outside of your homes in Beit Jala, Talbiyyeh, and Ramallah, now inhabited by occupants who are not us. I learned what you all lost to keep your children, my parents, safe.

To my mother, Dina Said, and my father, Yousef Bawalsa, thank you for all that you have sacrificed to give us a chance at a life undefined by more war and more loss. Thank you for teaching me to love who we are and who we always will be: Palestinians. I love you both with all my heart.

Notes

INTRODUCTION

1. Israel State Archives, Jerusalem, P-986/24.

2. Herbert Plumer succeeded Herbert Samuel. He served in this role from August 1925 until July 1928.

3. Israel State Archives, Jerusalem, P-986/24.

4. Rashid Khalidi, *Palestinian Identity: The Construction of Modern National Consciousness* (New York: Columbia University Press, 2008), 157.

5. Walter Shaw, *A Survey of Palestine* (Jerusalem: Government Printer, 1945–1946), 185.

6. There are documented cases of the Government of Palestine revoking Jewish immigrants' citizenship certificates, though only for those who did not relocate permanently to Palestine. The Zionist Federation in London regularly contested the revocations, arguing that the British authorities were obliged to respect the mandate and their promise to the Jews. See National Archives, London, CO 733/179/2.

7. For more about the citizenship legislation and how it was used to deny citizenship to thousands of Palestinian migrants, see Nadim Bawalsa, "Legislating Exclusion: Palestinian Migrants and Interwar Citizenship," *Journal of Palestine Studies*, 46:2 (2017): 44–59; and Lauren Banko, *The Invention of Palestinian Citizenship, 1918–1947* (Edinburgh: Edinburgh University Press, 2016).

8. Frederick Cooper and Ann Stoler have described the importance of assuming historical contingency when writing the histories of "coloniality." See Cooper and Stoler, eds. *Tensions of Empire: Colonial Cultures in a Bourgeois World* (Berkeley:

University of California Press, 1997). See also Sebastian Conrad, *Globalization and the Nation in Imperial Germany* (Cambridge: Cambridge University Press, 2014) for an analysis of the importance of transnationalism in the development of German nationalism in the nineteenth century.

9. Khalidi, *Palestinian Identity*, 205.

10. During a panel titled "Little Syria, NYC: History and Advocacy" at CUNY, New York, 20 May 2013, Nancy Foner included Syrians in what she termed "the last great wave of immigration" to the USA between 1880 and 1920. See Nancy Foner, *From Ellis Island to JFK: New York's Two Great Waves of Immigration* (New Haven: Yale University Press, 2002).

11. See Albert Hourani and Nadim Shehadi's edited volume *The Lebanese in the World: A Century of Emigration* (London: I. B. Tauris, 1992) for an example of the scope and depth of scholarly analysis surrounding the Lebanese diaspora.

12. Camila Pastor, *The Mexican Mahjar: Transnational Maronites, Jews, and Arabs under the French Mandate* (Austin: University of Texas Press, 2017), 3.

13. Andrew Arsan, John Karam, and Akram Khater, "On Forgotten Shores: Migration in Middle East Studies, and the Middle East in Migration Studies," *Mashriq & Mahjar* 1 (2013): 1.

14. Arsan, Karam, and Khater, "On Forgotten Shores," 3.

15. Arsan, Karam, and Khater, "On Forgotten Shores," 1.

16. Arsan, Karam, and Khater, "On Forgotten Shores," 5–6.

17. Pastor, *Mexican Mahjar*, 4. Emphasis in the original.

18. Arsan, Karam, and Khater, "On Forgotten Shores," 4.

19. Arsan, Karam, and Khater, "On Forgotten Shores," 6.

20. Khachig Tololyan, "Rethinking Diaspora(s): Stateless Power in the Transnational Moment," *Diaspora* 5:1 (1996): 3.

21. Tololyan, "Rethinking Diaspora(s)," 28.

22. Rogers Brubaker, "The 'Diaspora' Diaspora," *Ethnic and Racial Studies* 28:1 (2005): 1.

23. Brubaker, "'Diaspora' Diaspora," 5.

24. Christian Hess, "What Are 'Reverse Diasporas' and How Are We to Understand Them?" *Diaspora* 17:3 (2008): 290.

25. Brent Hayes Edwards, "The Uses of Diaspora," *Social Text* 66 19:1 (2001): 1.

26. Brubaker, "'Diaspora' Diaspora," 10.

27. Tololyan in Brubaker, "'Diaspora' Diaspora," 10.

28. Brubaker, "'Diaspora' Diaspora," 10.

29. Brubaker, "'Diaspora' Diaspora," 12.

30. Erik Olsson and Russell King, "Introduction: Diasporic Return," *Diaspora* 17:3 (2008): 256–57.

31. Daphne Winland, "Why We Come Back to Diasporas: Heterogeneous Groups and the Persistent Dream of Political Action," *Diaspora* 16:1/2 (2007): 263.

32. Notable theoretical discussions about the imbedded violence and authoritarianism of contemporary state structures when it comes to people's struggles over citizenship, identification, and subjecthood include James Scott, *Seeing like a State: How Certain Schemes to Improve the Human Condition Have Failed* (New Haven: Yale University, 1999), Wendy Brown, *Regulating Aversion: Tolerance in the Age of Identity and Empire* (Princeton: Princeton University Press, 2006), and Timothy Mitchell, "The Limits of the State: Beyond Statist Approaches and Their Critics," *American Political Science Review* 85:1 (1991): 77–96.

33. Keith Watenpaugh, "The League of Nations' Rescue of Armenian Genocide Survivors and the Making of Modern Humanitarianism, 1920–1927," *American Historical Review* 115:5 (December 2010): 1315–39. Also see Erez Manela, *The Wilsonian Moment: Self-Determination and the International Origins of Anticolonial Nationalism* (Oxford: Oxford University Press, 2009), for a discussion of the importance of the 1919 Peace Conference and the rhetoric of Woodrow Wilson for non-Western nationalists in Egypt, India, China, and Korea.

34. Pastor, *Mexican Mahjar*, 16.

35. Pastor, *Mexican Mahjar*, 10.

36. Pastor, *Mexican Mahjar*, 10.

37. Pastor, *Mexican Mahjar*, 9.

38. Beshara Doumani, *Rediscovering Palestine: Merchants and Peasants in Jabal Nablus, 1700–1900* (Berkeley: University of California Press, 1995), 10.

39. Jacob Norris's research on transnational Bethlehemite traders at the turn of the twentieth century is an excellent example of the importance of migration for Palestine's economic prosperity. Norris, "Return Migration and the Rise of the Palestinian Nouveaux Riches, 1870–1925," *Journal of Palestine Studies*, 46:2 (2017): 60–75.

40. Some notable works investigating the contradictory practices of European international law in the twentieth century include Antony Anghie, *Imperialism, Sovereignty and the Making of International Law* (New York: Cambridge University Press, 2007); Mark Mazower, "An International Civilization? Empire, Internationalism, and the Crisis of the Mid-Twentieth Century," *International Affairs* 82:3 (2006): 553–66; Caroline Elkins and Susan Pedersen, eds., *Settler Colonialism in the Twentieth Century: Projects, Practices, Legacies* (London: Routledge, 2005); Susan Pedersen, "The Meaning of the Mandate System: An Argument," *Geschichte und Gesellschaft* 32:4 (2006): 560–58; and Frederick Cooper and Ann Stoler, eds., *Tensions of Empire: Colonial Cultures in a Bourgeois World* (Berkeley: University of California Press, 1997).

41. For an explanation of collective national and civic consciousness in late Ottoman Palestine, see Michelle Campos, *Ottoman Brothers: Muslims, Christians, and*

Jews in Early Twentieth-Century Palestine (Stanford: Stanford University Press, 2010). Campos argues that Jews, Christians, and Muslims in Palestine shared a sense of "civic Ottomanism" that reflected the post-1908 revolutionary spirit of reform and imperial citizenship.

42. This practice also affected Palestinian migrants in Egypt, Syria, and elsewhere regionally who sought to return or to secure legal belonging to Palestine. See Lauren Banko, "Claiming Identities in Palestine: Migration and Nationality under the Mandate," *Journal of Palestine Studies* 182:46 (2017): 26–43.

43. Two notable works that deal with the history of emigration, settlement, and diaspora formation of Chinese and Indian migrants in the Caribbean and Latin America at the turn of the twentieth century are Kathleen Lopez, *Chinese Cubans: A Transnational History* (Chapel Hill: University of North Carolina Press, 2013); and Gaiutra Bahadur, *Coolie Woman: The Odyssey of Indenture* (Chicago: University of Chicago Press, 2013).

44. The editors of *al-Sharq* translated it into Latin script as "al-Shark." This book uses the *q*, not the *k*, to denote the Arabic letter *qaaf* in the word *al-Sharq*, to differentiate it from the Arabic letter *kaaf*.

CHAPTER 1: PALESTINIANS SETTLE THE AMERICAN MAHJAR

1. Nicole Saffie Guevara and Lorenzo Agar Corbinos, "A Century of Palestinian Immigration to Chile: A Successful Integration," in *Latin American with Palestinian Roots*, ed. Viola Raheb (Bethlehem: Diyar Publishers, 2012), 64.

2. Akram Khater and Antoine Khater, "Assaf: A Peasant of Mount Lebanon," in *Struggle and Survival in the Modern Middle East*, ed. Edmund Burke III and David Yaghoubian (Berkeley: University of California Press, 2006), 35–47.

3. Akram Khater has estimated that in 1890, silk accounted for 50 percent of the GDP of Mount Lebanon. Akram Khater, "Little Syria, NYC: History and Advocacy" (presentation at CUNY University, New York, 20 May 2013).

4. See Roger Owen, *The Middle East in the World Economy, 1800–1914* (London: I. B. Tauris, 1993), for an examination of the struggles of Middle Eastern economic systems during the nineteenth and early twentieth centuries. Owen pays particular attention to the role that European trade and the globalized economy played in altering economic traditions in the Middle East.

5. See Hasan Kayali, *Arabs and Young Turks: Ottomanism, Arabism, and Islamism in the Ottoman Empire, 1908–1918* (Berkeley: University of California Press, 1997), for an investigation of the rise and development of Arab and Turkish nationalisms before and during World War I.

6. Najib Saliba, "Emigration from Syria," in *Arabs in the New World*, ed. Sameer Abraham and Nabeel Abraham (Detroit: Wayne State University, 1983), 37.

7. Manzar Foroohar, "Palestinians in Central America; From Temporary Migrants to a Permanent Diaspora," *Journal of Palestine Studies* 40:3 (2011), 7.

8. Cecilia Baeza Rodriguez, "Les Palestiniens d'Amerique Latine et la cause Palestinienne: Chile, Brésil, Honduras, 1920–2010," PhD diss., Sciences Po (2010), 93.

9. Nancie Gonzalez, *Dollar, Dove, and Eagle: One Hundred Years of Palestinian Migration to Honduras* (Ann Arbor: University of Michigan Press, 1992), 28n.

10. Kemal Karpat, "The Ottoman Emigration to America, 1860–1914," *International Journal of Middle East Studies* 17:2 (1985): 179.

11. Saliba, "Emigration from Syria," 36.

12. Philip Hitti, *The Syrians in America* (Piscataway: Gorgias Press, 2005), 48.

13. Manzar Foroohar, "Palestinian Diaspora in Central America—A Story of Hardship and Success," in *Latin American with Palestinian Roots*, ed. Viola Raheb (Bethlehem: Diyar Publishers, 2012), 47.

14. Hitti, *Syrians in America*, 48.

15. Kathy Kenny, "The Power of Place: Katrina in Five Worlds," *Jerusalem Quarterly* 35 (2008): 8. Kenny has shared with me her grandmother's private letters.

16. Kenny, "Power of Place," 8.

17. Katrina Saade, quoted in Kenny, "Power of Place," 9. Kenny collected this information from audiotapes that her aunt, Mary (Farhat) Bond, Katrina's youngest daughter, and her husband Henry Bond had recorded in Wyoming during the mid-1970s. Katrina Saade, who was six when her family first left Palestine in 1906, also corresponded with different family members in letters throughout her travels that spanned over twenty years. For more information about Katrina Saade and her letters, see Nadim Bawalsa, "Trouble with the In-Laws: Family Letters Between Palestine and the Americas, 1925–1939," *Jerusalem Quarterly* 47 (2011): 6–27.

18. Kenny, "Power of Place," 8. Cotton and silk from Syria and Lebanon were the most affected crops in the region due to global competition from the Far East, and by World War I, production of both had "practically ceased," as Najib Saliba points out. Saliba, "Emigration from Syria," 34.

19. Karpat has argued against the idea that emigration was a phenomenon strictly of the Christian populations of the Arab provinces. "It must be stressed," he says, that the deterioration of the "socioeconomic conditions in the Ottoman state after 1860 . . . affected all population groups." That said, he continues, the proportion of Christians leaving their homes was relatively larger than that of Muslims, mainly because of the type of commodities they were selling abroad and because of their confessional ties with the Western world. Karpat, "Ottoman Emigration to America," 179.

20. Saliba, "Emigration from Syria," 39.

21. Karpat, "Ottoman Emigration to America," 185.

22. The Ottoman provinces of Greater Syria at the turn of the twentieth century included the vilayets of Aleppo, Beirut, Syria, and Deir al-Zor, and the Mutasarrifate of Jerusalem. Inhabitants of these provinces were collectively referred to as Syrians. A reasonable estimate of the combined populations of these provinces based on Ottoman census records from 1885, 1897, and 1900 is approximately 1.8 million around the turn of the century. Alixa Naff, "New York: The Mother Colony," in *A Community of Many Worlds: Arab Americans in New York City*, ed. Kathleen Benson and Phillip Kayal (Syracuse: Syracuse University Press, 2002).

23. Naff, "New York," 5. For a history of the settlement and assimilation of Syrians in the United States, see Alixa Naff, *Becoming American: The Early Arab Immigrant Experience* (Carbondale: Southern Illinois University Press, 1985).

24. Hitti, *Syrians in America*, 48.

25. Baeza, "Palestiniens d'Amerique," 97.

26. Israeli archives are notoriously inaccessible to researchers of Palestinian history. Until very recently, they have also been notoriously disorganized. My experience in the Israel State Archives in 2011 is an example of how difficult it is to locate sources on Palestinians before 1948. Boxes were filled with mislabeled and unlabeled files containing an assortment of undated or misdated documents. In Palestine, too, sources are scant and mostly located in private collections that are difficult to access. The absence of a Palestinian national archive also makes it impractical to pose conventional historical queries about this time period or to develop conventional research methodologies.

27. While the *turco* misnomer is the subject of arguably any historical foray into Arab migration to Latin America, Manzar Forhoohar offers a concise explanation of the significance of the term at a social level for incoming migrants. Manzar Foroohar, "Palestinians in Central America; From Temporary Migrants to a Permanent Diaspora," *Journal of Palestine Studies* 40:3 (2011): 6–22. Jeffrey Lesser and Ignacio Klich also analyze the emergence and evolution of the term *turco* in its application to the Arab migrant communities of Latin America. See Klich and Lesser, "Introduction: 'Turco' Immigrants in Latin America," in *The Americas* 53:1 (1996): 1–14.

28. Karpat, "Ottoman Emigration to America," 180.

29. Charles Issawi, "Migration from and to Syria, 1860–1914," in *The Economic History of the Middle East, 1800–1914*, ed. Charles Issawi (Chicago: University of Chicago Press, 1966), 272.

30. Adnan Musallam, *Folded Pages from Local Palestinian History in the Twentieth Century* (Bethlehem: WIAM/Palestinian Resolution Centre, 2002), in Mutaz Qafisheh, *The International Law Foundations of Palestinian Nationality: A Legal Examination of Nationality in Palestine under Britain's Rule* (Boston: Martinus Nijhoff Publishers, 2008), 104.

31. Saffie and Agar, "A Century of Palestinian Immigration," 65.

32. Foroohar, "Palestinian Diaspora," 45.

33. Roberto Marin-Guzman, "Political Participation and Economic Success of the Palestinians of Christian Origin in Central America," in *Latin American with Palestinian Roots*, ed. Viola Raheb (Bethlehem: Diyar Publishers, 2012), 27.

34. Issawi, "Migration from and to Syria," 271–72.

35. Pastor, *Mexican Mahjar*, 5.

36. Theresa Alfaro-Velcamp, *So Far from Allah, So Close to Mexico* (Austin: University of Texas Press, 2007), 52–53.

37. Alfaro-Velcamp, *So Far from Allah*, 53.

38. Alfaro-Velcamp, *So Far from Allah*, 53.

39. *Filastin*, 1911, microfilm, Elmer Holmes Bobst Library at New York University, New York, NY. Translated from Arabic. The principal boat companies that operated between the Mashriq and Europe were the French Messageries Maritimes and the Italian Rubattino Line. Both are mentioned in *Filastin*, though only Messageries is advertised on the front page.

40. Salim Tamari, "A Miserable Year in Brooklyn: Khalil Sakakini in America, 1907–1908," *Jerusalem Quarterly* 17 (2003): 19–40, 25.

41. Tamari, "Miserable Year in Brooklyn," 25.

42. Pastor, *Mexican Mahjar*, 5.

43. Issawi, "Migration from and to Syria," 271.

44. Saliba, "Emigration from Syria," 38.

45. Issawi, "Migration from and to Syria," 271.

46. Foroohar, "Palestinians in Central America," 9.

47. Foroohar, "Palestinians in Central America," 10.

48. Roberto Marin-Guzman argues similarly in *A Century of Palestinian Immigration into Central America: A Study of Their Economic and Cultural Contributions* (San Jose: Editorial de la Universidad de Costa Rica, 2000), 17. He adds that Palestinians found welcoming markets in Central America for their goods as early as the 1890s.

49. For a detailed examination of the CUP-lead coup and its impact on the Arab provinces, see Hasan Kayali, *Arabs and Young Turks: Ottomanism, Arabism, and Islamism in the Ottoman Empire, 1908–1918* (Berkeley: University of California Press, 1997).

50. Saliba, "Emigration from Syria," 36.

51. For a detailed account of the life and travails of Khalil Sakakini as analyzed from his diary, see Nadim Bawalsa, "Sakakini Defrocked," *Jerusalem Quarterly* 42 (2010): 5–25.

52. Khalil Sakakini, *Kadha Ana Ya Dunya* (Beirut: al-Ittihaad al-ʿAamm li al-Kuttab wa al-Sahafiyyin al-Filastiniyyin, al-Amaana al-ʿAamma, 1982), 89. Translated from Arabic.

53. Sakakini, *Kadha Ana Ya Dunya* , 89. Translated from Arabic.

54. Akram Khater, *Inventing Home: Emigration, Gender, and the Middle Class in Lebanon 1870–1920* (Berkeley: University of California Press, 2001), 8.

55. Baeza, "Palestiniens d'Amerique."

56. Endogamy was an essential component of socialization across many communities in the Mediterranean, including the Middle East. The emphasis on its importance in the Palestinian diaspora is not meant to detract from its importance elsewhere in the world but to suggest that the practice was so important that migrants brought it with them to the diaspora and depended on it in significant ways for the survival of their communities.

57. Baeza, "Palestiniens d'Amerique," 95. Translated from French. Villas and larger homes in and around Bethlehem and Beit Jala, the two main origins of most Palestinian migrants, were also built using migrants' remittances. For more about the construction of these neighborhoods, see Abdulla Lutfiyya, *Baytin, a Jordanian Village: A Study of Social Institutions and Social Change in a Folk Community* (Berlin: De Gruyter Mouton, 2011).

58. Baeza, "Palestiniens d'Amerique," 97. Translated from French.

59. Baeza, "Palestiniens d'Amerique," 100. Translated from French.

60. Baeza, "Palestiniens d'Amerique," 94. Translated from French.

61. Gonzalez, *Dollar, Dove, and Eagle*, 116.

62. Baeza, "Palestiniens d'Amerique," 95. Translated from French.

63. Baeza, "Palestiniens d'Amerique," 96. Translated from French.

64. Roberto Marin-Guzman has shown that during the Great Depression and with new job opportunities emerging in Palestine under the British mandate, many Palestinians in the United States sought to return to Palestine to secure jobs either in British mandate offices and other lower-level clerkships or doing translation and tutoring. See Marin-Guzman, *A Century of Palestinian Immigration into Central America: A Study of Their Economic and Cultural Contributions* (San Jose: Editorial Universidad de Costa Rica, 2000), 27. Unlike their counterparts in Latin America, these migrants faced direr economic circumstances and would have been happy to abscond from the debt of unsuccessful businesses. Suleiman Farhat was one of those men, and by 1930, he was urging Katrina to move back to Ramallah to invest what little money they had saved in his family's property in Ramallah. Katrina, on the other hand, did not wish to return to Palestine, having left it more than fifteen years earlier. This family drama persisted for nearly a decade and ended with Katrina escaping from her in-laws' home in Ramallah and boarding a ship back to the United States with two of the three children with whom she had returned to Palestine. Katrina and Suleiman divorced a few years later. For more information, see Nadim Bawalsa, "Trouble with the In-Laws: Family Letters Between Palestine and the Americas, 1925–1939," *Jerusalem Quarterly* 47 (2011): 6–27.

65. Alfaro-Velcamp, *So Far from Allah*, 49.

66. Alfaro-Velcamp, *So Far from Allah*, 53.

67. Alfaro-Velcamp, *So Far from Allah*, 54.

68. Alfaro-Velcamp, *So Far from Allah*, 46.

69. Sarah Gualtieri's book *Arab Routes: Pathways to Syrian California* (Stanford: Stanford University Press, 2020), examines the emergence in Los Angeles of a Syrian community in the early twentieth century. She highlights the centrality of Latin America, especially Mexico, in this development. For Gualtieri, the interconnectedness of Latin America in Middle Eastern migration to North America must be emphasized.

70. Alfaro-Velcamp, *So Far from Allah*, 61. Porfirio Diaz served seven terms, amounting to over three decades in office between 1876 and 1911. His dictatorial reign sparked the ten-year revolution which pitted the rising working class against the much smaller landowning elite. In 1910, an election year, opponents of Diaz and his regime took the opportunity to stage a political rebellion that soon spread to mining regions and the Mexican countryside. The revolution is considered a formative event in the history of Mexico. In addition to the 1917 Constitution which empowered the peasantry, the revolution contributed to the formation of the Institutional Revolutionary Party in 1929, a party which continues to hold great significance in Mexican politics to this day.

71. Alfaro-Velcamp, *So Far from Allah*, 69.

72. Pastor, *Mexican Mahjar*, 5. Lily Balloffet's recent book, *Argentina in the Global Middle East* (Stanford: Stanford University Press, 2020), explores the emergence of Syrian communities in Argentina throughout the twentieth century. She shows how through their expansive peddling networks and thanks to the arrival of the railroad to Argentina, Syrian migrants managed to spread credit-based businesses deep into the Argentinian interior.

73. Alfaro-Velcamp, *So Far from Allah*, 70.

74. Alfaro-Velcamp, *So Far from Allah*, 77.

75. Alfaro-Velcamp, *So Far from Allah*, 83.

76. Alfaro-Velcamp, *So Far from Allah*, 95.

77. Alfaro-Velcamp, *So Far from Allah*, 71.

78. Alfaro-Velcamp, *So Far from Allah*, 96–97.

79. Alfaro-Velcamp shows that of all registered Middle Eastern migrants in Mexico, 46 percent arrived between 1920 and 1929. Alfaro-Velcamp, *So Far from Allah*, 98.

80. Alfaro-Velcamp, *So Far from Allah*, 102. Restrictive immigration laws in Mexico emerged alongside similar legislation in the United States. In 1924, the US federal government enacted the Immigration Act of 1924, or the Johnson-Reed Act. It limited the annual number of immigrants who could be admitted to the US from any

country to 2 percent of the number of people from that country who were already living in the US. This was 1 percent down from the 3 percent cap set by the Immigration Restriction Act of 1921. Although the 1924 law was meant to limit the number of Eastern and Southern Europeans seeking entry into the United States after World War I, it outright banned Arabs and Asians under the pretext of preserving the "ideal of American homogeneity."

81. Alfaro-Velcamp, *So Far from Allah*, 103. Punctuation in the original. The Mexican government had been restricting or banning migrants from other origins starting in 1921 with Chinese migrants, then 1923 with Indians, 1924 with Africans, and 1926 with gypsies. These kinds of migration laws persisted throughout the 1920s and into the 1930s, and though new legislation emerged after World War II to limit racial discrimination, the Mexican government continued to promote the entry of "assimilable" foreigners who were either racially white or whiter, or socioeconomically successful. Other governments in the Americas, including in Chile, did the same.

82. Alfaro-Velcamp, *So Far from Allah*, 106.

83. Alfaro-Velcamp, *So Far from Allah*, 108.

84. Saffie and Agar, "A Century of Palestinian Immigration," 64.

85. Emilio Dabed, "A Constitution for a Non-State: The False Hopes of the Palestinian Constitutional Process, 1988–2007" (PhD diss., Sciences Po 2012), 23.

86. *Al-Watan*, 8 October 1927, Biblioteca Nacional, Santiago de Chile. Translated from Arabic.

87. Saffie and Agar, "A Century of Palestinian Immigration," 65.

88. Myriam Olguin Tenorio and Patricia Peña Gonzalez, *La Inmigracion arabe en Chile* (Santiago: Instituto Chileno Arabe de Cultura, 1990), 82. Translated from Spanish.

89. Olguin and Peña, *Inmigracion arabe*, 82. Translated from Spanish.

90. Saffie and Agar, "A Century of Palestinian Immigration," 65.

91. Baeza, "Palestiniens d'Amerique," 81. Translated from French.

92. Baeza, "Palestiniens d'Amerique," 81. It is not clear why Palestinians from Bethlehem and Beit Jala were leaving at a higher rate. Historians seem to agree that, since endogamy within the extended family or religious community was the primary form of socialization, the existence of a growing population of Bethelehemites and Bajjaalis in Chile would have ensured a steady outflow of migrants from those towns in Palestine.

93. See Balloffet, *Argentina in the Global Middle East*, for a discussion of the different social and cultural achievements of Syrian migrants in Argentina.

94. Baeza, "Palestiniens d'Amerique," 80.

95. Stacy Fahrenthold, *Between the Ottomans and the Entente: The First World War in the Syrian and Lebanese Diaspora, 1908–1925* (New York: Oxford University Press,

2019). In the opening pages to the book, Fahrenthold includes a list of the political organizations that formed throughout the Lebanese and Syrian diaspora.

96. See Baeza, "Palestiniens d'Amerique," for more information about the different organizations, sports clubs, and committees devoted to different Middle Eastern national and cultural causes that emerged in Chile, Honduras, and Brazil in the first two decades of the twentieth century.

97. Saffie and Agar, "A Century of Palestinian Immigration," 66.

98. Saffie and Agar, "A Century of Palestinian Immigration," 66.

99. Marco Allel, *Las industrias de las colectividades de habla Arabe in Chile* (Chile: Syrian-Palestinian Business Association, 1937), 35, as cited in Saffie and Agar, "A Century of Palestinian Immigration," 66.

100. *Al-Watan*, 8 October 1927. Translated from Arabic.

101. Saffie and Agar, "A Century of Palestinian Immigration," 66.

102. Saffie and Agar, "A Century of Palestinian Immigration," 70.

103. Alell, *Las Industrias*, 34, quoted in Saffie and Agar, "A Century of Palestinian Immigration," 69.

104. Saliba, "Emigration from Syria," 36.

105. Saliba, "Emigration from Syria," 36.

106. The blockade contributed to a famine in wartime Syria that led to massive casualties. In Mount Lebanon alone, approximately two hundred thousand perished, amounting to half the population.

107. Hitti, *Syrians in America*, 60–61.

108. For a thorough explanation of the different uses of citizenship and nationality in British legislation in the context of the mandate for Palestine, see Lauren Banko, *The Invention of Palestinian Citizenship, 1918–1947* (Edinburgh: Edinburgh University Press, 2016). Banko argues that British officials often used citizenship and nationality interchangeably in policy documents, but that they also differentiated between the two strategically: whereas citizenship more directly referred to the process of naturalizing Jewish immigrants to Palestine as Palestinians, nationality referred more broadly to the notions of belonging and rights that were associated with other colonial processes, as in India. This, she argues, contributed to separating the process of settling and naturalizing Jews in Palestine from other colonial contexts worldwide.

109. Hitti, *Syrians in America*, 58–59.

110. Hitti, *Syrians in America*, 60.

CHAPTER 2: THE TRADITION OF TRANSNATIONAL "PRO-PALESTINA" ACTIVISM

1. Emir Faisal was the son of Hussein bin Ali, the Sharif of Mecca, who was proclaimed King of the Arabs in June 1916. Emir Faisal played a critical role in the 1916 Arab Revolt, which contributed to the ouster of the Ottomans from the Middle East.

He made several agreements with British leaders to collaborate in defeating the Ottomans in order to achieve Arab independence. The Syrian National Congress in Damascus elected him King of Syria in March 1920, a position he held until July of that year, when the French ousted him and established their mandate over Syria. Subsequently, the British appointed him King of Iraq, a position he held from 1921 until his death in 1933.

2. National Archives, London, FO, 608/98/8.

3. The Sykes-Picot Agreement was also made public by the Russians after the Bolshevik Revolution, though, unlike Balfour's letter, it was never meant to be made public.

4. Keishiro Matsui, an ambassador from Japan, also attended the conference.

5. Transjordan and Palestine were governed as the same Palestine mandate until the 1921 Cairo conference, during which British forces decided to split the territory into two mandates in order to grant Transjordan to the Hashemites.

6. See Susan Pedersen, *The Guardians: The League of Nations and the Crisis of Empire* (New York: Oxford University Press, 2015) for an investigation into the emergence of the League of Nations and the Permanent Mandates Commission.

7. "Resolution of the General Syrian Congress at Damascus, 2 July 1919," in *The Middle East and North Africa in World Politics: A Documentary Record,* ed. J. C. Hurewitz (New Haven: Yale University Press, 1979), 180–82.

8. The Arab Kingdom of Syria was declared on 8 March 1920, but it soon dissolved after the French threatened Faisal, who surrendered, and defeated the Syrian army at the Battle of Maysalun on 24 July 1920.

9. Nadi Abusaada, "'Who Are We and What Are We Called?': Palestinians in Chile at the End of Ottoman Rule," 18 March 2020, Accessed 25 March 2020, https://www.nadiabusaada.com/blog/who-are-we-and-what-are-we-called.

10. Fahrenthold, *Between the Ottomans,* 28.

11. Fahrenthold, *Between the Ottomans,* 32–33.

12. Fahrenthold, *Between the Ottomans,* 42.

13. Fahrenthold, *Between the Ottomans,* 48.

14. Fahrenthold, *Between the Ottomans,* 51–79.

15. Fahrenthold, *Between the Ottomans,* 87–93.

16. Fahrenthold, *Between the Ottomans,* 87.

17. Fahrenthold, *Between the Ottomans,* 110.

18. Fahrenthold, *Between the Ottomans,* 103.

19. Fahrenthold, *Between the Ottomans,* 111.

20. National Archives, London, FO, 608/98/8. Translated from French.

21. National Archives, London, FO, 608/98/8. Translated from French.

22. National Archives, London, FO, 608/98/8. Translated from French.

23. National Archives, London, FO, 608/98/8. Translated from French.

24. National Archives, London, FO, 608/98/8. Translated from French.

25. Between July 1915 and January 1916, and in a series of letters, the high commissioner for Egypt, Henry McMahon, and the sharif of Mecca, Hussein bin Ali, agreed on a deal whereby in exchange for Arab support of British forces in the war against the Ottomans, Britain would recognize Arab independence upon defeating the Ottomans. In May 1916, however, French and British diplomats signed the Sykes-Picot Agreement and laid the plans for carving up the Middle East into British- and French-mandated territories. Therefore, the letters between Hussein and McMahon, referred to as the Hussein-McMahon Correspondence, are considered by many Arabs to be the most enduring example of British betrayal.

26. National Archives, London, FO, 608/98/8. Translated from French.

27. National Archives, London, FO, 608/98/8. Emphasis in the original.

28. National Archives, London, FO, 608/98/8. This refers to the Balfour Declaration of 1917, which made it clear that the establishment in Palestine of a Jewish "national home" would be carried out with the understanding that "nothing should be done which might prejudice the civil and religious rights of existing non-Jewish communities in Palestine."

29. National Archives, London, FO, 608/98/8.

30. Based on archival evidence, this is the earliest petition delivered to the Peace Conference from Palestinians.

31. National Archives, London, FO, 608/98/8.

32. National Archives, London, FO, 608/98/8.

33. National Archives, London, FO, 608/99.

34. National Archives, London, FO, 608/98/8. In April 1920, riots erupted in Jerusalem between Arabs and Jews in what became known as the Nabi Musa riots. The clashes coincided with religious festivities in and around Jerusalem during Easter. They lasted for four days and were followed by oppressive crackdowns on the Palestinian nationalist movement by the British authorities. Jewish immigration was also halted temporarily as a result. The Nabi Musa riots are considered the first of their kind in the modern history of Palestinian inter-confessional relations, and their effect was to harden divisions between the communities.

35. National Archives, London, FO, 608/98/8.

36. Eric Hooglund, *Crossing the Waters: Arabic-Speaking Immigrants to the United States before 1940* (Washington: Smithsonian Institution Press, 1987), 7.

37. Hitti, *Syrians in America*, 160.

38. Pastor, *Mexican Mahjar*, 6.

39. See John Torpey, "The Great War and the Birth of the Modern Passport System," *Documenting Individual Identity: The Development of State Practices in the*

Modern World, ed. Jane Caplan and John Torpey (Princeton: Princeton University Press, 2001), for a discussion of how passports were implemented in the aftermath of World War I.

40. For an examination of French citizenship legislation and Syrian and Lebanese migrants during the interwar period, see Fahrenthold, *Between the Ottomans*, chs. 5 and 6.

41. Pastor, *Mexican Mahjar*, 6.

42. Pastor, *Mexican Mahjar*, 16. Emphasis in the original.

43. Khater, *Inventing Home*, 10.

44. Reem Bailony, "Transnationalism and the Syrian Migrant Public: The Case of the 1925 Syrian Revolt," *Mashriq & Mahjar* 1 (2013): 9.

45. Akram Khater, "Becoming 'Syrian' in America: A Global Geography of Ethnicity and Nation," *Diaspora* 14:2/3 (2005): 299.

CHAPTER 3: THE 1925 PALESTINIAN CITIZENSHIP ORDER-IN-COUNCIL

1. Although the Treaty of Lausanne was signed on 24 July 1923, it was not ratified until 6 August 1924. Throughout this book, reference will be made to both dates.

2. For a thorough examination of the history of the legislation of Palestinian nationality following the defeat of the Ottomans, see Mutaz Qafisheh, *The International Law Foundations of Palestinian Nationality: A Legal Examination of Nationality in Palestine under Britain's Rule* (Boston: Martinus Nijhoff Publishers, 2008). Qafisheh also offers a comparative analysis of the development of Palestinian nationality under British rule in relation to other newly mandated territories both in the Middle East and across the world.

3. For a description of the impact of these changes on Jerusalem and its residents, see Salim Tamari, "City of Riffraff: Crowds, Public Space, and New Urban Sensibilities in War-Time Jerusalem, 1917–1921," in *Comparing Cities: The Middle East and South Asia*, ed. Kamran Asdar Ali and Martina Rieker (Oxford: Oxford University Press, 2009), 23–48.

4. Shaw, *Survey of Palestine*, 208.

5. Sir Harold Morris of the 1936 Peel Commission, which was sent to Palestine to investigate the causes of the unrest among Arab Palestinians that culminated in the Great Revolt of 1936–39, provided these estimates in a memorandum to London's Home Office. National Archives, London, CO, 733/347/4.

6. For an explanation of this process, see chapters 2 and 3 in Banko, *Invention of Palestinian Citizenship*, 2016.

7. For the full text of the 1925 Palestinian Citizenship Order-in-Council, see National Archives, London, CO, 733/179/2, or https://www.nevo.co.il/law_html/law21/PG-e-0147.pdf, pp. 460–78.

8. Qafisheh, *International Law Foundations*, 76.

9. Lauren Banko notes the distinction between legislation put forth by His Majesty's Government in England versus that proposed by colonial offices themselves. See Banko, "The Creation of Palestinian Citizenship under an International Mandate: Legislation, Discourses and Practices, 1918–1925," *Citizenship Studies* 16:5/6 (2012): 641–55.

10. The economic developmentalist and modernist foundations of the British Mandate for Palestine are explored in detail in the works of Jacob Norris and Fredrik Meiton. See Norris, *Land of Progress: Palestine in the Age of Colonial Development, 1905–1948* (Oxford: Oxford University Press, 2013); and Meiton, *Electrical Palestine: Capital and Technology from Empire to Nation* (Berkeley: University of California Press, 2019).

11. National Archives, London, CO, 733/35.

12. Fahrenthold, *Between the Ottomans*, 163.

13. National Archives, London, CO, 323/831.

14. A condensed version of this chapter was published in the *Journal of Palestine Studies* as part of a special issue on Palestinian circulations before 1948. See Bawalsa, "Legislating Exclusion," 2017.

15. National Archives, London, CO, 733/179/2.

16. Banko, *Invention of Palestinian Citizenship*, 85.

17. National Archives, London, CO, 733/55.

18. Walter Shaw, *Report of the Commission on the Palestine Disturbances of August, 1929* (London: His Majesty's Stationary Office, 1930), 133–34.

19. National Archives, London, CO, 733/271–273.

20. National Archives, London, CO, 733/271–273.

21. National Archives, London, CO, 733/110.

22. National Archives, London, CO, 733/103.

23. National Archives, London, CO, 733/103.

24. National Archives, London, CO, 733/103.

25. National Archives, London, CO, 733/104.

26. National Archives, London, CO, 733/104.

27. National Archives, London, CO, 733/98.

28. National Archives, London, CO, 733/98.

29. National Archives, London, CO, 733/121.

30. National Archives, London, CO, 733/121.

31. National Archives, London, CO, 733/121.

32. National Archives, London, CO, 733/142/8.

33. National Archives, London, CO, 733/142/8.

34. National Archives, London, CO, 733/142/8.

35. National Archives, London, CO, 733/142/8.

36. National Archives, London, CO, 733/142/8.

37. Anna Wicksell joined the PMC in 1921 as a Swedish diplomat. "Annex 9, Petitions. A. Palestine; Petitions from Certain Turkish Subjects of Palestinian Origin, now living some in Honduras, others in El Salvador and others in Mexico, dated April 23rd, June 10th, and September nineteenth, 1927," in League of Nations PMC Minutes of the 15th Session, 1927, accessed June 30, 2012, http://biblio-archive.unog.ch/suchinfo.aspx.

38. Pedersen, *Guardians*, 403.

39. National Archives, London, CO, 733/142/8.

40. National Archives, London, CO, 733/142/8.

41. This decision reiterated the declaration made in a dispatch from London to the British consulate on the island of San Salvador on 29 June 1927. The final sentence of the dispatch stated that, regarding the case of Palestinians desiring permits to travel to states other than Palestine, "Sir Austen Chamberlain proposes to return a negative answer." National Archives, London, CO, 733/142/8.

42. For a comparative analysis of the theme of managing difference across empires in world history, see Jane Burbank and Frederick Cooper, *Empires in World History: Power and the Politics of Difference* (Princeton: Princeton University Press, 2011).

43. Ihsan al-Jabiri was born in Aleppo in 1879. His father was the mufti of Aleppo, and so al-Jabiri received a prestigious education in law in Istanbul. In 1919, he was appointed mayor of Aleppo, and he proceeded to call for the independence of Greater Syria as one of the trustees of King Faisal. When King Faisal was deposed in 1920, al-Jabiri left with him, taking exile in Paris. Shortly thereafter, he fled Paris and took refuge in Geneva in 1920. There, he joined the newly formed Syro-Palestinian Delegation, which fought for the rights of Palestinians to self-determination in the face of the Zionist movement. The delegation was composed of notable Palestinian nationalists as well as representatives from the Arabic-speaking diaspora in South America. The delegation met in Geneva until 1923, and al-Jabiri spent the 1920s and 1930s traveling between the Middle East and Europe protesting French rule in Syria and agitating for the rights of Palestinians to self-determination. While European authorities never officially recognized the delegation, al-Jabiri and his colleagues continued to protest European rule in the region and especially in Palestine under the name the Syro-Palestinian Delegation, which by the early 1930s had relocated to Cairo. Throughout his life, al-Jabiri was imprisoned several times and sentenced to death by French authorities in Syria. He died in Cairo in 1980 and was buried in Aleppo.

44. National Archives, London, CO, 733/262/11.

45. National Archives, London, CO, 733/262/11.

46. National Archives, London, CO, 733/262/11. Emphasis in the original.

47. National Archives, London, CO, 733/262/11.

48. National Archives, London, CO, 733/262/11. See Banko, *Invention of Palestinian Citizenship*, 2016, for an examination of the amendments made to the Palestinian Citizenship Orders-in-Council in 1925 and 1931. The amendments were insignificant regarding migrants' applications for citizenship.

49. National Archives, London, CO, 733/262/11.

50. National Archives, London, CO, 733/262/11.

51. National Archives, London, CO, 733/347/4.

52. The Peel Commission Report can be found at https://unispal.un.org/pdfs/Cmd5479.pdf

53. National Archives, London, CO, 733/347/4. "King Hussein" here refers to the sharif of Mecca, Hussein bin Ali, who colluded with the British in 1916 to revolt against the Ottoman Empire in exchange for an independent Arab state. His descendants would rule over parts of Greater Syria and Iraq for varying lengths of time during the twentieth century, and still in Jordan today.

54. National Archives, London, CO, 733/347/4.

55. National Archives, London, CO, 733/347/4.

56. National Archives, London, CO, 733/347/4.

57. National Archives, London, CO, 733/347/4.

58. National Archives, London, CO, 733/347/4.

59. National Archives, London, CO, 733/347/4.

60. National Archives, London, CO, 733/347/4.

61. National Archives, London, LO, 3/898.

62. Antony Anghie, *Imperialism, Sovereignty and the Making of International Law* (New York: Cambridge University Press, 2007), 312.

63. Anghie, *Imperialism*, 311–12.

64. Rogers Brubaker and Frederick Cooper, "Beyond Identity," *Theory and Society*, 29:1 (2000): 16.

65. Brubaker and Cooper, "Beyond Identity," 16.

66. Brubaker and Cooper, "Beyond Identity," 14.

67. Brubaker and Cooper, "Beyond Identity," 15.

68. Cooper and Stoler, *Tensions of Empire*, 35. See other chapters in this book for analyses of the intricate and imbricated processes of constructing colonial dynamics in a variety of contexts, including South Africa, Algeria, and Southeast Asia.

69. Timothy Mitchell, *Questions of Modernity* (Minneapolis: University of Minnesota Press, 2000).

70. Pedersen, *Guardians*, 406.

CHAPTER 4: MEXICO'S PALESTINIANS TAKE ON BRITAIN'S INTERWAR EMPIRE

1. A search on www.ancestry.com yields interesting information about Salamon Canavati and his family. On 15 May 1930, Canavati and his family were registered in the population census of the Mexican Department of National Statistics. The census indicated that Canavati was forty-seven in 1930, placing his birth in 1883. Under "Place of birth," the Mexican authorities wrote "Arabia," and under "Nationality," an X indicating yes was not placed under "Mexicana." Rather, "*sirio*" was written in the second sub-column, which was headed with "If a foreigner, mention actual nationality." The column beside it asked whether the individual had a "former nationality" to which the Mexican authorities indicated yes with a check mark but did not provide further information (though it can be surmised that this nationality was assumed to be *sirio*). The same status was indicated for all of Canavati's family members. As for languages spoken, Canavati and his family members all spoke Spanish, but they also all evidently spoke "*arabe*." Under religion, Canavati registered as a Catholic, and under employment, he registered as "Industrial." Canavati also owned real estate in the city of Monterrey, in the state of Nuevo Leon.

Several members of Canavati's family were listed underneath his name, including his wife Sultana (38) and their three children Jorge (20), Espiridion (18), and Consuela (16). Espiridion's application for Palestinian citizenship was also denied in 1926, and he also worked in industry. Apart from Sultana, whose place of birth was likely also "Arabia" since she came after Salamon in the list and a check mark was placed in the box, the three children were born in the state of Nuevo Leon, Mexico. This suggests that by the time Salamon was petitioning Plumer in Jerusalem in February 1927, he had been in Mexico for at least twenty years and had amassed sufficient wealth to own property in the city of Monterrey through his work in industry. It also shows that three years after the applications for citizenship were submitted and denied, Canavati and his children were still considered foreigners without Mexican nationality. The children's birth in Mexico did not guarantee them Mexican nationality. By 1930, then, Palestinians were registered in Mexican population censuses without nationalities.

2. Israel State Archives, Jerusalem, P-986/24.

3. Pedersen, *Guardians*, 78.

4. Pedersen, *Guardians*, 78.

5. League of Nations Archive, 1/16448/2413, as cited in Pedersen, *Guardians*, 82.

6. Pedersen, *Guardians*, 83.

7. Pedersen, *Guardians*, 83.

8. Pedersen, *Guardians*, 79.

9. Pedersen, *Guardians*, 78–79.

10. Pedersen, *Guardians,* 78.

11. Natasha Wheatley, "Mandatory Interpretation: Legal Hermeneutics and the New International Order in Arab and Jewish Petitions to the League of Nations," *Past and Present* 227:1 (2015): 207–209.

12. Israel State Archives, Jerusalem, M-233/38.

13. Israel State Archives, Jerusalem, M-233/38.

14. Wheatley, "Mandatory Interpretation," 208.

15. Wheatley, "Mandatory Interpretation," 208.

16. Natasha Wheatley, "The Mandate System as a Style of Reasoning: International Jurisdiction and the Parceling of Imperial Sovereignty in Petitions from Palestine," in *The Routledge Handbook of the History of the Middle East Mandates,* ed. Cyrus Schayegh and Andrew Arsan (New York: Routledge, 2015), 106.

17. Wheatley, "Mandate System," 107.

18. Wheatley, "Mandatory Interpretation," 210.

19. Pedersen, *Guardians,* 4. Emphasis in the original.

20. Mark Mazower, "An International Civilization? Empire, Internationalism, and the Crisis of the Mid-Twentieth Century," *International Affairs* 82:3 (2006): 553–66.

21. Israel State Archives, Jerusalem, M-223/38.

22. Israel State Archives, Jerusalem, M-223/38.

23. Susan Pedersen, "The Meaning of the Mandate System: An Argument." *Geschichte und Gesellschaft* 32:4 (2006): 571.

24. See chapters 1–3 in Anghie, *Imperialism,* 2007.

25. Pedersen, *Guardians,* 87. Emphasis in the original. The figure of 3,000 represents petitions reaching Geneva between 1919 and 1940. In order from highest to lowest percentage from each mandated territory, the PMC received petitions from Palestine/Transjordan (43.4%), Syria/Lebanon (40.6%), South West Africa (4.8%), French Togo (2.3%), Iraq (2.3%), British Tanganyika (2.2%), French Cameroon (1.3%), and Western Samoa (1.2%). Petitions that amounted to less than 1 percent included those from New Guinea, Japanese islands, Ruanda/Urundi, British Cameroon, Nauru, and British Togo. See table 4 in Pedersen, *Guardians,* 87.

26. Wheatley, "Mandatory Interpretation," 208.

27. Cooper and Stoler, *Tensions of Empire,* 3.

28. Brubaker, "'Diaspora' Diaspora," 13.

29. Israel State Archives, Jerusalem, P-986/27. Letter reproduced as written; ellipses in the original.

30. Israel State Archives, Jerusalem, P-986/24. Emphasis in the original. See Israel State Archives, Jerusalem, M-233/38 for a list of the signatures of the members of the Centro Social Palestino de Monterrey.

31. Wheatley, "Mandatory Interpretation," 214.

32. Israel State Archives, Jerusalem, P-986/24. The terms *citizenship* and *nationality* were used interchangeably in the petition, a fact that mirrors their usage in both legal and policy documents at the time. Qafisheh explained that "Employing both terms was consistent with Article 7 of the Palestine Mandate, which used the two terms synonymously. Moreover, as it has been evident in several cases, Palestinian courts did not make a clear distinction between both terms. In law and practice of Palestine, therefore, 'nationality' and 'citizenship' were designed to have the same meaning." See Qafisheh, *International Law Foundations*, 77.

33. Ronald Storrs, British military general of Palestine, replaced Musa Kazim with Ragheb Bek Nashashibi as mayor of the city in 1920 since the latter was evidently more tractable and obedient. Musa Kazim proceeded to spearhead the Palestinian nationalist movement through his work in the Arab Executive.

34. Israel State Archives, Jerusalem, P-986/24.

35. The telegrams from Mexico's Palestinian collectives, with the original lists of handwritten signatures, can be found in the Israel State Archives, Jerusalem, M-233/38.

36. Israel State Archives, Jerusalem, M-233/38. Translated from Spanish. N.L. is the abbreviation for Nuevo Leon, a state in northeast Mexico.

37. Israel State Archives, Jerusalem, M-233/38. Translated from Arabic.

38. Israel State Archives, Jerusalem, P-986/24.

39. Israel State Archives, Jerusalem, M-233/38. Emphasis in the original. Linares was not included in this list as its Palestinian members submitted their telegram three days later on 26 February. However, the Centro submitted their telegram to the office of the Consulate General in Mexico City, and it was sent to Jerusalem as part of the same dispatch.

40. Several of the signatures included "and his family" or "and his children," indicating that the Centro's estimate of three hundred was an approximation, but that it counted families and children.

41. Israel State Archives, Jerusalem, M-233/38.

42. Israel State Archives, Jerusalem, M-233/38.

43. Israel State Archives, Jerusalem, M-233/38. The Covenant of the League of Nations was signed in 1919 and put into effect in January 1920.

44. Israel State Archives, Jerusalem, M-233/38.

45. Israel State Archives, Jerusalem, M-233/38.

46. Israel State Archives, Jerusalem, M-233/38. Translated from Arabic.

47. Qafisheh, *International Law Foundations*, 68.

48. Qafisheh, *International Law Foundations*, 68.

49. Israel State Archives, Jerusalem, M-233/38. In addition to the Treaty of Lausanne, the petitioners also referred to the 1920 Treaty of Sèvres.

50. Israel State Archives, Jerusalem, M-233/38. Translated from Arabic.

51. Israel State Archives, Jerusalem, M-233/38. Translated from Arabic.

52. Israel State Archives, Jerusalem, P-986/24. Translated from Arabic.

53. Israel State Archives, Jerusalem, M-233/38. Translated from Arabic.

54. Israel State Archives, Jerusalem, P-986/27. Translated from Arabic.

55. *Al-mawla* refers to God.

56. Israel State Archives, Jerusalem, M-233/38.

57. Israel State Archives, Jerusalem, M-233/38. Translated from Arabic.

58. Wheatley, "Mandate System," 118.

59. Pedersen, "Meaning of the Mandate System," 571–72.

60. Pedersen, *Guardians*, 91.

61. Pedersen, *Guardians*, 93.

62. The 4 May dispatch included the letters and petitions of Jesus Talamas, president of the Comité Hijos de Palestina, to the Arab Executive and to Vice-Consul Jeffrey, on 27 March and 12 April, respectively. The dispatch also included another petition, written in Spanish, from the Comité Hijos de Palestina in Torreon, Mexico. This four-page petition protested the high commissioner's decision to refuse citizenship to Palestinians in Torreon. It included two extra pages with forty-four signatures. Israel State Archives, Jerusalem, M-233/38.

63. Israel State Archives, Jerusalem, M-233/38.

64. Pedersen, *Guardians*, 102.

65. Pedersen, *Guardians*, 100.

66. Pedersen, *Guardians*, 100.

67. Pedersen, *Guardians*, 102, 358.

68. Pedersen, *Guardians*, 93–94.

69. Pedersen, *Guardians*, 94.

70. Timothy Mitchell, "The Limits of the State: Beyond Statist Approaches and Their Critics," *American Political Science Review* 85:1 (1991): 94.

CHAPTER 5: THE CHILEAN ARABIC PRESS AND THE STORY OF PALESTINOS-CHILENOS

1. *Al-Watan*, 26 December 1925. Translated from Arabic.

2. Saffie and Agar, "A Century of Palestinian Immigration," 73.

3. In August 2014, the late Professor Eugenio Chahuan of the Centro de Estudios Arabes at the Universidad de Chile in Santiago spoke to me about the dearth of Arabic speakers in Chile. For this reason, most Chileans, even those of Middle Eastern descent, are unaware that these microfilms exist. The newspapers are filled with hitherto unexplored historical information on different aspects of the daily lives of Chile's early Arabic-speaking migrants; the rich literary and social history of this community, Chahuan lamented, could very well remain untold.

4. Brubaker, "'Diaspora' Diaspora," 13.

5. Narbona's doctoral dissertation focuses on the transnational elements of the development of Lebanese and Syrian national modes of identification between 1915 and 1929. She examines the Arabic press in Argentina and Brazil to highlight their relevance in developing "nationalist identities" before and following the arrival of French forces in Lebanon and Syria. See Maria del Mar Logroño Narbona, "The Development of Nationalist Identities in French Syria and Lebanon: A Transnational Dialogue with Arab Immigrants to Argentina and Brazil, 1915–1929" (PhD diss., University of California, 2007).

6. For more about the Arab press in Brazil and Argentina, see Narbona, "Development of Nationalist Identities," 2007.

7. Bailony, "Transnationalism and the Syrian Migrant Public," 10.

8. Stacy Fahrenthold, "Transnational Modes and Media: The Syrian Press in the Mahjar and Emigrant Activism during World War I," *Mashriq & Mahjar* 1 (2013): 48.

9. Bailony, "Transnationalism and the Syrian Migrant Public," 10.

10. For an analysis of the role of newspapers and print capitalism in the construction of national communities since the nineteenth century, see Benedict Anderson, *Imagined Communities* (London: Verso, 1983). In the case of Palestine, see Weldon Matthews, *Confronting an Empire, Constructing a Nation: Arab Nationalists and Popular Politics in Mandate Palestine* (London: I. B. Tauris, 2006), for an examination of how the nationalist Istiqlal Party utilized newspapers to mobilize Palestinians against British rule throughout the 1930s.

11. Bailony, "Transnationalism and the Syrian Migrant Public," 10. The 1925 Great Syrian Revolt was a collective effort by multiconfessional groups throughout Syria and Lebanon to end French mandate rule. Though decentralized and ultimately put down by the French, the revolt was effective in mobilizing residents of the new mandates in a common goal. Approximately six thousand Syrians were killed as a result of the revolt, and France remained in Syria and Lebanon until 1943.

12. Bailony, "Transnationalism and the Syrian Migrant Public," 9.

13. *Al-Sharq*, 9 September 1928. Translated from Arabic.

14. *Al-Watan*, 28 February 1925. Translated from Arabic.

15. *Al-Sharq*, 22 January 1927. Translated from Arabic.

16. *Al-Watan*, 21 February 1925. Translated from Arabic.

17. *Al-Watan*, 21 February 1925. Translated from Arabic.

18. *Al-Watan*, 21 February 1925. Translated from Arabic.

19. *Al-Watan*, 21 February 1925. Translated from Arabic.

20. *Al-Watan*, 28 March 1925. Translated from Arabic.

21. *Al-Watan*, 29 October 1927. Translated from Arabic.

22. *Al-Watan*, 29 October 1927. Translated from Arabic.

23. *Al-Watan,* 29 November 1927. Translated from Arabic.

24. *Al-Watan,* 29 November 1927. Translated from Arabic.

25. Sarah Gualtieri's book, *Between Arab and White: Race and Ethnicity in the Early Syrian American Diaspora* (Berkeley: University of California Press, 2009), examines the development of race issues among Syrian migrants in the United States during the early twentieth century. Similarly, Camila Pastor explores the establishment in Mexico of an Arab migrant middle class during the 1920s and 1930s. Part of this process of assimilation, she explains, meant that many Arabs registered themselves as "white" in Mexican state registers. Pastor, *Mexican Mahjar,* 2017.

26. *Al-Watan,* 29 November 1927. Translated from Arabic.

27. *Al-Watan,* 23 August 1924. Translated from Arabic.

28. "Estatutos: Sociedad Juventud Palestina," 26 May 1924, in the periodicals of Biblioteca Nacional, Santiago, Chile. Translated from Spanish.

29. Olguin and Peña, *Inmigracion arabe,* 127.

30. *Al-Sharq,* 5 August 1928. Translated from Arabic.

31. *Al-Watan,* 20 June 1925. Translated from Arabic.

32. *Al-Watan,* 11 February 1925. Translated from Arabic.

33. *Al-Watan,* 11 February 1925. Translated from Arabic.

34. *Al-Watan,* 11 February 1925. Translated from Arabic.

35. *Al-Watan,* 11 November 1925. Translated from Arabic.

36. *Al-Watan,* 5 March 1926. Translated from Arabic.

37. *Al-Watan,* 5 March 1926. Translated from Arabic.

38. *Al-Sharq,* 29 January 1927. Translated from Spanish. Punctuation in the original.

39. *Al-Sharq,* 29 January 1927. Translated from Spanish.

40. *Al-Sharq,* 29 January 1927. Translated from Spanish.

41. *Al-Sharq,* 29 January 1927. Translated from Spanish.

42. *Al-Sharq,* 29 January 1927. Translated from Spanish.

43. *Al-Sharq,* 29 January 1927. Translated from Spanish.

44. *Al-Watan,* 19 November 1927. Translated from Arabic.

45. *Al-Sharq,* 22 January 1927. Translated from Arabic.

46. *Al-Sharq,* 22 January 1927. Translated from Arabic.

47. *Al-Sharq,* 22 January 1927. Translated from Arabic.

48. *Al-Watan,* 20 August 1927. Translated from Arabic.

49. *Al-Watan,* 20 August 1927. Translated from Arabic.

50. *Al-Watan,* 20 August 1927. Translated from Arabic.

51. *Al-Watan,* 8 April 1928. Translated from Arabic.

52. *Al-Watan,* 8 April 1928. Translated from Arabic.

53. *Al-Watan,* 8 April 1928. Translated from Arabic.

54. *Al-Watan,* 8 April 1928. Translated from Arabic. Punctuation in the original.

55. *Al-Watan,* 8 April 1928. Translated from Arabic. Punctuation in the original.

CHAPTER 6: BRINGING THE RIGHT OF RETURN HOME TO PALESTINE

1. Issa Bassel Bandak (1891–1984) served in several roles throughout his life in Palestine. Most importantly, he produced two publications after World War I, *Bethlehem* and *Sawt al-Sha'b*; the latter was in circulation until 1957. A nationalist, he was also a member of Bethlehem's Muslim-Christian Association, as well as the Arab Executive. In addition, he served as mayor of Bethlehem in the 1930s and, after 1948, as Jordan's ambassador to Spain and commissioner in Chile.

2. Banko, *Invention of Palestinian Citizenship,* 96.

3. Banko, *Invention of Palestinian Citizenship,* 97.

4. Banko, *Invention of Palestinian Citizenship,* 99.

5. Banko, *Invention of Palestinian Citizenship,* 99.

6. Banko, *Invention of Palestinian Citizenship,* 100.

7. Adnan Musallam, "The Formative Stages of Palestinian Arab Immigration to Latin America and Immigrants' Quest for Return and for Palestinian Citizenship in the Early 1920s" in *Latin American with Palestinian Roots,* ed. Viola Raheb (Bethlehem: Diyar Publishers, 2012), 21.

8. Issa Bassel Bandak, *Hayaatahu, A'maalahu, Mudhakkaraatahu; 1898–1984,* ed. Adnan Musallam (Bethlehem: Diyar Publishers, 2013), 58. Translated from Arabic.

9. Musallam, "Formative Stages," 22–23.

10. Banko, *Invention of Palestinian Citizenship,* 103.

11. Israel State Archives, Jerusalem, M-223/38.

12. Israel State Archives, Jerusalem, M-223/38.

13. Israel State Archives, Jerusalem, M-223/38.

14. "Arab emigrants" refers to Palestinians residing abroad who were applying for Palestinian citizenship.

15. Israel State Archives, Jerusalem, M-223/38.

16. Israel State Archives, Jerusalem, M-233/38.

17. Israel State Archives, Jerusalem, M-223/38.

18. Israel State Archives, Jerusalem, M-223/38.

19. Israel State Archives, Jerusalem, M-233/38.

20. Israel State Archives, Jerusalem, M-223/38.

21. Israel State Archives, Jerusalem, M-223/38.

22. Israel State Archives, Jerusalem, M-223/38.

23. National Archives, London, CO, 733/142/18.

24. National Archives, London, CO, 733/142/18.

25. National Archives, London, CO, 733/142/18.

26. National Archives, London, CO, 733/142/18.

27. Israel State Archives, Jerusalem, M-233/38.

28. Israel State Archives, Jerusalem, M-233/38.

29. Israel State Archives, Jerusalem, M-233/38.

30. Banko, *Invention of Palestinian Citizenship*, 105.

31. Ayoub Musallam, *Ihyaa' Dhikra Faqeed al-Watan wa al-Mahjar, Ayoub Musallam Yaqoub Musallam, 1905–2001*, ed. Adnan Musallam (Bethlehem: Diyar Publishers, 2016), 56–57. Translated from Arabic.

32. During the 1948 war, the offices of *Filastin* in Jaffa were relocated to East Jerusalem, which was annexed by Jordan. The newspaper continued to be published in Jerusalem until 1967, when it was merged with *al-Manar* to produce *al-Dustour* newspaper in Amman, still operational to this day. For more on *Filastin*, see R. Michael Bracy, *Printing Class: 'Isa al-'Isa, Filastin, and the Textual Construction of National Identity, 1911–1931* (Lanham, MD: University Press of America, 2011); and Rashid Khalidi, *The Iron Cage: The Story of the Palestinian Struggle for Statehood* (Boston: Beacon Press, 2006).

33. This petition from the Centro Social Palestino in Monterrey is different from the one analyzed in chapter 4. For more information about Canavati, see note 1 in chapter 4.

34. *Filastin*, 16 August 1927. Translated from Arabic.

35. See chapter 1 for more information about how migrants' remittances were used to build comparatively large homes and upscale neighborhoods in Bethlehem, Beit Jala, Ramallah, and other towns throughout Palestine.

36. *Filastin*, 16 August 1927. Translated from Arabic. Punctuation in the original.

37. *Filastin*, 16 August 1927. Translated from Arabic.

38. *Filastin*, 5 August 1927. Translated from Arabic.

39. *Filastin*, 5 August 1927. Translated from Arabic.

40. *Filastin*, 5 August 1927. Translated from Arabic.

41. *Filastin*, 5 August 1927. Translated from Arabic.

42. For an examination of the troubled Palestinian nationalist movement in the interwar period, see Khalidi, *Palestinian Identity*, 2008.

43. *Filastin*, 12 August 1927. Translated from Arabic.

44. *Filastin*, 9 August 1927. Translated from Arabic.

45. *Filastin*, 9 August 1927. Translated from Arabic.

46. *Filastin*, 9 August 1927. Translated from Arabic.

47. *Filastin*, 9 August 1927. Translated from Arabic.

48. *Filastin*, 30 August 1927. Translated from Arabic.

49. *Filastin*, 30 August 1927. Translated from Arabic.

50. *Filastin*, 30 August 1927. Translated from Arabic.

51. *Filastin,* 12 August 1927. Translated from Arabic.

52. Sebastian Conrad, *Globalization and the Nation in Imperial Germany* (Cambridge: Cambridge University Press, 2014), 4.

CONCLUSION

1. Conrad, *Globalization,* 1.

2. Conrad, *Globalization,* 5.

3. Israel State Archives, Jerusalem, M-223/38.

Bibliography

SECONDARY LITERATURE

Abusaada, Nadi. "'Who Are We and What Are We Called?': Palestinians in Chile at the End of Ottoman Rule." 18 March 2020. Accessed 25 March 2020, https://www.nadiabusaada.com/blog/who-are-we-and-what-are-we-called.

Alfaro-Velcamp, Theresa. "From '*Baisanos*' to Billionaires: Locating Arabs in Mexico." In *Between the Middle East and the Americas: The Cultural Politics of Diaspora*, edited by Ella Shohat and Evelyn Alsultany, 96–107. Ann Arbor: University of Michigan Press, 2013.

———. *So Far from Allah, So Close to Mexico*. Austin: University of Texas Press, 2007.

Allel, Marco. *Las industrias de las colectividades de habla Arabe in Chile*. Santiago: Syrian-Palestinian Business Association, 1937.

Anderson, Benedict. *Imagined Communities*. London: Verso, 1983.

Anghie, Antony. *Imperialism, Sovereignty and the Making of International Law*. New York: Cambridge University Press, 2007.

Arsan, Andrew, John Karam, and Akram Khater. "On Forgotten Shores: Migration in Middle East Studies, and the Middle East in Migration Studies." *Mashriq & Mahjar, Journal of Middle East Migration Studies* 1 (2012): 1–7.

Baeza Rodriguez, Cecilia. "Les Palestiniens d'Amerique Latine et la Cause Palestinienne: Chile, Bresil, Honduras, 1920–2010." PhD diss., Sciences Po, 2010.

———. "Palestinians in Latin America: Between Assimilation and Long-Distance Nationalism." *Journal of Palestine Studies* 43:2 (2014): 59–72.

Bahadur, Gaiutra. *Coolie Woman: The Odyssey of Indenture*. Chicago: University of Chicago Press, 2013.

Bailony, Reem. "Transnationalism and the Syrian Migrant Public: The Case of the 1925 Syrian Revolt." *Mashriq & Mahjar, Journal of Middle East Migration Studies* 1 (2013): 8–29.

Balloffet, Lily. *Argentina in the Global Middle East*. Stanford: Stanford University Press, 2020.

Bandak, Issa Bassel. *Hayaatahu, Aʿmaalahu, Mudhakkaraatahu; 1898–1984*. Edited by Adnan Musallam. Bethlehem: Diyar Publishers, 2013.

Banko, Lauren. "Citizenship Rights and Semantics of Colonial Power and Resistance: Haifa, Jaffa, and Nablus, 1931–1933." In *Violence and the City in the Modern Middle East*, edited by N. Fuccaro. Stanford: Stanford University Press, 2016.

———. "Claiming Identities in Palestine: Migration and Nationality under the Mandate." *Journal of Palestine Studies* 182:46 (2017): 26–43.

———. "The Creation of Palestinian Citizenship under an International Mandate: Legislation, Discourses and Practices, 1918–1925." *Citizenship Studies* 16:5/6 (2012): 641–55.

———. *The Invention of Palestinian Citizenship, 1918–1947*. Edinburgh: Edinburgh University Press, 2016.

———. "The Invention of Citizenship in Palestine." In *The Routledge Handbook of Global Citizenship Studies*, edited by E. Isin and P. Nyers, 317–24. London: Routledge, 2014.

———. "The Palestinian Citizen vs. the Palestinian National: Past and Present." In *Membership of Palestine in the United Nations: Legal and Political Implications*, edited by Mutaz Qafisheh, 363–78. Cambridge: Cambridge Scholars Press, 2013.

Bawalsa, Nadim. "Citizens from Afar: Palestinian Migrants and the New World Order, 1920–1930." In *The Routledge Handbook of the History of the Middle East Mandates*, edited by Cyrus Schayegh and Andrew Arsan, 123–35. London: Routledge, 2015.

———. "Legislating Exclusion: Palestinian Migrants and Interwar Citizenship." *Journal of Palestine Studies* 46:2 (2017): 44–59.

———. "Palestine West of the Andes." *NACLA Report on the Americas* 50 (2018): 34–39.

———. "Sakakini Defrocked." *Jerusalem Quarterly* 42 (2010): 5–25.

———. "Trouble with the In-Laws: Family Letters between Palestine and the Americas, 1925–1939." *Jerusalem Quarterly* 47 (2011): 6–27.

Bawardi, Hani. *The Making of Arab Americans: From Syrian Nationalism to US Citizenship*. Austin: University of Texas Press, 2014.

Bracy, Michael. *Printing Class: ʿIsa al-ʿIsa, Filastin, and the Textual Construction of National Identity, 1911–1931*. Lanham, MD: University Press of America, 2010.

Brown, Wendy. *Regulating Aversion: Tolerance in the Age of Identity and Empire*. Princeton: Princeton University Press, 2006.

Brubaker, Rogers. "The 'Diaspora' Diaspora." *Ethnic and Racial Studies* 28:1 (2005): 1–19.

Brubaker, Rogers, and Frederick Cooper. "Beyond Identity." *Theory and Society*, 29:1 (2000): 1–47.

Burbank, Jane, and Frederick Cooper. *Empires in World History: Power and the Politics of Difference*. Princeton: Princeton University Press, 2011.

Campos, Michelle. *Ottoman Brothers: Muslims, Christians, and Jews in Early Twentieth-Century Palestine*. Stanford: Stanford University Press, 2010.

Chatty, Dawn. *Displacement and Dispossession in the Modern Middle East*. Cambridge: Cambridge University Press, 2010.

Conrad, Sebastian. *Globalization and the Nation in Imperial Germany*. Cambridge: Cambridge University Press, 2014.

Cooper, Frederick, and Ann Stoler, eds. *Tensions of Empire: Colonial Cultures in a Bourgeois World*. Berkeley: University of California Press, 1997.

Dabed, Emilio. "A Constitution for a Non-State: The False Hopes of the Palestinian Constitutional Process, 1988–2007." PhD diss., Sciences Po, 2012.

Doumani, Beshara. *Rediscovering Palestine: Merchants and Peasants in Jabal Nablus, 1700–1900*. Berkeley: University of California Press, 1995.

Eckstein, Susan, and Adil Najam, eds. *How Immigrants Impact their Homelands*. Durham, NC: Duke University Press, 2013.

Elkins, Caroline, and Susan Pedersen, eds. *Settler Colonialism in the Twentieth Century: Projects, Practices, Legacies*. London: Routledge, 2005.

Fahrenthold, Stacy. *Between the Ottomans and the Entente: The First World War in the Syrian and Lebanese Diaspora, 1908–1925*. New York: Oxford University Press, 2019.

———. "Transnational Modes and Media: The Syrian Press in the Mahjar and Emigrant Activism during World War I." *Mashriq & Mahjar, Journal of Middle East Migration Studies* 1 (2013): 30–54.

Fleischmann, Ellen. *The Nation and Its "New" Women: The Palestinian Women's Movement, 1920–1948*. Berkeley: University of California Press, 2003.

Foner, Nancy. *From Ellis Island to JFK: New York's Two Great Waves of Immigration*. New Haven: Yale University Press, 2002.

———. *In a New Land: A Comparative View of Immigration*. New York: New York University Press, 2005.

Foroohar, Manzar. "Palestinian Diaspora in Central America—A Story of Hardship and Success." In *Latin American with Palestinian Roots*, edited by Viola Raheb, 45–62. Bethlehem: Diyar Publishers, 2012.

———. "Palestinians in Central America: From Temporary Migrants to a Permanent Diaspora." *Journal of Palestine Studies* 40:3 (2011): 6–22.

Gelvin, James. *Divided Loyalties: Nationalism and Mass Politics in Syria at the Close of Empire.* Berkeley: University of California Press, 1998.

Gonzalez, Nancie. *Dollar, Dove and Eagle; One Hundred Years of Palestinian Migration to Honduras.* Ann Arbor: University of Michigan Press, 1992.

Gualtieri, Sarah. *Arab Routes: Pathways to Syrian California.* Stanford: Stanford University Press, 2020.

———. *Between Arab and White: Race and Ethnicity in the Early Syrian American Diaspora.* Berkeley: University of California Press, 2009.

Hayes Edwards, Brent. "The Uses of Diaspora." *Social Text* 66 19:1 (2001): 45–73.

Hess, Christian. "What Are 'Reverse Diasporas' and How Are We to Understand Them?" *Diaspora* 17:3 (2008): 288–315.

Hitti, Philip. *The Syrians in America.* Piscataway, NJ: Gorgias Press, 2005.

Hooglund, Eric. *Crossing the Waters: Arabic-Speaking Immigrants to the United States before 1940.* Washington, DC: Smithsonian Institution Press, 1987.

Hourani, Albert, and Nadim Shehadi. *The Lebanese in the World: A Century of Emigration.* London: I. B. Tauris, 1992.

Hurewitz, J. C., ed. *The Middle East and North Africa in World Politics; A Documentary Record.* New Haven: Yale University Press, 1979.

Issawi, Charles. "Migration from and to Syria, 1860–1914." In *The Economic History of the Middle East, 1800–1914,* edited by Charles Issawi, 269–73. Chicago: University of Chicago Press, 1966.

Karam, John T. "*Turcos* in the Mix: Corrupting Arabs in Brazil's Racial Democracy." In *Between the Middle East and the Americas: The Cultural Politics of Diaspora,* edited by Ella Shohat and Evelyn Alsultany, 80–95. Ann Arbor: University of Michigan Press, 2013.

Karpat, Kemal. "The Ottoman Emigration to America, 1860–1914." *International Journal of Middle East Studies* 17:2 (1985): 175–209.

Kayali, Hasan. *Arabs and Young Turks: Ottomanism, Arabism, and Islamism in the Ottoman Empire, 1908–1918.* Berkeley: University of California Press, 1996.

Kenny, Kathy. "The Power of Place: Katrina in Five Worlds." *Jerusalem Quarterly* 35 (2008): 5–30.

Khalidi, Rashid. *The Iron Cage: The Story of the Palestinian Struggle for Statehood.* Boston: Beacon Press, 2006.

———. *Palestinian Identity: The Construction of Modern National Consciousness.* New York: Columbia University Press, 2008.

Khater, Akram. "Becoming 'Syrian' in America: A Global Geography of Ethnicity and Nation." *Diaspora* 14:2/3 (2005): 299–331.

———. *Inventing Home: Emigration, Gender, and the Middle Class in Lebanon 1870–1920.* Berkeley: University of California Press, 2001.

Khater, Akram, and Antoine Khater. "Assaf: A Peasant of Mount Lebanon." In *Struggle and Survival in the Modern Middle East*, edited by Edmund Burke III and David Yaghoubian, 35–47. Berkeley: University of California Press, 2006.

Klich, Ignacio, and Jeffrey Lesser, eds. *Arab and Jewish Immigrants in Latin America: Images and Realities*. London: Routledge, 1998.

———. "Introduction: 'Turco' Immigrants in Latin America." *The Americas* 53:1 (1996): 1–14.

Lesser, Jeffrey. *Immigration, Ethnicity, and National Identity in Brazil*. Cambridge: Cambridge University Press, 2013.

Lopez, Kathleen. *Chinese Cubans: A Transnational History*. Chapel Hill: University of North Carolina Press, 2013.

Lutfiyyeh, Abdulla. *Baytin, a Jordanian Village: A Study of Social Institutions and Social Change in a Folk Community*. Berlin: De Gruyter Mouton, 2011.

Manela, Erez. *The Wilsonian Moment: Self-Determination and the International Origins of Anticolonial Nationalism*. Oxford: Oxford University Press, 2009.

Marin-Guzman, Roberto. *A Century of Palestinian Immigration into Central America: A Study of Their Economic and Cultural Contributions*. San Jose: Editorial Universidad de Costa Rica, 2000.

———. "Political Participation and Economic Success of the Palestinians of Christian Origin in Central America." In *Latin American with Palestinian Roots*, edited by Viola Raheb, 25–44. Bethlehem: Diyar Publishers, 2012.

Matthews, Weldon. *Confronting an Empire, Constructing a Nation: Arab Nationalists and Popular Politics in Mandate Palestine*. London: I. B. Tauris, 2006.

Mazower, Mark. "An International Civilization? Empire, Internationalism, and the Crisis of the Mid-Twentieth Century." *International Affairs* 82:3 (2006): 553–66.

Meiton, Fredrik. *Electrical Palestine: Capital and Technology from Empire to Nation*. Berkeley: University of California Press, 2019.

Mitchell, Timothy. "The Limits of the State: Beyond Statist Approaches and Their Critics." *American Political Science Review* 85:1 (1991): 77–96.

———. *Questions of Modernity*. Minneapolis: University of Minnesota Press, 2000.

Morawska, Ewa. "Return Migrations: Theoretical and Research Agendas." In *A Century of European Migrations, 1830–1930*, edited by Rudolph Vecoli and Suzanne Sinke, 277–92. Urbana: University of Illinois Press, 1991.

Musallam, Adnan. *Folded Pages from Local Palestinian History in the Twentieth Century*. Bethlehem: WIAM/Palestinian Resolution Centre, 2002.

———. "The Formative Stages of Palestinian Arab Immigration to Latin America and Immigrants' Quest for Return and for Palestinian Citizenship in the Early

1920s." In *Latin American with Palestinian Roots*, edited by Viola Raheb, 15–24. Bethlehem: Diyar Publishers, 2012.

Musallam, Ayoub. *Ihyaa' Dhikra Faqeed al-Watan wa al-Mahjar, Ayoub Musallam Yaqoub Musallam, 1905–2001*. Edited by Adnan Musallam. Bethlehem: Diyar Publishers, 2016.

Naff, Alixa. *Becoming American: The Early Arab Immigrant Experience*. Carbondale: Southern Illinois University Press, 1985.

———. "New York: The Mother Colony." In *A Community of Many Worlds: Arab Americans in New York City*, edited by Kathleen Benson and Philip Kayal, 3–10. Syracuse, NY: Syracuse University Press, 2002.

Narbona, Maria del Mar Logroño. "The Development of Nationalist Identities in French Syria and Lebanon: A Transnational Dialogue with Arab Immigrants to Argentina and Brazil, 1915–1929." PhD diss., University of California, Santa Barbara, 2007.

Norris, Jacob. *Land of Progress: Palestine in the Age of Colonial Development, 1905–1948*. Oxford: Oxford University Press, 2013.

———. "Return Migration and the Rise of the Palestinian Nouveaux Riches, 1870–1925." *Journal of Palestine Studies* (2017) 46 (2): 60–75.

Olguin Tenorio, Myriam, and Patricia Peña Gonzalez. *La inmigracion arabe en Chile*. Santiago: Instituto Chileno Arabe de Cultura, 1990.

Olsson, Erik, and Russell King. "Introduction: Diasporic Return." *Diaspora* 17:3 (2008): 255–61.

Owen, Roger. *The Middle East in the World Economy, 1800–1914*. London: I. B. Tauris, 1993.

Pastor de Maria y Campos, Camila. *The Mexican Mahjar: Transnational Maronites, Jews, and Arabs under the French Mandate*. Austin: University of Texas Press, 2017.

Pedersen, Susan. *The Guardians: The League of Nations and the Crisis of Empire*. New York: Oxford University Press, 2015.

———. "The Meaning of the Mandate System: An Argument." *Geschichte und Gesellschaft* 32:4 (2006): 560–58.

———. "Samoa on the World Stage: Petitions and Peoples before the Mandates Commission of the League of Nations." *Journal of Imperial and Commonwealth History* 40:2 (2012): 231–61.

Qafisheh, Mutaz. *The International Law Foundations of Palestinian Nationality: A Legal Examination of Nationality in Palestine under Britain's Rule*. Boston: Martinus Nijhoff Publishers, 2008.

Raheb, Viola, ed. *Latin Americans with Palestinian Roots*. Bethlehem: Diyar Publisher, 2012.

Saffie Guevara, Nicole, and Lorenzo Agar Corbinos. "A Century of Palestinian Immigration to Chile: A Successful Integration." In *Latin American with Palestinian Roots,* edited by Viola Raheb, 63–82. Bethlehem: Diyar Publishers, 2012.

Sakakini, Khalil. *Kadha Ana Ya Dunya.* Beirut: al-Ittihaad al-ʿAamm li al-Kuttab wa al-Sahafiyyin al-Filastiniyyin, al-Amaana al-ʿAamma, 1982.

Saliba, Najib. "Emigration from Syria." In *Arabs in the New World,* edited by Sameer Abraham and Nabeel Abraham, 31–43. Detroit: Wayne State University, 1983.

Sanchez, George. *Becoming Mexican American: Ethnicity, Culture, and Identity in Chicano Los Angeles, 1900–1945.* New York: Oxford University Press, 1993.

Scott, James. *Seeing like a State: How Certain Schemes to Improve the Human Condition Have Failed.* New Haven: Yale University, 1999.

Shakir, Evelyn. *Bint Arab: Arab and Arab American Women in the United States.* Westport, CT: Praeger, 1997.

———. *Remember Me to Lebanon: Stories of Lebanese Women in America.* Syracuse, NY: Syracuse University Press, 2015.

Shaw, Walter. *Report of the Commission on the Palestine Disturbances of August, 1929.* London: His Majesty's Stationary Office, 1930.

———. *A Survey of Palestine.* Jerusalem: Government Printer, 1945–1946.

Shohat, Ella, and Evelyn Alsultany, eds. *Between the Middle East and the Americas: The Cultural Politics of Diaspora.* Ann Arbor: University of Michigan Press, 2013.

Smith, Barbara. *The Roots of Separatism in Palestine: British Economic Policy, 1920–1929.* Syracuse, NY: Syracuse University Press, 1993.

Tamari, Salim. "City of Riffraff: Crowds, Public Space, and New Urban Sensibilities in War-Time Jerusalem, 1917–1921." In *Comparing Cities: The Middle East and South Asia,* edited by Kamran Asdar Ali and Martina Rieker. Oxford: Oxford University Press, 2009.

———. "A Miserable Year in Brooklyn: Khalil Sakakini in America, 1907–1908." *Jerusalem Quarterly* 17 (2003): 19–40.

Thompson, Elizabeth. *Colonial Citizens: Republican Rights, Paternal Privilege, and Gender in French Syria and Lebanon.* New York: Columbia University Press, 2000.

Tololyan, Khachig. "Rethinking Diaspora(s): Stateless Power in the Transnational Moment." *Diaspora* 5:1 (1996): 3–36.

Torpey, John. "The Great War and the Birth of the Modern Passport System." In *Documenting Individual Identity: The Development of State Practices in the Modern World,* edited by Jane Caplan and John Torpey. Princeton: Princeton University Press, 2001.

Tsuda, Takeyuki. *Diasporic Homecomings: Ethnic Return Migration in Comparative Perspective*. Stanford: Stanford University Press, 2009.

Watenpaugh, Keith. *Being Modern in the Middle East: Revolution, Nationalism, Colonialism, and the Arab Middle Class*. Princeton: Princeton University Press, 2006.

———. "The League of Nations' Rescue of Armenian Genocide Survivors and the Making of Modern Humanitarianism, 1920–1927." *American Historical Review* 115:5 (2010): 1315–39.

Wheatley, Natasha. "The Mandate System as a Style of Reasoning: International Jurisdiction and the Parceling of Imperial Sovereignty in Petitions from Palestine." In *The Routledge Handbook of the History of the Middle East Mandates*, edited by Cyrus Schayegh and Andrew Arsan. New York: Routledge, 2015.

———. "Mandatory Interpretation: Legal Hermeneutics and the New International Order in Arab and Jewish Petitions to the League of Nations." *Past and Present* 227:1 (2015): 205–48.

Winland, Daphne. "Why We Come Back to Diasporas: Heterogeneous Groups and the Persistent Dream of Political Action." *Diaspora* 16:1/2 (2007): 254–64.

ARCHIVES

Biblioteca Nacional de Chile, Santiago.

Elmer Holmes Bobst Library, New York.

Israel State Archives, Jerusalem.

National Archives, London.

NEWSPAPERS

al-Islaah, Santiago, Chile. Preserved in microfilm at the Biblioteca Nacional de Chile.

al-Murshed, Santiago, Chile. Preserved in microfilm at the Biblioteca Nacional de Chile.

al-Shabeebah, Santiago, Chile. Preserved in microfilm at the Biblioteca Nacional de Chile.

al-Sharq, Santiago, Chile. Preserved in microfilm at the Biblioteca Nacional de Chile.

al-Watan, Santiago, Chile. Preserved in microfilm at the Biblioteca Nacional de Chile.

Filastin, Jaffa, Palestine. Preserved in microfilm at Elmer Holmes Bobst Library.

Mundo Arabe, Santiago, Chile. Preserved in microfilm at the Biblioteca Nacional de Chile.

Index

Page numbers in italics refer to figures. Those followed by n refer to notes, with note number.

WORLDING THE MIDDLE EAST

Emily Gottreich and Daniel Zoughbie, editors
Center for Middle East Studies, University of California, Berkeley

This series investigates the "worlding" of the Middle East and the ever-changing, ever-becoming dynamism of the region. It seeks to capture the ways in which the region is reimagined and unmade through flows of world capital, power, and ideas. Spanning the modern period to the present, Worlding the Middle East showcases critical and innovative books that develop new ways of thinking about the region and the wider world.

Carel Bertram, *A House in the Homeland: Armenian Pilgrimages to Places of Ancestral Memory*
2022

Susan Gilson Miller, *Years of Glory: Nelly Benatar and the Pursuit of Justice in Wartime North Africa*
2021

Amélie Le Renard, *Western Privilege: Work, Intimacy, and Postcolonial Hierarchies in Dubai*
2021

Made in United States
North Haven, CT
14 September 2023